THE RAIDERS

Cinderella Champions of Pro Football

BY LOU SAHADI

FOREWORD BY HANK STRAM

DIAL PRESS   NEW YORK

The author expressly wishes his sincere thanks to Al LoCasale of the Raiders, not only for his time and patience under an excruciating deadline, but for his remarkable efficiency; and to Fran Connors and Pete Abitante of the National Football League.

Photography Credits:
Color: Fred Kaplan and Michael Zagaris.
Black and White: Russ Reed, Dan Honda, and Norm Fisher.

Published by The Dial Press, 1 Dag Hammarskjold Plaza, New York, New York 10017

Manufactured in the United States of America

First printing

Library of Congress Cataloging in Publication Data

Sahadi, Lou.
    The Raiders: Cinderella Champions of Pro Football.

    1. Oakland Raiders (Football Club)a   I. Title.
GV956.024S23   796.332′64′0979466   81-9887
ISBN 0-385-27192-1   AACR2

CONTENTS

INTRODUCTION   v

FOREWORD   1

AL DAVIS   3

TOM FLORES   13

JIM PLUNKETT   23

THE OFFENSE   35

TED HENDRICKS   55

THE DEFENSE   69

THE 1980 SEASON   89

HOUSTON PLAYOFF   121

CLEVELAND PLAYOFF   133

AFC CHAMPIONSHIP SAN DIEGO   147

SUPER BOWL XV   165

To Tony and Stella:
Two Raider fans who live high on a hill in San Francisco overlooking Oakland Bay, which provided an expansive panorama of inspiration.

INTRODUCTION

They are unique. They are unique, and colorful, and controversial; and there has never been a team quite like them. In 1980 the Oakland Raiders defied all logic to produce one of the most awesome chapters in the history of professional football. They not only won the AFC Championship, but they crowned their Cinderella season by winning the biggest bauble of all—Super Bowl XV. And they did it in a way that literally captured the imagination of every pro football fan in America. Love them or loathe them, one has to marvel at what they achieved. No one can deny them their place in the sun.

Damon Runyon would have loved them with their puckish genius for an owner and players who answer to such offbeat nicknames as Tooz, Sparky, Kickem, Uppie, Dante, Spike, Double D, Tooch, Judge, Plunk, Duke, and Disco. Individually, they are flamboyant personalities—playful, colorful, prideful, too. More important though, collectively, they are a team with a unique character all its own.

The fact remains, the Raiders won against all the improbable odds. Before the 1980 season even began, they were written off as losers. The experts diagnosed their ailment as a case of decline, quickly referring to the golden past of Raider excellence and then to their last two mediocre seasons. The prognosis looked grim. Those who hated the Raiders applauded. They loved it when Al Davis traded a favorite All-Pro quarterback and an All-Pro tight end. That was considered panic.

Actually it wasn't panic, but design. The basic premise behind the Raider attack down through the years has been the big play. It had been missing from the Raider scheme for the past two years. Instead of a long, vertical attack, the Raiders were resorting more to a horizontal one. It was out of character for them. Their attack was always predicated on exerting pressure on opposing secondaries. The big-play pressure often would force the secondary into mistakes. That was the offensive theory that Davis introduced to the team when he took over a woeful franchise back in 1963 and designed pass routes for four and even five receivers at one time.

Since then, the Raiders have been an extension of Davis's personality. He is one of the two owners in professional football who knows the game as a former coach and strategist. E.W. McGah is the sole remaining partner since the Raiders first began in 1960 to look on with satisfaction at what Davis accomplished. In a sense, the Raiders have been structured from the top down. Their commitment to excellence is a working credo that has been fostered by the fact that the Raiders are the only team in the 61-year-old history of the NFL to produce 16 consecutive winning seasons. Despite a 9-33 beginning, the Raiders over the last 21 years have attained the phenomenal status of pro football's winningest team with a 188-101-11 record. They have maintained such excellence with a system all their own, disdaining scouting combines and working the college lodes themselves. It is Davis's way.

"We all know each other so well that we communicate in ways the computer just doesn't allow," explained Davis. "If I have a question, I don't look at a piece of paper. I ask the man who's seen the player in action. Also, with a computer, nobody has to take the responsibility for making a choice. If a player is a bust, the information's at fault. In our system our guys are responsible for their recommendations, so they make doubly sure they're right. We always know what we're getting because we have personally seen everybody we pick.

"The Raider organization is the most respected, imitated, and feared in pro football. If I had my choice, I'd rather be feared. We have a total commitment to excellence."

Excellence in 1980 was attained in the wake of great adversity. Five games into the season, they were 2-3 and had to turn to rusty Jim Plunkett to replace injured Dan Pastorini at quarterback. Davis's faith in Plunkett, who had sat dejectedly on the bench for two years, never wavered. True to Davis's trust, Plunkett climaxed one of the most courageous comebacks in sports by leading the Raiders in their struggle against all odds to achieve the championship of professional football. This book is about that struggle, that victory. There may never be another team quite like the Raiders, or people like Sparky, Dante, and Tooz. . . .

Lou Sahadi

FOREWORD

It is very unusual that an adversary of the Oakland Raiders for a period of fifteen competitive years would be asked to write the foreword to this book. I do so because of the great respect and admiration I have for Al Davis, former assistant coach, head coach, Commissioner of the American Football League, and now owner of the most successful franchise in the National Football League. It is a team that has distinguished itself by being the "winningest" team in professional football over a twenty-year period. The Raiders are an extension of their dynamic leader, a man who has devoted his life to football—and winning.

The Super Bowl Champions are a unique organization. They have a strong philosophy and literally exercise the true meaning of what they believe. They do not belong to the scouting combine. They have a big-play passing approach at a time when most teams are thinking possession passes. They have man-for-man coverage when most teams are employing zones. They have the great capacity to take players from the scrap heap and make them winners. Their success story is the end result of the execution of the feelings expressed above.

Winning World Championships in the National Football League is a tremendous task and a great challenge. It basically involves three things: assessing talent, accumulating talent, and making the talent play up to its potential.

Tom Flores and his staff, along with Executive Vice President Al LoCasale, Personnel Director Ron Wolfe, and the scouting department, did a tremendous job of making it all happen.

You will enjoy reading Lou Sahadi's exciting book on the 1981 World Champions.

Hank Stram

1

AL DAVIS

Down below, Al LoCasale had made his way onto the field in the waning moments of the game. It has been his ritual the past several years as executive assistant of the Oakland Raiders. He was appropriately dressed in a gray shirt with a black sweater and trousers. He had all he could do to control his emotions. This game was bigger than any of the others. The Raiders were only minutes away from embarrassing the Philadelphia Eagles in Super Bowl XV.

High above the Superdome crowd sat LoCasale's boss, Al Davis. He viewed the extravaganza, not in a private owner's box but from the press box. Since his announced move of the Oakland franchise to Los Angeles over a year ago, Davis had not endeared himself to the remaining twenty-seven owners of Pete Rozelle's sports lodge. Far from it. He was looked upon as the enemy.

No one could deny him his hour. In what was the most improbable of all professional football seasons, the renegade Raiders were about to become the champions of football. In a tumultuous season that included such things as court tests, allegations of all sorts, and contempt charges, somehow Al Davis at this moment was enjoying himself more than anyone.

He, too, was appropriately dressed in a white silk shirt with a light grey V-neck sweater and pants to match. His Raiders, who were eschewing the Eagles amidst the glitter of the Superdome, were of course similarly attired in white and gray battle gear. It is almost as if Davis were involved in the game itself, scribbling notes on a pad, making remarks, and regularly glancing at the clock that would officially signal the Raiders' Super Bowl triumph. It was indeed his finest hour.

Jim Heffernan, the National Football League's director of public relations, approached Davis, asking him if he needed security guards to accompany him to the Raider dressing room to accept the silver Vince Lombardi Trophy, emblematic of football supremacy. Commissioner Rozelle would present it. Davis quickly looked around and just as quickly riveted his steely eyes on the scoreboard.

"Jim," exclaimed Davis, while shaking his head at the intrusion, "the game's still got seven minutes to go!"

It was typical of Davis. He is known as a worrier—it almost consumes him. In all his twenty-one years in football he has worried. There wasn't any way the Eagles could win now in the remaining minutes, yet Davis refused to leave. This was no time to change his ways.

There were countless others worrying, too, concerned perhaps that Davis would refuse to accept the Super Bowl trophy from Rozelle. Their feud was known to everyone. On Friday, two days before the game, Rozelle had branded Davis as an outlaw at his press conference. Now even Heffernan had some reservations about Davis's participation in the brief locker room ceremony.

It was not until a Raider aide shouted: "It's over, Al. We did it!" that Davis got up. He thrust his right arm in the air and began heading for the elevator that would take him to the dressing room. Before he reached the door, he was surrounded by several writers. They wanted a quick comment.

"I've been quiet all along," said Davis. "Let Tom Flores and the players tell you. They did it. They're a funny bunch. They're the most unique group we've ever had. It doesn't matter where they had the ball, they just played. On our thirty, on their forty—it didn't matter. They attacked all day."

"Are you going to accept the trophy?" someone asked.

Davis cracked a smile for the first time all day.

"I love professional football," he replied. "We're going to accept the trophy, and we're going to be proud of it."

A horde of reporters was trying to get into the Raider dressing room when Davis finally arrived. Somehow, Davis ever so slowly snaked his way through the maze of bodies. Offensive line coach Sam Boghosian was the first to greet him.

"You knew it in training camp," smiled Boghosian as he hugged Davis.

High on a platform Rozelle and NBC sportscaster Bryant Gumbel waited ever so patiently for Davis to join them. Holding the silver trophy with two hands, Rozelle expounded on the virtues of the Raiders' successful season. He handed the trophy to Davis with both hands, obviating any chance for a customary handshake.

"Call him an obscenity, Al," one of the Raider players shouted.

Davis wouldn't hear of it. He wasn't about to tarnish the moment they had all worked for.

"This is the proudest hour in the history of the Raiders," claimed Davis as he looked around the room at his players. "You were magnificent out there today, you really were."

Davis got down from the platform.

"I just want to talk to my players," he remarked. "I want to be with them."

He wasn't on camera now. Slowly, searching out player after player, he went around the hot, crowded room. One by one, he shook their hands. Some he hugged. He was one of them. He would worry about the courts another time. No one could take this day away from him.

It was undoubtedly the greatest event in Davis's career in football. The 1980 season was perhaps the most painful he had experienced. He incurred the wrath of Oakland fans by his determined efforts to move the franchise and then by trading two of the most popular players, quarterback Ken Stabler and tight end Dave Casper, both All-Pros. Davis also was subjected to abuse by the media for the way he operated. He was likewise looked upon with disdain by his peers, the owners of the other pro teams. There would never be a testimonial dinner for Al Davis.

Yet, it was all part of the Davis mystique—one that he perpetuates. It is, in a word, charisma, and it is something Davis has more than any other owner in professional football. He is feared, yet respected; he is hated, yet also loved. He is clever, even cunning. He is hard and he is understanding. He is all these things and more. He wins—and that to Davis is the bottom line. For all the hyperbole about the Dallas Cowboys, the Raiders are the most successful team in pro football history.

That success is no accident. Nobody works harder to win than Al Davis. He has always been a street fighter. Anyone from Brooklyn where Davis was raised will tell you that if you have street smarts you can survive anywhere. Davis is the leading disciple of this city-spawned philosophy. Coach Sam Rutigliano of the Cleveland Browns would agree. He was a classmate of Davis's at Brooklyn's Erasmus Hall High School.

Executive assistant Al LoCasale, left, joins Al Davis on the practice field.

"Al always had information nobody else had," recalled Rutigliano. "He was always looking for an edge. He's a very smart man. Hey, he's probably the only one who knows the serial number of the Unknown Soldier."

He got his start in the streets. It gave him endurance. It made him clever and it made him tough. Once as a youngster he found a screwdriver in the street. He picked it up, looked it over, and stuck it in his pocket. He was approached by a man who had watched the episode.

"Did you find my screwdriver, boy?" he asked Davis.

"Yes, sir," answered Davis. "Did it have a red handle?"

"That's right," came the answer.

"I'm sorry," smiled Davis, "this one has a green handle."

Davis applied himself in college. He attended Wittenberg and later Syracuse University where he earned a degree in English. In college he participated in three major sports: football, basketball, and baseball. After graduating in 1950, he joined the coaching staff at Adelphi College as a line coach. That was the beginning. He wrote highly technical articles on football that were published in a number of

5

coaching magazines. He was so well versed in football skills that *Scholastic Coach* magazine singled him out as "the most inventive mind in the country."

Davis's promising coaching career was interrupted by a stretch in the Army, but he was fortunate in being able to coach the football team at Fort Belvoir, Virginia. Though he was only a private, he wasn't timid about telling the brass what he needed.

"If we want a winner, you've got to get me this player from that other camp," Davis would say.

He was very successful. He developed a national rivalry among the service teams and achieved a milestone one year in a squad game by defeating the University of Maryland, who were the national collegiate champions.

While only twenty-four, Davis worked in the player personnel area with the Baltimore Colts in 1954 after his release from the Army. He went back to amateur athletics the next two years as line coach and recruiter for the Citadel, a military school in South Carolina. One player he recruited at the time was Paul Maguire, who later played professional ball as a linebacker and punter with the Buffalo Bills and San Diego Chargers. Maguire remembers it well.

"When he recruited me, Al told me that he would help get me a cheap car. I found one for about three hundred fifty dollars and told Al about it. He said, 'I said I'd help you find one, not buy one.'"

Later Davis coached at the University of Southern California for three years, first as a line coach and then as head of the defense. In 1960 Sid Gillman, the head coach of the Los Angeles Chargers (which was newly formed in the first year of the American Football League) hired Davis as his offensive end coach. A year later the Chargers relocated to San Diego.

It didn't take Davis long to rise in the pro ranks. In 1963 he was hired as the head coach of the floundering Oakland Raiders, a team that had won three games in two years and was derided because they played their games on a high school field. The first year in Oakland Davis transformed the club from perennial

A visible part of the Raider organization, Davis gets involved on the field.

losers to overnight winners with a 10-3 record and he was voted Coach of the Year.

Since its inception it had been an uphill struggle for the AFL. In the spring of 1966 the owners decided that they had to take an assertive course of action and get a dynamic new commissioner. Led by Gillman, the owners selected thirty-six-year-old Davis. Reluctant to leave the coaching lines, Davis was persuaded that the existence of the league depended on his leadership. The challenge was too much to decline.

In the eight weeks that he was commissioner Davis had the complacent National Football League asking for a truce. Davis's plan for the AFL's survival was strong, quick action. He had decided to sign the older league's star quarterbacks. That would give the AFL instant star quality and immediate credibility. John Brodie of San Francisco and Roman Gabriel of the Los Angeles Rams were among the first to sign AFL contracts. Two months later the NFL agreed to a merger. However, there are those who would tell you that Davis didn't want to

Former Raider great George Blanda, left, spends a quiet moment with Davis.

merge, that he quickly had the older league on the run. The conservative NFL wasn't ready for someone like him. They voted to retain Pete Rozelle as commissioner and Davis returned to Oakland where he developed the Raiders into the league's most successful team.

Davis's tenacity, his guile, his persistence, his penchant for winning cast him in the role of a loner. As much as the other owners respected his knowledge, they were wary of him. More often than not they were reluctant to do business with him. Somehow he always seemed to come out on top.

"Characterizing me as a maverick, well, I don't know if I agree with that," says Davis. "I honestly don't think I'm a maverick per se. For example, within the realm of football I have a great relationship with players. It's just a cer-

tain clique of owners who don't go for my way, for my approach. I've never been one of the crowd."

Many of Davis's players haven't been part of the crowd, either. Davis's way has been to judge a player on his abilities and not on the reputation he may have earned with other teams. Over the years Davis has signed players as free agents with reputations for being or having been difficult—players like Art Powell, Ben Davidson, Ike Lassiter, John Matuszak, Jim Plunkett, and Burgess Owens. All have contributed to the Raiders' success and to Oakland's being known as the halfway house of the NFL.

"I've always believed that environment is the most important thing. I believe you can motivate a man and make him work," rationalizes

Davis manages a smile for NBC's Bryant Gumble. Coach Tom Flores is center.

Davis. "My belief has always been that unless somebody proves to me he can't play, I'm not going to take anybody else's word for it."

It is not unusual to discover Davis at the practice sessions of many college all-star games, like the East-West shrine game in San Francisco or the Senior Bowl game in Mobile, Alabama. It was at one of the East-West games several years ago that Davis discovered a player nobody thought much of.

"I saw a guy who will really help us," he told John Madden.

"I thought the East-West practice got rained out yesterday," remarked Madden.

"Yeah, but I watched him run around the gym," continued Davis. "I'm telling you this kid can play. His name is Mark Van Eeghen from Colgate."

"You just watched him run around?" asked Madden.

"That's all I needed," answered Davis.

Madden coached the Raiders for ten years during which they won 103 games—a remarkable achievement. It took Madden a long time to earn a reputation as an outstanding coach. The story that often circulated was that Davis was coaching the team from the background and that Madden was only a puppet. Madden corrected the misconception.

"In all my time as a head coach Al never once told me, 'Do it this way,'" disclosed Madden. "Of course he had input. Any coach would be out of his mind not to listen to suggestions from someone with his insight. He would say, 'Have you thought of . . . ?' If you didn't happen to take certain advice, it was

A happy Davis raises the team's 1981 Super Bowl trophy.

okay with him.

"I've often said that the status of your coaching job in the NFL depended on how many people you had over you. Some clubs have four or five people over the head coach. At Oakland there was always one—Al Davis. When I started out, I was only thirty-two years old. I needed all the help I could get. He was always available. I never asked for anything and got turned down by him. Having a guy like that who understands the game is so much easier for a head coach. Everyone has that old image of Al Davis from the 'war' years. That stuff is so old. That's not the way he is.

"I remember an incident with Houston a few years ago; it's just one more example of Al's hyped-up image. Do you know Bum Phillips was convinced that something was up with the air in the football. He took one of the footballs and carried it to Rice University to have it examined. I saw Bum later, and I asked him to consider how a ball filled with helium would react on the center snap. Can't you see it sailing over the punter's head? That's how it goes. If the field in Pittsburgh is not in shape, it's the maintenance men's fault. If the field is in Oak-land, it's Al's fault."

Perhaps Sid Gillman had the best reason why Davis is so unpopular in NFL circles. He, too, like Davis, was an innovator in the early days of the AFL. Now, years later, other teams have asked Gillman for help with their offensive schemes, especially in the passing game.

"There are a lot of people who dislike folks who work harder than they do, who are smarter and wiser, who do their homework, and who work every edge in the book to win," reasoned Gillman. "In this business we live and die by winning and losing."

Davis does work. He is only one of two owners in the NFL who has been a coach. It isn't unusual for Davis to work long hours at home. He is constantly looking at films, making notes well into the night. He is up early the next morning doing the same thing. It isn't until after lunch that he leaves for the Raiders' offices. Only once, two years ago, did Davis put football in the background. His wife, Carol, suffered a near-fatal heart attack. Davis remained at her side while she was in the hospital's intensive care unit, sleeping next to her in a makeshift bed. He didn't go back to football

10

until she was completely out of danger several weeks later.

"I always said it would take a life-or-death situation to get me away from football, and she put me to the test," said Davis. "She made a remarkable recovery after the doctors said she wouldn't. It certainly makes you believe in the guy upstairs. I don't care what people think, but I certainly believe."

His players believe in him. That also gives him satisfaction. They see him as a person, and many of his critics don't.

"Al Davis is a very special man," exclaimed John Matuszak, who was given a chance by Oakland when no other team would. "Nobody wanted me, but Al took me in. I'll never forget what he did for me. That's the world's greatest man. He cares about players. He cares about those who can make him win, who play when they're hurt, who don't bitch, and who are strong enough to provide leadership for younger players."

It almost sounds like Davis himself. Yet it is that type of philosophy that has made the Raiders a winning team down through the years. Despite his strong personality, Davis has had only three coaches during his reign: John Rauch, John Madden, and Tom Flores.

"John Rauch quit after a few years of coaching here because he said I interfered with his coaching," Davis asserted. "I do interfere. I feel it is my right because of the position I have with the team. My role, however, is to assist, not direct; but I'm more director than inspector. I watch a lot of game films. . . . Tom Flores is a new coach, and I help him. He is bright and intelligent, but I have a right to utilize my intelligence."

The mystique that surrounds Davis will always be there. It doesn't bother him in the least. Those who know him and understand him aren't affected by it at all. Al LoCasale, the Raiders' executive assistant, has been with Davis for twelve years, longer than anyone.

"Mystique, like beauty, is in the eye of the beholder," said LoCasale philosophically. "Al has said many times that we are feared, imitated, respected; and if he had his choice of any of these, he would rather be feared. Al is a forever coach and probably knows as much

football as anybody in this game. He understands players and empathizes with them, and they realize that.

"He knows it's not easy to play football. A quarterback for instance has to keep a lot of

things within himself. He can't go out and have a lot of beers and cuss people out. Al respects the feelings of his football players. There's a closeness. He's not one of those guys who say to a play, 'Hey, tiger, great job,' and won't even know what the player's name is."

TOM FLORES

He was alone now. It gave him an eerie feeling. He looked up and slowly glanced around the Superdome, not seeing anyone. It was only six o'clock in the morning. Even if there was to be a game that day, nobody would be up at that hour. Yet, just twelve hours earlier there had been a game and eighty thousand people yelling on every play in Super Bowl XV. He looked over to where he had stood for over three hours in front of the Oakland bench, easily identifiable in his black sweater and gray slacks. That's how most people recognized Tom Flores, coach of the Oakland Raiders.

It had been a long night or maybe a short one for Flores, depending on how you looked at it. In any event, he'd had to sleep fast. After celebrating the Raiders' storybook victory over the Philadelphia Eagles, Flores did not get to bed until three o'clock. He'd awakened two hours later so that he could be in the Superdome at six for an appearance on *Good Morning, America*. Flores, without a doubt, had to sleep in a hurry, but it was only the beginning of a long day.

When he had finished his interview, Flores looked at his watch. It was only seven o'clock. He still had two hours to kill before his nine o'clock press conference across the street at the Hyatt Regency hotel, which had been bedlam for the past five days, overrun with the nation's press and the usual Super Bowl revelers. Flores seemed to enjoy the morning quiet. He decided to drink several cups of coffee at the hotel's coffee shop until his scheduled press conference. Then all the questions would begin all over again.

"I half expected Ricardo Montalban to tap me on the shoulder with a wake-up call and tell me it was all a fantasy," Flores said, smiling. "I just get a warm feeling all over when I reflect on what's happened to us this season. Winning the Super Bowl was the greatest moment I ever had, and we deserved to win. We didn't do it with any flukes, and we didn't go through any back doors. As a head coach this is the ultimate experience because it's something you yourself have molded. Just a few hours before, I had lived through the greatest moment of my life and being there alone was a lonely feeling. I don't suppose I have much of an image. I've been asked how I feel about getting out from behind John Madden's shadow. I don't know. Have I?"

Few early risers in New Orleans that morning recognized Flores. Only a couple of people thought to ask for his autograph. It didn't seem to bother him. All season long he'd remained one of the more anonymous members of the Raiders. Sadly enough, hardly any of the pro football historians who covered the scene all year even recognized what Flores had accomplished. He wasn't even seriously considered for Coach of the Year—a profound oversight.

No one who has ever coached for Al Davis has ever surfaced as a commanding personality. First there was John Rauch. Ask who coached the Raiders in their first Super Bowl game in 1968, and the answer invariably comes back "Davis." Then there was John Madden who coached the Raiders for a decade during which they won their first Super Bowl in 1977. He has become a much more recognizable personality in the last two years as a television sportscaster. It is commonly accepted that the Raiders are an extension of Davis's personality. This at times could be a hardship for a Raider coach.

In all the years he toiled until a bleeding ulcer forced him into retirement, Madden never fully emerged from Davis's shadow. When Flores replaced Madden, the same stories were heard. The truth is that Davis's presence is so overpowering that the public assumes he is the one orchestrating through a conductor-coach.

"That will always be," said Flores. "Al is such a dynamic person, a tremendous fighter. We talk a lot about philosophies and ideas, like we did when I was assistant coach. I said when I took this job that I would welcome his ideas. I have a good relationship with him."

Actually when Flores was made head coach of the Raiders on February 8, 1979, he honestly had better credentials than Madden. Not only was Flores a past player, but he put in an eight-year apprenticeship as an assistant coach at Buffalo and Oakland. He was on Madden's staff for seven years. Interestingly enough, Davis kept Flores waiting five weeks before naming him to replace Madden.

"Tom is ready to be head coach," said Madden at the time. "He has a lot of experience as a player and a coach. He knows everyone involved—the players, the administration, the setup. These things are important."

The Raiders' philosophy has always been to promote coaches from within the organization. Yet, Davis kept Flores waiting.

"I just wanted to see how he handled pressure," winked Davis. "Tom has strong credentials. He is farther along, football-wise, than any coach we've hired. John Madden was farther along with people. I think you'll find that Tom has an inner strength as tough as anyone from any walk of life. Tom is destined for greatness as a football coach."

Flores's strength was severely tested during the early part of the 1980 season. During his first season, in 1979, he produced a 9-7 record. However, after that lackluster record, the Raiders made several major personnel changes, most notably at quarterback. Ken Stabler was traded to Houston for Dan Pastorini. The new quarterback was being tested and so was Oakland. They had lost two straight games, and the record fell to 2-3. Rumors began circulating around the Bay area that Flores's days as the Raiders' coach were numbered.

"I'd by lying if I said it wasn't disturbing," admitted Flores, "but you have to put those games on the side. You never know how rumors start."

The rumors motivated Gene Upshaw, the veteran guard who is the club's spokesman, to call a team meeting and ask the players to evaluate their contributions. They all agreed that they were easing up late in the week in practice. They were not showing the required degree of intensity which reflected on the team as a whole both mentally and physically on Sunday. The meeting cleared the air. The Raiders began to win, and Flores's job was safe.

"A lot of motivation comes from within," explained Flores. "The biggest thing on this team is that we believe in ourselves. We have from day one. You try to find out why you lost. Did you lose because they were better or because you played poorly? It's hard when

you're not playing consistently, but you have to practice consistently. You don't close up the book after Sunday."

After the players' meeting, the squad became more united in their efforts. Perhaps they needed time to adjust to a different temperament. Madden hollered. Flores was quiet. While Madden was outgoing, Flores was introspective. Flores put in longer practice time which the players frowned on for a while. He concerned himself more with the technical aspect of the game—the X's and O's which involve time and quiet concentration. Flores's workday began at 7:00 A.M., and he never got home much before 11:00 P.M.

Along with all his strategy Flores's major contribution was the amazing turnabout he produced in Jim Plunkett. After Oakland was embarrassed at home by the Kansas City Chiefs, 31–17, for their third defeat in five games, several significant things happened. Plunkett, who had sat on the Oakland bench for two years, became the new quarterback. The players rallied behind both Plunkett and Flores, and Davis decided against a coaching change.

Nobody knew what to expect from Plunkett. He was a crestfallen quarterback who had been on the verge of retiring before the season began. Being a former quarterback himself for a decade, Flores knew how to handle Plunkett. He extended himself, talking with Plunkett for hours at a time, attempting to restore his confidence. He stayed with him after some questionable performances. Slowly, week after week, Plunkett improved, and week after week the Raiders won.

Not that it was so easy. Plunkett started strong, went into a slump for about a month, but came back stronger than ever at the end of the season, into the playoffs, and right through the Super Bowl. All the while, Flores had to keep Plunkett's confidence high and defend his quarterback.

"First he showed us something, then he worried us, then he came on stronger than ever," said Flores. "When we brought Jim in for a tryout in 1978, I ran him through all the quarterback drills there are—the short passes, intermediate, long ones, rollouts, and everything else. He could do it all as well as ever.

"There was a point before Pastorini got hurt when I was considering possibly making a change. Dan was having some problems. He was really pressing. There was a lot of pressure on Dan because he had come into a situation where he was to replace an Oakland legend—Kenny Stabler. Everybody was expecting him to come up with the big play, and I think Dan was trying to do that.

"You don't learn a new system right away, and he was having a few problems moving the ball. So there were a few times when I was contemplating not just making a change but using Jim more. Dan worked hard at trying to be a leader, but Jim had been with us and the players knew him better. He knew the system better and, I think in this respect, leadership comes from that knowledge. Dan was not as knowledgeable about our system as Jim was."

The players responded to Flores after learning, firsthand, how he thought. They learned that a quiet person ought not to be misjudged as a weak one. They realized that as calm as Flores appeared on the surface, especially during a game, he was tense inside. They sensed that since Flores himself had been a player, he knew what their moods and feelings were.

"John Madden had forty-seven different personalities, and he adjusted to us," explained right guard Mickey Marvin. "Coach Flores said, 'I'm going to let them adjust to me.' He was right in the way he handled us. He might not look it, but he's really intense on the sideline. Underneath, he's ready to explode. He's totally into the game. He's thinking three or four plays ahead."

It was Flores's team now. He had them thinking his way. The entire squad was loose, and they began to play that way without feeling any pressure. Still, with all his accomplishments, Flores never truly got the recognition he deserved, especially from the media. If they wrote and said that it was Al Davis's team, then that's what the public believed; but Flores had the respect of his players, and that's all he really cared about.

"They're always going to say that Al Davis runs the team," remarked wide receiver Cliff Branch. "Mr. Davis is a pretty powerful man. He's Oakland's genius. He gets the top publicity. Tom Flores really runs the team. He is the head coach. I resent it when they say Al Davis runs the show. It's not the truth. That's why we hired a head coach—to be a head coach."

Few remember that as a player Flores was the first quarterback Oakland ever had. When the team started in 1960, no fewer than eleven quarterbacks tried out. Flores earned the starting job and was backed up by Babe Parilli. The strong-armed Flores quarterbacked the Raiders during their formative years from 1960 through 1966. He was thereafter traded to Buffalo for Daryle Lamonica. He has some fond memories of the early halcyon years of the old American Football League.

"People would always ask, 'Are you a team?'" recalled Flores. "'Are you professionals?' and 'Where is Oakland?' We'd say: 'You know where San Francisco is? We're right across the bay.' Once, in New York we were paged as the Oklahoma Raiders."

Actually the Raiders played their home games during the first year of their existence in Kezar Stadium, which is in San Francisco. They didn't draw fans. Friends and relatives just barely outnumbered the seagulls. They had to play another year in San Francisco before the Raiders secured a high school field in Oakland for their home games. Flores earned $10,000 his first year, that is, when the checks didn't bounce. But Oakland was home, and he loved playing football.

The league wasn't very organized at its inception. The Raiders had to make a trip to Amherst, Massachusetts, to play the Boston Patriots in the last exhibition game before the league's first season. Arrangements were made for the team to stay and practice at Amherst College, yet nobody told the players.

"We drove around looking for a hotel," said Flores. "Then we looked for a field to practice on. We found a Little League field, but we were kicked off. We taped up in a public facility—a toilet. On another trip to the East, we took a train from New York to Boston, and no one knew where to get off. So we all got off at the wrong spot. We all took cabs from the station to the hotel. Our end, Charlie Powell, missed the train in New York, and he took a

Flores as he appeared when he was the Raiders' quarterback in 1967.

A day after Super Bowl XV, Flores addresses the press.

cab all the way to Boston. We were leaving the hotel and he pays the guy, jumps out of the cab, and goes to practice.

"When we played in New York, you could never see the fans at the Polo Grounds because it was so dark. You'd hear some semblance of a crowd. You'd never know how many people were there, and then they'd announce twenty-five thousand. We had a couple of characters on the team. One was Dan Manoukian. He quit and became a pro wrestler because he could make more money. Another was Dan Birdwell. He was just a big teddy bear or a bull in a china shop. He didn't know his own strength. He'd always step on your shoes in the huddle. If you needed a dollar, he'd give you his last one and then go borrow one. One time he had a knee injury. He got tired of the cast, so he took it off."

Flores played with Buffalo for two years and finished his playing career with the Kansas City Chiefs the next two years. He didn't play much as a backup to Len Dawson but Hank Stram, who coached the Chiefs then, remembered Flores.

"I never saw anyone stay in the pocket as long as Tom did," said Stram. "He would hold the ball and take the shot. Right before he got the shot, he'd get rid of the ball. He was utterly fearless. Tom was a very keen student of the game. He had a good understanding of the passing game—very logical, low-key in his approach.

"One day we were playing Houston on a sloppy, muddy day in Kansas City. There was a real torrential storm going on. Dawson was out with an injury that day, and Tom was the holder for kicks. We decided to fake a field

Offensive line coach Sam Bogoshian, center, looks concerned as Flores gives instructions to quarterback Jim Plunkett.

Biting his lip, Flores waits to answer announcer Bryant Gumble's question.

goal. Flores took the snap, rolled to his left, and hit Bobby Holmes, who went all the way for the touchdown. In the process Flores got a shot in the 'smoosh,' and it broke his nose. That's the only pass he threw for us, and it went for a touchdown."

The broken nose Stram talked of wasn't the only one Flores suffered as a quarterback. He had several others, and it reached a point where the doctors couldn't do anything anymore. Despite the crooked nose, which makes him resemble a young Jake LaMotta, Flores has boyish good looks.

Broken noses and injuries were all a concern to his mother, Nellie, when Flores signed to play with the Raiders that first year. She remembers her son being carried off the field on a stretcher when he played at the College of the Pacific.

"He told me not to worry because they aren't allowed to touch the quarterback in the pros," recalled his mother. "Well, it didn't take long before I found out that he was only trying to make me feel good. Football was always the love of Tom's life. But, to tell you the truth, Tom made me nervous when he played.

I know he's a coach now and can't get hurt, but he still makes me nervous.

"Sonny—that's what we called him—never mentioned to us that he wanted to play pro ball. That is just something that happened. He went to college to become a teacher. Sonny was always a quiet boy who kept everything to himself. He once had a bad stomachache and went to the doctor. The doctor told him he was going to develop an ulcer. Instead of giving him medication, the doctor told him to lock himself in the garage and bang on the walls for a while."

There was a time during Flores's youth when there weren't any walls to bang on. His father, Tom, Sr., was born in Guadalajara, Mexico. His mother was born in Sanger in California's San Joaquin Valley. Both parents were farm workers. Flores remembers his childhood when he joined his parents in the field picking fruit for three cents a tray.

"I picked plums, peaches, apricots, apples—you name it," said Flores. "We worked in the farm areas of the San Fernando Valley. I did it through elementary school and junior high. We had a very proud family, and

we all had to work together to make a way of life. I guess one of the reasons that I am quiet is that I think about the way that I established myself. When I worked the field, the family knew that we were on the right track. You acquired good habits because you had so little time for anything else.

"I was five or six when I first began picking grapes. There were no child labor laws then, and I didn't think it was strange for little kids to be picking fruit. Everyone did it. It was what was done."

Ironically Flores and Plunkett have similar backgrounds. Both were born of poor Mexican-American parents and rose in the pro ranks as quarterbacks. It could be the reason why Plunkett related to Flores during that critical period when he had to turn the Raiders around. The chemistry was there from the beginning.

"When I first came up as a quarterback, nobody paid any attention to the fact that I was Hispanic," said Flores. "Times have changed. The Hispanic community has changed; it's grown more vocal. They have some heroes—a Lee Trevino, a Trini Lopez. It's all a lot bigger now.

"I feel very good about it . . . very proud about being the first Chicano quarterback, the first Chicano coach. I can sense there are people who care about what I do because of what I am. I get the feeling they are very proud and happy. They see me on *Monday Night Football*. That means something, to be recognized by your people. Not 'your people' really, but people of your background. I came to realize that there are people who identify with me."

Most of Flores's players, especially Plunkett, feel that he needs to receive more recognition for what he has achieved.

"Tom doesn't get all the credit he deserves," remarked Plunkett. "He is the coach, and he's done a great job."

"I think the reason Tom doesn't get the publicity is that he doesn't promote himself," observed wide receiver Bob Chandler. "You hear about Don Coryell and San Diego, and Chuck Knox and Buffalo, but you don't hear about Tom. He suffers from it in the long run, but I

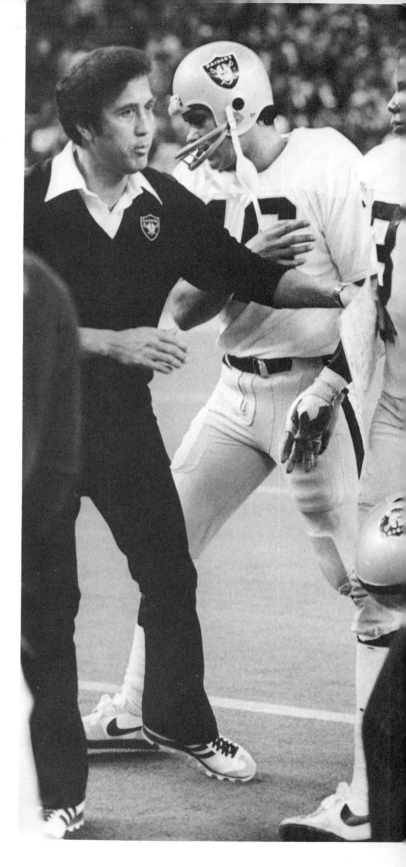

don't know if it is that important to him. I think the most important thing to him is that the players appreciate him, and they do. I have never, never heard anybody say anything bad about Tom Flores."

JIM PLUNKETT

All week long he couldn't sleep. He was too excited. During the long hours of the night he would lie awake creating different game situations. He would read a blitz and then throw a quick pass for a big gain or maybe a touchdown. In his mind he would see a cornerback playing too tight; he'd throw a long one over his head for a touchdown. The adrenaline was flowing ever so quickly at a time when sleep wasn't that important. After all, he hadn't felt this excited in ten years. It was almost as if he was a rookie again. That's when football is fun—full of hopes and dreams. All too quickly they can disappear into doubts and anguish, torment and pain. Jim Plunkett knew it well. He'd lived through it all, but at the age of thirty-two he was dreaming again.

During the week before Super Bowl XV Plunkett was the busiest athlete in New Orleans. He was the one most sought after by the news media, wanting to know all about his Cinderfella story . . . about how he rose from the junkyard of broken dreams to lead the Oakland Raiders on what seemed to be an impossible journey to the top of the football world. Patiently, quietly, he answered their hundreds of questions. Only in the quiet of his room could he relax and dream.

"I've been waiting for this one for a long time," sighed Plunkett. "I lie awake in bed at night thinking of situations in the game, things I'll do. I think of how sweet this tastes, no matter what happens. It comes down to one game now, and whatever happened before doesn't mean much anymore—just what we do on Sunday. This is the best team I've ever played with. They're a bunch of guys with talents and experience.

"Ten years at the bottom is tough to take. It's been a long road, and I haven't had time yet to sit down and reflect on what has really happened. It's all come so fast, and been so good, and I've been too busy. Maybe later I will."

No doubt he will. Plunkett is a deeply sensitive man who didn't believe the cheers of the crowd could ever change so quickly to demoralizing boos. In one year he had plummeted from being an idol to being a bum. It had been a new experience for him, and he'd been shaken by it. The entire world of professional football had been strange to him. An introvert by nature, Plunkett wanted to withdraw even more. He couldn't understand how the fans in New England could cheer him when he was Rookie of the Year in 1971, then turn around and boo him the next season. He didn't complain; he just wondered. It was only when he would leave the Boston area after the football season and return to the area around San Jose and Atherton, California, that he would find inner peace.

Plunkett was a special person. He had to be to rise from the poverty-scarred streets of San Jose to a level of football excellence that few have known. His parents were Mexican-American, but what made them different was the fact that they both were blind. Although they were on welfare, Jim's father operated a newsstand in the San Jose post office building. He worked and saved enough to buy a modest home near the barrio and provide for his son and two daughters.

Plunkett's childhood memories aren't very pleasant. He doesn't talk too much about them. He worked all sorts of odd jobs to help out: delivering newspapers, stacking groceries at a local market, and pumping gas when he got older. All the time Plunkett's security blanket was athletics.

"I used to work at a grocery store after school," Plunkett recalled. "I did odd jobs, made deliveries, and helped clean the place up. At other times I sold newspapers and also worked at a gas station. When I got older, I did construction work. That was hard. We were always digging, or lifting, or carrying heavy things; but I made more money, so the work was worth it."

Plunkett was big for his age. He was also popular. Since he was a good athlete, he was a leader in the playground and in school. Although he played baseball and basketball, he preferred football. However, as a fifth-grader he still didn't engage in contact football at school.

"We only played touch and flag football then," said Plunkett. "They didn't let ten- and eleven-year-olds play tackle. That was good. We could learn about the game and not risk a serious injury. It was still a rough game. I hurt my ankle in the sixth grade and had to play guard because I couldn't run well enough to

play in the backfield."

At the time, Plunkett's knees began bothering him. When he finally went to a doctor to have them checked, he was told that he had a temporary bone disease that at times affects children who grow too fast. Plunkett didn't play football again for about a year.

Entering eighth grade Plunkett was already five eleven and weighed 150 pounds. Instead of a lineman he was now the quarterback simply because he could throw a football better than anyone else. He became the school's star player and led them to the county championship. Plunkett earned a reputation in other sports. He skillfully participated on the wrestling and basketball teams and competed on the track team as a high jumper. Because of his strong arm he was also pitcher for the baseball squad.

When Plunkett entered James Lick High School, he was a highly regarded athlete. Naturally he gravitated to football. His coach back then, Al Cementina, is still coaching there. He completed his twenty-fifth year in 1980. He remembers the first time he saw Plunkett on the field.

"He was standing on the twenty yard line at one end of the field, and he threw the football right through the goal posts on the other end," recalled Cementina. "Later he looked up at me and said, 'I guess a hurricane just came up.' He wasn't a loud guy. He never went 'Hey, hey, hey' and slapped guys on the butt or anything like that. He was just a natural leader.

"Jim was a five-sport athlete: football, wrestling, baseball, basketball, and track. He was an athlete three hundred sixty-five days a year. I used to play a trick on the other teams we'd play. I'd walk Jim past their dressing room and holler: 'Hey, you guys, this is our quarterback. Wait until you see our tackles.' By the time he was a senior he was six three and weighed two hundred fifteen pounds."

In his final year Plunkett led his team to a 9-0 record. He was named to the all-league team. He earned a spot playing in the North-South Shrine Game in Los Angeles. The coaches were so impressed with his size that they played Plunkett at defensive end. He got to throw only two passes. Yet he didn't complain. That wasn't his nature.

Plunkett had a number of college offers, from Stanford, Santa Clara, North Carolina, and the University of California, to name a few. He chose Stanford.

"I picked Stanford for two reasons," Plunkett revealed. "It was close to home. I could be near my parents, plus the school had a great academic reputation. It really wasn't a difficult choice for me. I consulted with my coach, Al Cementina, but it was my decision. Cementina was like a father to me, and I'll never forget all the help he gave me during my high school years. I was lucky to have someone who took such a personal interest in me. He was a good friend who always had my interests at heart. He gave me his opinion, but he felt I was capable of making the ultimate decision, and he was right."

It was a big decision for Plunkett, but he made it. He realized early in life that although he worked to help his parents out and enjoyed family life with them, he had to seek out opportunities for himself. Football was only part of it. Making certain that he got an education was the other part.

"I knew back then that I would have to work hard for everything that I got," said Plunkett. "I figured the only way I could compete with everybody else was to work a little harder than they did. I felt I needed something extra to get by. So I went out for cross-country, and I ran track. I just did everything to get into a little better shape. I clearly remember something that was said to me. It sticks in the back of my mind. My junior high coach said: 'Wait until you get some coordination. Then we'll see what you can do.' "

Cementina remembered when he first talked to the Stanford coaches about Plunkett. They had some reservations about him; still Plunkett got his scholarship.

"I remember talking to John Ralston, who was the head coach at the time, and to Dick Vermeil, who was his assistant; and I was telling them about how well Jim would perform at Stanford," said Cementina. "Vermeil said, 'Yeah, but he's never performed before ninety thousand spectators.' "

At the beginning it wasn't easy. When Plunkett arrived at Stanford for his physical, the

Plunkett's pro career began with the New England Patriots.

In college, Plunkett won the Heisman Trophy, 1970 his final year at Stanford.

doctors discovered a tumor on his neck. They told him he would have to have an operation. Frightened at first, Plunkett refused. However, the doctors convinced Plunkett that he would be able to play football. As it happened, Plunkett missed most of his freshman season and only managed to play in the final three games. He wasn't impressive at all on the frosh team. His timing wasn't quite right, and he couldn't seem to connect with his receivers.

"The operation really shook me up," admitted Plunkett. "The doctors told me that if it was cancerous, I could forget football. At that time I couldn't imagine my life without it. I was scared, really scared. At first I said I wouldn't have the operation. I guess I thought if I ignored it, it would go away, but my parents understood the situation and talked me into going through with it. Well, they operated, and fortunately it was benign."

Disappointed with his showing as a freshman, Plunkett was determined to make up for it in his sophomore season. He couldn't wait for spring practice and a new beginning. After all, he still had three years of varsity ball ahead of him. However, his disappointment continued through the spring; he still didn't appear ready.

"I really had a poor spring," revealed Plunkett. "Nothing seemed to work right. I wasn't throwing the ball as well as I knew I could, and it was obvious that I had a long way to go. I still thought I could play in the fall, but the quarterback position was jammed up, and I really didn't get an opportunity to break into the lineup.

"When Coach Ralston told me I wouldn't make the trip to Oregon State for the opener, I was really down. During the season when one of the quarterbacks got hurt, I thought I'd finally get a chance to play even though there were just two games left. The coaches talked to me, and we all decided it was silly to throw away a whole year of eligibility so late in the season. So I red-shirted, which still left me with three years of football.

"The whole thing seemed like a bad dream. I went to Stanford with such high hopes, and

A big Raider welcome for Plunkett.

after two years I had nothing to show for it. Football had been awful, my grades weren't as good as I had hoped, and I wasn't even making friends. I guess all three were related, but it was a definite low point."

By 1968 it all started to fall into place for Plunkett. He was established as the team's regular quarterback, and he led Stanford to a 6-3-1 season. The next year he picked up right where he'd left off, leading Stanford to a 7-2-1 record and establishing several Pac Eight passing records along the way. Because he had red-shirted, Plunkett was eligible for the NFL draft. There was some speculation that he might declare himself a prospect. Plunkett didn't hesitate in saying that he would return to Stanford for his final year of football. The Stanford coaches were relieved. They were thinking ahead to the Rose Bowl.

"I didn't look upon it as a big deal," claimed Plunkett. "The press people made a big fuss about the whole thing, writing about the big contract I'd get and how good it was. The way I looked at it, I wanted to go back and finish my last year. I knew we had a shot at the conference title and the Rose Bowl. Those things were really on my mind.

"Also, there were some other people to consider. All of my coaches and teammates had been building something for three years. If I left, I would always have the feeling that I let them down. Besides, we were always telling kids not to drop out, to finish their schooling, to achieve the goals they work for. What would they think if I dropped out to play pro ball?"

Plunkett had a most memorable season his final year at Stanford. He sparked the Indians to an 8-3 record and into the Rose Bowl for the first time since 1952. Personally, Plunkett continued his assault on the Pac Eight record books as well as the NCAA ledgers. He was awarded numerous national honors, the most distinguished of which were the Heisman Trophy and the Maxwell Award. He wasn't done yet. He saved his best for last. Plunkett carried Stanford to a 27–17 upset over number 1-ranked Ohio State in the Rose Bowl.

There was some concerned speculation about whether or not the lowly New England Patriots would make Plunkett the top pick in the 1971 draft. Finishing another losing season with the worst record in the NFL, the Patriots earned the distinction of having the first draft choice because of their 2-12 record. Speculation centered around two avenues of thought. One was that if the Patriots traded their choice, they could obtain two or possibly three proven veterans who could give them instant help. The other was that since New England obtained the veteran Joe Kapp in a trade with the Minnesota Vikings, they wouldn't need another quarterback.

It's a recognized fact in the demanding world of professional football that quarterbacks coming out of college in their first year with the pros never lead winning teams. There's no way they can be expected to do so. With the real possibility that the Patriots were thinking along these lines, a local Boston newspaper ran a poll among its readers. The result was that out of 763 persons questioned seventy-four percent wanted the Patriots to draft the Stanford star.

"You'd better tell them to keep him here," said one. "I think owner Billy Sullivan has pulled enough boners already."

"Keep Plunkett, keep Kapp, and trade the rest of the crummy team," another disillusioned fan said.

If the Patriots' management harbored any doubts, then Kapp himself dispelled them.

"If you ask me whether they should draft Plunkett, I'll tell you," remarked Kapp. "When you've got the first draft pick, you take the best player in the country. I've watched Plunkett. He was by far the best I saw."

The Patriots were convinced. Besides, Kapp was thirty-four years old, and Plunkett could learn from the veteran who had led the Vikings to the Super Bowl in 1970. It was quite logical. However, a startling turn of events took place which upset the entire timetable. While Plunkett was in Chicago preparing to play in the College All-Star Game, Kapp left the Patriots' training camp. The NFL ruled that since Kapp didn't sign the mandatory standard NFL player contract, he could not indeed sign a contract with New England. The headstrong Kapp refused and filed a lawsuit against the NFL.

When Plunkett finally arrived at the Patriots' training camp he was shocked to learn of Kapp's departure. He had no illusions about being the number one quarterback, but he had expected to play and learn from Kapp in the process. Besides the rookie Plunkett, all that New England had in quarterback talent was backup veteran Mike Taliaferro. New England fans looked upon Plunkett as the savior. It was indeed a lot to ask of a rookie. Plunkett sensed a different atmosphere.

"I had to cram to catch up," said Plunkett. "I felt as if I was preparing for final exams. I had to learn the Patriots' plays and terminology. It's natural that quarterbacks carry a degree of authority, but to be completely effective the quarterback must have the full respect of his team. That kind of confidence can't be gained from a playbook.

"I could see how Terry Bradshaw felt frustrated. There are things I did in college that you feel you can do up here, but when you first try them they just don't work. I knew there were going to be setbacks, and I also knew there would be progress. As long as the frustration didn't linger on and bother me too much, it was okay.

"That's what happened to Bradshaw. The frustration just overwhelmed him. He began thinking so much about his performances that he couldn't concentrate on the ball game. I didn't know whether his unfortunate experience would help me out or not. Since we were different people with different ball clubs, you couldn't really compare the situation, but I knew what to watch out for."

For a rookie, especially one in the hot seat, Plunkett had a remarkable year. He led the Patriots to a 6-8 season, their best performance since 1966. Plunkett also set a rookie record for touchdown passes with 19. Since he threw only 16 interceptions, it was indeed a productive first year.

"I didn't know what to expect when I came into professional football," reflected Plunkett. "As a result I didn't know what I could or couldn't do, especially as a rookie. At times I thought I was doing a good job, doing good things on the field, things I knew should be done during a ball game. The coaches showed me the basics as far as play calling and defense were concerned.

"But there were still times when I felt I wasn't throwing the ball as well as I should. It might have been because of my concentration. I was often split between mechanics, reading defenses, and thinking about the offense. I always had great confidence in my passing. I thought I could pass against anyone, but you just couldn't do it against certain teams and certain defenses. I had to become better at reading defenses and exploiting them. Overall, I wish I had done a lot better."

It didn't get better. Although he started every one of the Patriots' games the first four seasons, statistically Plunkett didn't improve. He threw more interceptions than he did touchdown passes, and only once, in 1974, did he match the 19 touchdowns he threw his rookie season. During that time he was sacked a total of 112 times. When Chuck Fairbanks arrived to lead the Patriots out of the wilderness with his option plays, Plunkett ended up with a shoulder separation. Physically Plunkett

A quarterback's job isn't always a glamorous one.

was taking more than his share of blows. The Patriots' overall team performance diminished each year, and Plunkett couldn't carry the team alone. No player could. Then the injuries began to mount—now a shoulder, then a knee—and the aches and pains came with greater intensity. His back bothered him; his ribs were caved in. He was becoming a physical wreck. Psychologically, his confidence was being shattered. He appeared timid and unsure of himself. After being injured again during the 1975 season, he asked the Patriots to trade him. He couldn't take the beatings anymore and wanted a fresh start somewhere else.

Through it all Plunkett never complained. Game after game he would stand in front of his locker and answer the hard questions about the sacks, the interceptions, the defeats. He never once pointed the finger of blame at anyone else. Somehow Plunkett managed to survive. Only now it was time to leave.

The spring of 1976 gave Plunkett new hope. The Patriots traded him to San Francisco. Plunkett was going back home. The price was high. The 49ers surrendered quarterback Tom Owens and four draft choices. However, when a new general manager, Joe Thomas, took over the fortunes of the 49ers, he didn't look too favorably on Plunkett. He wanted to install an entire new offense, and the thirty-year-old Plunkett didn't figure in his plans. In the two years Plunkett played for the 49ers, he continued to take a beating. Each year he threw more interceptions than touchdowns. The booing continued. It left Plunkett demoralized. It was New England all over again. Was this the end?

The coaching changes in San Francisco could be compared to the proverbial revolving door. In his first season there, in 1976, Plunkett played under Monte Clark. The following season it was Ken Meyer. After the 1977 season Pete McCulley took over. A short time later Plunkett was gone. He was placed on waivers, and none of the other twenty-seven teams would claim him for the paltry sum of $100. Plunkett had hit bottom. It was a shocking fact for him. He wasn't worth a lousy $100.

Dejected, he went home. There was no other place for him to go. He couldn't believe he'd ended up by the side of the road, unwanted. He tried to sort out his options. It all came up the same. He wanted to play football. He knew he could still play, and hey, he was only thirty years old. Some quarterbacks never begin to peak until then. All he wanted was a chance, just one opportunity to prove that he still could play.

Finally, after a week someone called. It was Al Davis. He invited Plunkett to try out for the Oakland Raiders. Plunkett said that he would come out. He had too much pride to be cast aside without showing what he really could do. Still, it would be traumatic to be put on trial again.

"When San Francisco let me go, that was the real low point in my life," disclosed Plunkett. "It was probably the most depressing in my life. I had to have the help of some people, particularly my mother, to keep my spirits up. There were times when I'd given up hope. I had thought about retiring. I had some businesses, but I wanted to give football another try. Oakland was near home, so . . ."

Plunkett tried out with the Raiders under the watchful eyes of Davis, coach John Madden, and quarterback coach Tom Flores. After the session the Raider braintrust conferred. Davis and Flores wanted to sign Plunkett. Madden didn't. He was perfectly content with Ken Stabler and David Humm. Who needed another quarterback, much less one nobody else wanted?

By 1978 Plunkett had become a Raider. He sat behind Stabler and Humm, never getting into a game, never throwing a pass. Davis told him to be patient, to learn the system and rest his weary body. The Raiders finished 9-7 that year and missed the playoffs for the first time in six years. All Plunkett did was wear the headsets and walk the sidelines like a forgotten mannequin.

After the season Madden retired, and Flores was made head coach. Oakland was still Stabler's town. However, Flores hadn't forgotten about Plunkett.

"I remember Plunkett's first season with the Raiders," Flores confided. "I called across the field for him, and he didn't respond. Maybe it

Before joining the Raiders, Plunkett played for the San Francisco 49ers for two years.

was the way I asked for him. I called, 'Hey, rookie.' "

That was the approach the Raiders took. Psychologically, it was vital. They wanted to impress Plunkett with the idea that his new opportunity with the Raiders would be as if he was first starting in pro football. It seemed to relax Plunkett. He understood what it would take, and he accepted it.

"When he first came to us, I could see he'd had enough pressure to last him awhile," continued Flores. "Everybody expected him to produce immediately at New England as a kid right out of Stanford. When he got to San Francisco, everybody expected him to produce right away there, too, even though they didn't have enough talented players for any quarterback to be successful. It seemed to us the best way to let him know that the pressure was off was to treat him like a rookie.

"He learned the system at his own pace. We made him feel at home. We wanted him to be eager to play before he had to play."

In 1979 Plunkett, still in a remote backup role, threw a total of 15 passes and saw action in four games. That was hardly encouraging. The Raiders again finished with a 9-7 record and missed the playoffs for the second straight year. Stabler was still considered the leader, and Plunkett had resigned himself to being strictly a reserve.

During the spring of 1980 in a surprise move, Stabler was traded to Houston for Dan Pastorini. Coincidentally enough, Plunkett's and Pastorini's careers corresponded. Like Plunkett, Pastorini had a strong arm; like Plunkett, Pastorini was from the Bay area. When Plunkett was at Stanford, Pastorini was playing at Santa Clara; and, like Plunkett, Pastorini wanted to be traded to another team. While the trade sent tremors through the Oakland area, Plunkett wondered what it all meant as far as he was concerned. He waited until training camp to find out.

It seemed only logical that no one would trade a first-string quarterback to another team for someone who would be considered a good backup. Davis told him again to be patient, to keep plugging. His friends also encouraged him while he patiently tried to determine his status. Plunkett went to training camp that summer with the determination to compete for the starting job. However, when it was obvious that Pastorini would be the starter, Plunkett felt it was time to talk with Flores.

"They announced that he'd be the starter," remarked Plunkett, "but I thought I'd still have a chance to compete for the job. It didn't work out that way, and after the second preseason game I went to Tom and asked him to trade me. I wanted to play somewhere, I didn't care where; but Tom said he was happy with the way I was working, and he didn't want me to leave. So I was still the backup. I didn't feel I'd gotten a proper shot, but I figured, okay, I'll stay around and see what happens."

Then fate intervened. In the fifth game of the season against Kansas City, Pastorini broke his leg. Plunkett replaced him. He wasn't exactly the Raiders' ray of hope. He threw 5 interceptions as the Raiders suffered their third defeat in five games. With Pastorini finished for the year, everyone in football wrote Oakland off. The Raiders turned to Plunkett to help them turn the season around. Fans were not optimistic.

Plunkett hung tough until, week after week and little by little, his confidence grew. The Raiders rallied around him. Plunkett was earning their respect. In his first start in three years Plunkett led the Raiders to an upset over the favored San Diego Chargers, who were picked to win the Western Division by just showing up every week. Then he led them over Pittsburgh, Seattle, Miami, Cincinnati, and Seattle again. Before anyone could ask if Plunkett was for real, Oakland had won six straight games.

The momentum was building every week. When the season finally ended, Plunkett had won ten of the twelve games in which he'd started and had gotten the Raiders into the playoffs. As always, there were the skeptics.

They all seemed to agree that he would fold in the playoffs, that he would revert to the "old" Plunkett—timid and unsure. In all three play-off games in which they appeared, the Raiders were the underdog. All three times Plunkett led them to victory, with a spectacular performance against San Diego in the AFC championship game.

After the game he really felt he belonged . . . that he was part of the Raiders. George Blanda, a former Raider hero for many years, walked into the Raider dressing room to congratulate Plunkett. As former quarterback, in addition to being an outstanding kicker, Blanda appreciated the game Plunkett played.

"I've never seen a quarterback play a better game," Blanda praised. "Statistically, he was almost perfect. He scrambled for a touchdown, he scrambled for first downs, he threw the ball as accurately as it could be thrown. He was just outstanding."

Blanda extended his congratulations to Plunkett.

"Everybody in Oakland still thinks number sixteen is you," laughed Plunkett.

"I don't have that big a butt," needled Blanda.

"I need it," Plunkett answered, smiling.

Cliff Branch was dressing at the locker next to Plunkett. He saw Blanda and shook his head.

"The ghost still lives," remarked Branch, referring to the fact that Plunkett wore the same number that Blanda had. "You don't win a Heisman Trophy if you're not a winner, and Jim Plunkett was a winner today. He brought us to the Super Bowl. Jim had been playing too much with people who didn't have enough talent, but now he's with the Raiders. I knew his chance would come, even if he didn't. Pastorini didn't know the system, and Jim does."

Davis came by. He had a smirk on his face.

"Plunkett did it, huh?" he said almost sarcastically. "He thought he was winning the Rose Bowl again."

Not quite. Plunkett had one more game to win—the Super Bowl.

"Even if I hadn't gotten this far, I think this year I proved that I can play," remarked Plunkett.

THE OFFENSE

Although the players change, the pattern is the same. Down through the years the Raiders have always advocated the big play. It was the catalyst that Al Davis added to the chemistry of Oakland's offense. Davis had mastered the "big bomb" offense while serving as an assistant for three years under Sid Gillman at San Diego. When he took over the Raiders in 1963, Davis brought that highly volatile passing attack with him. It is still the single most explosive element in the Oakland repertoire.

The Raiders have never been a team to make changes at quarterback. First there was Tom Flores, then Cotton Davidson for a year, followed by the Daryle Lamonica and Ken Stabler eras. All had the same characteristic—a strong arm that could throw the ball deep to a fast wide receiver. Not that the offense was geared strictly to facilitate the long bomb, but it was there in the Raiders' arsenal and it was an ominous threat every moment. The Raiders always worked the short and intermediate passing game. However, the thought of the long pass would occupy the minds of the opposing defenders, which made the shorter passing game that much more effective.

The blueprint for the passing game required certain types of receivers. There were the speedy ones like Warren Wells, Art Powell, and Cliff Branch, and the pattern runners like Fred Biletnikoff and Bob Chandler. It also called for the heavy duty backs like Clem Daniels, Hewritt Dixon, Marv Hubbard, and Mark van Eeghen who could provide extra blocking, plus the quicker backs like Charlie Smith and Kenny King who could run or receive. Blend them together with a big, protective offensive line, mix in a pass-catching tight end, and that's what the Raiders look like even today.

"To stop Oakland, the first thing you have to do is take away the bomb," explained receiver coach Lew Erber. "A lot of people don't have the threat, and some others don't believe in it. Our philosophy has always been to attack. How many times do you have to run the ball to gain fifteen yards? Four times? Five times? We'll get that in one shot. We'll always throw the football, and we'll throw it up the field. Very rarely do our quarterbacks even look laterally.

"You need three things to make it work. You've got to have a line that can protect; you've got to have a quarterback that can see the whole field, and you've got to have re-

ceivers that can get open. The Raider quarterback has always called his own plays. We put a lot of pressure on our quarterbacks.

"We always go for a speed guy like Branch, a move guy like Chandler, and a tight end like [Ray] Chester who can go deep down the middle. We've always had that threat deep up the middle with our tight end. Pittsburgh is about the only other team that does some of the things we do with our tight end. Everywhere else they just expect them to catch hooks and cuts.

"The Raider fullback has to be a good blocker. We keep the fullback in the pocket a good fifty percent of the time to insure that added time the quarterback needs to pass. We've broken more big plays since Kenny King has been here, but basically we're a tackle-to-tackle team. The fullback has always been the workhorse. There is never any substitute for speed, and that's why we want to get our halfbacks one-on-one with a linebacker. We always want to get the halfback out in the pattern to use his running ability."

Nobody has more of an understanding of what the Oakland offensive scheme is than Gene Upshaw. The veteran guard completed his fourteenth season in 1980, more than any other Raider. Upshaw has played in 202 consecutive games and 24 postseason contests. He has never missed a Raider game, during regular season or preseason, which is quite an accomplishment for a thirty-five-year-old star.

It's an established fact that the Raiders like to run left. They have demonstrated that characteristic down through the years, and it's not difficult to understand why. In Upshaw and tackle Art Shell the Raiders probably have the two best linemen in the NFL playing next to each other. Upshaw and Shell are the leaders of the line. Both are big, strong, and quick. Gene Upshaw joined the Raiders in 1967 as a first-round draft pick from Texas A & I. He is considered one of the finest pulling guards in the league.

"I've played every game since 1967, and they are certainly adding up," said Upshaw. "I'm afraid to talk about it because something might happen. I think the key to staying

healthy is not what you do during the season but in the off-season. I remember when I was a rookie that John Madden told me that football players are made from January to July, not from July to September. It's true. I've always remembered that. You have to maintain what you have."

What Upshaw has is a great deal of pride. He enjoys the battle on the line and looks forward to getting the job done, whether it's on the field or in the locker room. Upshaw has been the Raiders' captain for over a decade and as the team's spokesman has quite a bit to do with maintaining harmony. It was Upshaw

Veteran running back Mark van Eeghen has not only demonstrated durability but also dependability.

Quarterback Dan Pastorini broke his leg during the fifth game of the season.

37

who called a team meeting after the Raiders dropped their third game of the 1980 season; and it was Upshaw who kept reminding the players that they hadn't won anything yet during the playoffs, only the chance to play again next week.

He speaks with authority because he has lived through the experience. He is the only Raider to have been in all three Super Bowl games in which Oakland played—Super Bowls II, XI, and XV—and he still has vivid memories of that first 1967 battle against the Green Bay Packers when he was a twenty-one-year-old rookie.

"What came out of that game was the knowledge that it's pretty tough on a team that doesn't know what it's like to be in the playoffs," recalls Upshaw. "We treated it like a college bowl game. We didn't know what to do. We had never even been to the playoffs before. I was just happy as hell to be playing. I didn't have anything else to do. I didn't have the slightest idea what it would be like. It was a growing thing.

"We weren't in awe of the Packers, although they may have been the best football team in the world at the time. We were just in awe of being there. Hell, I stood out and watched halftime. They had those two big guys wearing Packer and Raider uniforms walking around

Acquired before the 1980 season, running back Kenny King gave the Raider ground attack an added dimension.

blowing smoke. It was great. I was out there looking at all that stuff.

"We forgot that we were players; but you know, we never thought we were in trouble until Herb Adderley intercepted that pass and ran for a touchdown that made the score 33-7 in the fourth quarter. Even though we lost, we felt we just hadn't shown what we could do. I really thought that we would go to seven or eight Super Bowls in a row, but it didn't work out that way. When we finally got back to the second one, I decided we'd be players this time."

And they were. In 1977 the Raiders thrashed the Minnesota Vikings 32–14 in Super Bowl XI. It was a picture-book victory. The Raiders were practically perfect, both offensively and defensively. A lot of experts felt that Upshaw and Shell should have been named the game's most valuable players for the way they handled Minnesota's defensive line. The Raiders ran left whenever they wanted, and the ample pass blocking practically allowed Stabler to sit back in a rocker and throw.

"I realized the game was under control when we took over on the two yard line and drove all the way down there in the fiirst period," remembered Upshaw. "You have to make them pay for it. That's what it is all about—a pit battle—and we took it to them. You can talk all you want about your Biletnikoffs and Tarkentons and Stablers, but if you can't dominate the line of scrimmage, nobody makes a yard.

"We didn't make any adjustments. We just played our game. We knew if we tired them out, things would start happening. You get to the line, and you see one of their guys blowing hard. You see his jersey moving up and down. You know you're wearing him out. You know you've got him."

It is this kind of leadership that Upshaw brought to Super Bowl XV. It is what makes him so valuable to the Raiders. He embodies the spirit of the Raiders, and his influence is formidable. He is looked up to and respected by the younger players even though he is considered the "old guard." Upshaw realizes that there is a new breed of athlete in the game

Scat back Arthur Whittington.

today.

"I haven't gotten that purse to carry around like they do," teases Upshaw, referring to the bag that players prefer instead of an old-fashioned wallet. "They think a lot differently than we did. I don't sit in a corner like a grouchy old man, but they do talk a different language."

Still, during the week of Super Bowl XV, Upshaw set the tone. He kept reminding the players where it was all at—especially the ones who had never appeared in a Super Bowl before. He didn't want a repeat of 1967. The thought of failure moved him to make certain none of the others lost perspective.

"We have to realize that we haven't done anything yet," Upshaw told them. "There will be a carnival atmosphere down there. We have guys who have never been interviewed, and soon they'll be asked questions by guys who can't even speak English. We all have to remember we're still football players. We're not there to enjoy that carnival atmosphere. You can't forget you're there with a helmet, not a ticket. We're there drinking Gatorade, not beer. We're not there for the parties, we're there to make history."

Upshaw also wants to make history on another front. He has serious thoughts about running for governor of the state of California when he retires. His teammates already address him as such, but while he is still active in football, he also wants to be the first two-term president of the National Football League Players Association. He strongly believes that the only reason why his activities with the players' union haven't cost him his job is that Al Davis wouldn't allow such a thing to happen. His brother Marvin, who had been a starter with the Kansas City Chiefs, was suddenly out of a job. Marvin had also been active in the association and Upshaw puts the blame on the pro football establishment.

"They figured when they did that, I would get softer at the bargaining table, but I didn't. I got tougher."

Right guard Mickey Marvin.

Part of the harder line Upshaw took was on the free agent system. It is not as prevalent in football as it is in baseball. In football, compensation is awarded to the team which loses a player to another club. The amount of compensation is decided by the commissioner. Upshaw claims the players are not advocating more liberal compensation terms.

"That's the biggest crock of bull I've ever heard," remarked Upshaw. "None of us control how many tickets are sold. The Super Bowl will still sell out regardless of whether Jim Plunkett, Ron Jaworski, or I am there. We're not interested in free agency. We are interested in a percentage of gross income.

"Free agency doesn't work. The owners aren't going to bid for players. Why should a guy go out and increase his payroll. He's not going to make any more money. They've already got a certain amount for tickets, television, NFL Properties. They're all in business together. It's not like any other sport. There's no incentive to win in the NFL. There's a number of owners who think winning is more important than gross profit, but there aren't enough of those guys."

There also aren't enough guys like Art Shell. Most of the time when people talk about Upshaw, they mention Shell in the same breath. It's natural. After all, they've played next to each other for over ten years. Some marriages don't even last that long.

"To me, offensive tackle is the toughest position in the league as far as line play is concerned," said Shell. "It's a very lonely world out there. I kid Gene about this. If you're playing guard, you've got someone on each side of you. You've got the tackle for a cushion and the center to help you out in case you get into trouble.

"If you're a tackle and you set up to pass-block, the defensive end has two lanes in which to beat you. He can beat you inside, and he can beat you outside. It's the worst feeling in the world when this happens. I feel like I've let the whole team down. If you know what you've done wrong, however, you shouldn't make the same mistake the next time."

It wasn't always that easy for Shell. Whe he reported to the Raiders in 1968, he had a big

Guard Gene Upshaw has played longer than any other Raider.

adjustment to make. He wasn't skilled in pass blocking, principally because he didn't get the experience in college. Most of the football he played at University of Maryland, Eastern Shore was geared to running. There is quite a difference. Shell recognized that the very first summer he joined the Raiders.

"When we did pass-block in college, it was taking the guy right there on the line of scrimmage in what you call a short set," explained Shell. "In the pros, you can't do it that way every time. Some guys can get away with it, but I have to change up. By that, I mean drop back deep, medium, and short."

The Upshaw-Shell combination is devastating. Upshaw is quick, tall at six five, and rangy, with the strength of someone who weighs more than 225 pounds. Shell is like a rock with his bulk—six five, 280 pounds—and has incredible strength. Upshaw and Shell lift weights together. They have great respect for one another. Ollie Spencer, who was at one time the Oakland line coach, saw it many years ago.

"They communicate on the field beautifully," remembers Spencer. "They know what each is going to do without saying anything. They are great athletes—fine competitors.

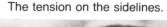

The tension on the sidelines.

Center Dave Dalby.

They play together as well as any guard-tackle combination I've ever seen."

Yet, it's only been in the last several years, since 1976 perhaps, that Shell has gotten the notice he deserves. Sometimes it was a case of mistaken identity.

"Guys started to come up to me and ask if I was Gene Upshaw," revealed Shell. "I just accept things as they are. It really doesn't bother me that much. It used to be worse. I'd shower and dress while people talked to Uppy, and

then I'd go home. I just never had anybody stop and talk to me before. I'm still not the type to go out and promote myself. I just go out and try to do my job and let that speak for me. Very seldom do I say anything; so when I do, it has impact. Most times when I say something, it sinks in."

No one is as quiet as center Dave Dalby. Few realize that he is the one who replaced the legendary Jim Otto. In fact, Otto and Dalby are the only two centers the Raiders have ever

had. At six three and 250 pounds, Dalby has played in 136 straight games at center since joining in 1972. Strong and rugged, Dalby may have a chance to match Otto's fifteen-year career if he desires.

"Dalby doesn't make mistakes very often," pointed out Stabler, who took his snaps for eight years. "That's why he's such a great center."

While Upshaw is an outspoken individual, Oakland's other guard, Mickey Marvin, is just the opposite. Marvin is awesome for a guard, six four and 270 pounds, but he has never been known to lose his temper. Upshaw calls him Sparky because he reminds him of a feisty dog he once had. A regular churchgoer, Marvin wouldn't even bark, much less bite.

"I would rather say I'm a Christian than say I'm religious," explains Marvin. "A lot of people are religious."

Henry Lawrence, the right tackle, has much the same quiet manner as Shell. He is nicknamed Killer, most likely because of his size, six four and 270 pounds. He has strong memories of his childhood, being raised by parents who were migrant farm workers. Now Lawrence owns his own farm in Florida and hires migrant farmhands to look after his vegetable crops.

"In this game you can't be like a cabbage— all head and no butt," said Lawrence.

The return of Raymond Chester gave the Raiders a tight end who could go deep. Chester was Oakland's number one pick in 1970. However, three years later he was traded to Baltimore. Oakland got him back in 1978, and in 1979 Chester led all tight ends in the league with 58 receptions. He also had the most Raider touchdown catches that year—eight.

The years Chester spent in Baltimore weren't happy ones. The Colts were going through all kinds of turmoil, and Chester wondered why he was caught up in the front-office war. During his first season in Baltimore he caught only 18 passes. He was practically forgotten. However, the players didn't forget him—defensive tackle Joe Ehrmann, for one.

"Raymond Chester is a great leader," said Ehrmann. "More than that, he's got character. He came from Oakland where he was All-Pro,

and here he hardly ever had the ball thrown to him. He could have quit, but he kept our spirits up. You knew he was meant to be a winner; he had that charisma."

Chester never forgot the day he got traded. It was a shock to him. In his first three years with the Raiders Chester had caught 104 passes, 22 for touchdowns. It was no secret why he was a genuine All-Pro.

"I remember the day I was traded from Oakland to Baltimore," remarked Chester. "It was the day before practice was to start, and I was out buying some track shoes. When I got home, my wife, Sharon, said I had a call from Al Davis's secretary. I got this sick feeling in the bottom of my stomach because I knew that I'd see him the next day. There was only one reason to call me. I knew it before I called him back, but I didn't want to admit it. So, I called Al Davis; and as soon as he got on, I said, 'Where to?' He said, 'Baltimore.' I thought, 'God.' My family didn't go for it, either. It was rough."

Right tackle Henry Lawrence.

Tackle Art Shell.

Now that he was back, he didn't disappoint the Raiders. Together with Dave Casper, Chester introduced Oakland's two-tight-end-offense to football. The other Raider receiver who could go deep was Cliff Branch. It was something he had been doing ever since he joined the club in 1972. Over the years the speedy wide receiver hasn't lost a step. When the Raiders picked him fourth in the draft, he had a reputation for being a sprint champion, and the Raiders first looked at him as strictly a kick-return specialist. They were wary because other track stars like John Carlos and Jimmy Hines never made it in pro football.

Even though he caught only 13 passes his final year at the University of Colorado, Branch made a big impression with the coaches in his rookie pro season. He looked so good running under a football that he started the opening game that year. Unfortunately, he dropped a long pass that game and was promptly benched and practically forgotten. He did manage to see some action again late in the season, catching a crucial third-down pass that clinched the Western Division title for the Raiders. It was the most significant catch of the three that Branch caught all year.

"I always had faith that I could do it," claimed Branch, "but nobody said anything to me when I wasn't playing, and it was hard to keep mentally prepared."

The Raiders felt that it wasn't a matter of ability. Rather, they felt that Branch didn't concentrate enough. Branch shared the same opinion. He worked hard to correct it.

"I would walk around the house dropping a football and trying to catch it before it hit the ground again," recalled Branch. "I also worked in practice a great deal, concentrating on making one-hand catches. My left hand was a problem because I was used to doing everything right-handed. Our receiver coach at the time, Tom Flores, used to work with me a lot on catching the ball with just my left hand. I finally mastered it so I could coordinate my left hand with my right hand when catching the football."

In 1974 Branch got his big break. Mike Siani got hurt, and Branch replaced him. Madden told Branch that the Raiders were

Tight end Raymond Chester can go deep.

counting on him because there was no one else. It was a tough assignment, but Branch came through. He finished the season with 60 receptions for 1,092 yards and 13 touchdowns. The Raiders had a long-ball threat at last.

"My biggest improvement was just playing," contends Branch. "I really started to get confidence, and I could feel the team getting confidence in me, also. It was just a matter of learning and applying.

"I learned how to use my speed, when to go full out, and when to glide—like when I'm running a comeback. I go out full speed because I want the defensive back to think I'm running an up. But when I run a hook, I go into a glide and then accelerate after I catch

the ball."

Branch realized that he needed more than speed to make it as a receiver. The rest was up to him. Running fly patterns straight downfield was one thing. That's something nobody can take away from him. Learning to be a receiver, however, was another. He was willing to learn how to run patterns and play off a defender, after first learning the proper way to catch and get hit. Preparing for a hit is very important for any receiver.

"I asked George Atkinson, who at the time was our cornerback, about it," said Branch. "He was the kind of guy who hits people hard for a living. I asked him about footsteps once. He told me: 'Clifford, you know that defensive man is going to hit you whether you catch the ball or not. He's going to hit you because you're there, but you're responsible for the ball. That's what they are paying you for, so you got to catch it.' That's the way it is. So I catch it."

Another who can catch it is Bob Chandler. He's the classy receiver who was needed as a perfect complement to Branch's deep patterns, and the Raiders didn't hesitate to trade Phil Villapiano to Buffalo to get him before the 1980 season. Chandler is a precise pattern receiver, much like Biletnikoff. In 1979 he was out the entire season with a shoulder separation. However, from 1975 to 1978 Chandler caught 220 passes, more than anyone else in the NFL during that four-year span. In his first year with Oakland, Chandler led the club in receptions with 49 and touchdowns with 10.

Chandler doesn't have many fond memories of the nine years he spent with Buffalo. In his first year there (in 1971) the Bills were still playing in antiquated War Memorial Stadium. It was a horror and far below professional standards. There weren't any parking facilities, even for the players. They had to park at a supermarket a half mile from the stadium, and the players had to pay a $2.50 parking charge. It wasn't uncommon for the players to return after a game to find their tires stolen.

"I got a hit about what to expect when I reported to Buffalo's rookie camp and checked into the hotel," chuckled Chandler.

"Everyone's key fit everyone else's room. The girl at the front desk was a hooker, and there were rats a foot long in the hall. They made more noise than the humans. We said, 'This is pro football?'

"One of the first things they told me was to be certain to wear my helmet both on and off the field because the fans threw things. I remember walking back one day and seeing a set of dentures on the ground. Someone had thrown their teeth at us.

"In my first five years there I lived at the Buffalo-South Motor Inn, Exit Fifty-six. It was a truck stop. I bought a fifty-three Chevy for a hundred dollars. It had no heat, and the radio only worked sporadically."

Chandler felt that everything would change when the Bills moved into their new field, Rich Stadium. The largest crowd in Buffalo history—some eighty thousand fans—turned out.

"Everything was upbeat," recalled Chandler. "It was a packed house, a new stadium, and an improved team. We kicked off, and they returned it ninety-seven yards for a touchdown. Just that fast, all those fans turned on us."

In 1976 the Raiders turned to Mark van Eeghen to spark the running game. Marv Hubbard had retired after the 1975 season, and the Oakland ground game was shaky. Fortunately, that year Pete Banaszak filled in admirably for the injured Hubbard, but age shortened Banaszak's career. Oakland desperately needed the big, heavy-duty fullback to complete its offensive picture.

After the final game of the 1976 season Van Eeghen sat in front of his locker holding a football. He sat there with a smile on his face. The ball had a special meaning for him. Just a short while before, Van Eeghen had run the ball 95 yards against the San Diego Chargers. That performance had given him a total of 1,012 yards for the season. It was the first time Van Eeghen had gone over the 1,000-yard mark in his brief three-year career in which he had played mostly a reserve role. It meant a great deal to him.

Before the season began, the Raiders had

not less than ten running backs in camp and Van Eeghen wasn't even listed as a starter. He was figured as the backup to Hubbard who was coming back from a 1975 injury that limited his playing. His injury had enabled Van Eeghen to gain some valuable experience in 1975, but Hubbard was still considered the number one fullback. However, in an early preseason game against St. Louis, Hubbard separated his shoulder. It was the third time in eleven months that Hubbard had injured the same shoulder. Hubbard was through for the year and in fact his career was ended. There was concern in the Raiders' camp that summer because Hubbard had been the key to the Oakland running game since 1971.

"This will be the first Raider opener I'll miss in eight years," Hubbard had noted, "but Van Eeghen will get the job done. He broke all my records at Colgate. Maybe he can break my pro record, too."

Still, no one expected that Van Eeghen would gain 1,000 yards his first year as the club's starting fullback. He was still young and had only a little experience. Neither Van Eeghen nor anyone else on the Raiders was thinking in terms of a 1,000-yard season. They were just concerned with winning and developing the running attack. After ten weeks the Raiders were 10-1. The following week Van Eeghen had his biggest day as a pro, running for 133 yards against Philadelphia.

"I didn't think about one thousand yards until then," admitted Van Eeghen. "After that game I had seven hundred fifty with three games to go and began thinking the opportunity was there. I said to myself, 'I can do it.'"

Before the final game of the year, Van Eeghen's teammates were thinking the same way. In fact, they wanted to make sure he accomplished it.

"The entire offensive line thinks this is important," said Upshaw. "We want him to get it, not only because this team hasn't had a thousand-yard rusher in a few years but because it is the best way to get recognition for an offensive line."

Against the Chargers Van Eeghen needed 83 yards to achieve his goal. With five minutes left in the third quarter, on his twentieth carry

Veteran running back Mark van Eeghen.

of the game, Van Eeghen got it.

"When I got within five yards of the thousand, the fans started to react," remembered Van Eeghen. "It was great the way the fans were behind me. They wanted me to do it as much as my teammates did. In the huddle the linemen kept saying: 'Give it to Mark. Give it to Mark.' The fans started yelling so loud I couldn't hear the signals, but I knew I was going to make it."

Oakland had surprised some people by drafting Van Eeghen on the third round of the 1974 college draft. Most of the pro scouts

Rookie quarterback Marc Wilson saw brief action in 1980.

figured Van Eeghen wasn't big enough, or strong enough, to make it in the pros, but by his third year he was both. It took Hubbard's injury to give Van Eeghen the opportunity to play.

"He worked hard to help the team when we needed it," pointed out Upshaw. "He deserved the one thousand yards, and that's why we wanted to be sure he got it."

The soft-spoken Van Eeghen took it from there. He was accepted by his teammates in that 1976 season, and he hasn't disappointed them since. He put together two more 1,000-yard seasons: 1,273 in 1977 and 1,080 in 1978. No one in the history of the Raiders had ever done that. He is the leading rusher in the club's history, and every yard he gains will only add to his mark.

"I'm not flashy," said Van Eeghen, "but I've only lost one fumble in 1980. I stay mentally alert in the game and don't make many mistakes. I pride myself on that."

Another running back was needed to blend with Van Eeghen, one who could go to the outside. The Raiders found Kenny King. Nobody knew much about him after his first year in Houston, nobody except the Raiders. They were willing to give up Jack Tatum for him. They way it turned out, the trade was a steal.

"It's the best deal Al Davis ever made," exclaimed Upshaw.

In his first year with the Raiders, King ran for 761 yards on only 172 carries, an average of 4.4 yards a run. He probably would have made the magic 1,000-yard circle if injuries hadn't sidelined him near the end of the season. He gave Oakland the outside speed they had lacked since Clarence Davis. Arthur Whittington helped but at 170 pounds he couldn't be expected to take the pounding for an entire game. No back that size could.

At Houston King seemed to be at a dead end. There wasn't any future in being Earl Campbell's backup. Campbell was young and so was King, and it could get pretty lonely standing on the sidelines knowing that Campbell had all those years ahead of him. The trade gave King a whole new world to look forward to.

"I feel great," snapped King. "I'm glad Oakland has given me a chance to show my ability. Earl's a great back, and I had come to the realization that I wasn't going to play much. I didn't have much of a future at Houston. I was extremely disappointed, but now I feel like I'm having a second life. I haven't been this happy in a long time."

Even at the University of Oklahoma, King had always been in the shadows. First there was Elvis Peacock and then Billy Sims, and King must have wondered if he would ever get his chance or if he was always going to be the back who did the blocking.

"I didn't mind playing that role at Oklahoma," admitted King. "It helped discipline me, and it made my job easier with the Raiders. You can't be a one-dimensional running back in this league. You must be able to block."

Van Eeghen appreciates King's contribution to the Raiders' running game.

"Kenny has the potential to be a great running back," said Van Eeghen. "We've got to get him the ball as much as possible. I'll block for the guy any time."

In the 1973 college draft Oakland had everyone wondering. Their first pick that year was Ray Guy, a punter at little Mississippi Southern. Although he also played defensive back, the Raiders drafted him strictly for punting. So Guy was the first punter ever selected on the first round in the history of the draft. Oakland thought so highly of Guy that they weren't the least concerned that he had broken his left ankle in the final game of the season and that the cast wasn't removed from his ankle until two days before the draft.

Over the years there has been no other punter in the NFL who has demonstrated the consistency that Ray Guy has. Nobody kicks the ball higher, and his hang time is such that his punts aren't easily returned. Because of his outstanding kicking ability most scouts regard Guy as an offensive weapon. For example, in the 1980 AFC championship game against San Diego Guy was called upon to punt four times and averaged 56 yards a kick. His longest was

Punter Ray Guy shows his form.

71 yards, which established an AFC title game record. His kicks gave the Chargers poor field position throughout the game. His consistency was evident throughout the playoffs. He averaged 48.6 yards during the regular season and that was minimized somewhat by the 38.3 average he produced in Cleveland on nine punts in subzero weather.

"Those last three weeks I was prouder of my punting than I have ever been," says Guy.

Some were even suspicious of his punting skill. Several years ago the Houston Oilers checked one of the balls that Guy used in a game against them. They were convinced that the ball was pumped with helium. That's how high and how far Guy booted the ball that day. Yet, there are a great many others who contend that Guy is simply the greatest punter the game has ever seen.

"I just do my job," he says. "I don't think about anything like that. So far, I've had no complaints. I must be doing something right, but if somebody came up and challenged me, then I'd meet the challenge."

Although he appears calm in any kicking situation no matter how perilous, Guy does admit to feeling pressure at times. It causes his palms to become sweaty. There were even times when he vomited before some games.

"I've tried to calm myself down," said Guy. "I sat myself down in camp this past summer and said that if I got a bad punt, I wouldn't let it bother me like it has the last seven years."

As far as Mickey Marvin is concerned, Guy can never make a bad punt. "I've said this lots of times, but Guy is the best offensive weapon we've got. He keeps getting us out of holes." Marvin's confidence is supported by the fact that Guy has been picked on the All-Pro team in seven of his eight years.

"Nobody really recognizes that special teams play an important role," according to Guy. "You're talking about field position. That has a tremendous effect. It influences what kind of plays you call. If the defense comes out on the field inside the twenty, that pumps them up."

Another expert at getting the players pumped up is field goal kicker Chris Bahr. The Raiders had been experiencing problems in that area for the past two years. Errol Mann

Place kicker Chris Bahr.

wasn't the answer, and neither was Jim Breech, so Oakland sought out Bahr, who was cut by Cincinnati after four years, and signed him as a free agent before the 1980 season opened. He had some shaky moments during the year. One game he'll never forget was late in the season against the Denver Broncos on *Monday Night Football*. He missed four field goals and the only extra point he attempted. Like all good kickers, Bahr snapped his slump. He finished with 98 points on 41 of 44 conversions and 19 of 37 field goals. All kickers need time to adjust—a new atmosphere, a new holder—and Bahr didn't miss in the playoffs or the Super Bowl.

"I've always said that I can tell how good a game I had by reading the newspapers the next day," confided Bahr. "If I don't find my name mentioned anywhere, I know I had a great day. If I'm mentioned a lot, it means that I had a bad game."

Oakland's offense didn't have many bad games in 1980.

TED HENDRICKS

He's unusual, to say the least. Some players are as big but not nearly as light in weight. He has curly hair and a thick moustache and looks more like a basketball player. Physically, he doesn't appear strapping—not at six seven, 225 pounds. Most football players that height weigh at least 265 pounds. They are big on weight conditioning, lifting the heavy iron with a consuming passion during the season and in the off months.

It's not that Hendricks isn't similarly dedicated. Far from it. It's just that he is such a free spirit, he doesn't seem a typical professional football player. He has been called Twiggy and the Mad Stork and is very often misunderstood, not by his teammates and the competition, but by the upper echelons of the sport's establishment. Certainly they didn't understand him in Baltimore, or later in Green Bay. Perhaps management wasn't used to dealing with such a refreshing personality as Ted Hendricks. One important thing they couldn't deny, however, is that Hendricks may just be the finest outside linebacker in football. He is such a commanding force that he can dramatically influence the flow of a game.

Yet during his first season with the Raiders, Hendricks got more splinters sitting on the bench than bruises playing. In 1975 Oakland had Phil Villapiano and Gerald Irons as outside linebackers and Monte Johnson in the middle. The Raiders used the more conventional defense consisting of three linebackers and four down-linemen. There wasn't any room for Hendricks except in some passing situations or on kicking downs.

"The first year I wasn't happy about not playing," admits Hendricks, "but I eventually got a chance to start, and it's been the same ever since."

There isn't any way that Hendricks could be kept out of the lineup. He has never missed a game in the twelve years he's been in the NFL. Hendricks has played in 178 games in a career that started in Baltimore, had a stopover in Green Bay, and is now alive and roaring in Oakland. He became a vital force in the Raiders' defense because linebacker coach Charlie Sumner decided to keep Hendricks on the field in passing situations. He would either drop back into coverage because of his range or blitz the quarterback. Hendricks usually made the choice.

"We decided during the off-season that we had to play Ted every down if possible," revealed Flores. "He's such a dominating player.

His moves are all designed. He moves around a lot and disguises it. He ends up in the right spot. When he lined up, teams were accounting for him, and that's when we started moving him around. It creates confusion for the opposition."

Hendricks's first start as a Raider was a big one. It came in a playoff game against the Cincinnati Bengals. Defensive end Tony Cline was sidelined with an injury, so for the game the Raiders went with a 3-4 alignment, inserting Hendricks on the outside. Before the game was over, Cincinnati quarterback Ken Anderson got to know Hendricks fairly well as Ted sacked him four times to help preserve Oakland's 31-28 victory.

The Raiders signed Hendricks that year as a free agent on August 6, well after training camp opened. Al Davis signed him to a three-year contract; twenty-seven-year-old Hendricks didn't come cheap. Besides a healthy six-figure salary, the Raiders also had to compensate the Green Bay Packers. The crafty Hendricks had signed only a one-year contract with the Packers which contained no option clause. After that one season Hendricks was free. Packer fans have never forgiven Dan Devine, who was the club's general manager and coach back then, for the omission, even going so far as to accuse Devine of sabotaging the team's future.

Hendricks was an invaluable acquisition for any team and a number of other clubs wanted the man who had been an All-Pro in his years with Baltimore. It was even feared that Hendricks wouldn't remain in the NFL. The Jacksonville Sharks, of the ill-fated World Football League, had their jaws open, waiting, but before the 1975 season opened, the Sharks were beached by financial woes and went out of business. Davis, unhappy with the tackling displayed during the previous season—especially in the AFC championship loss to Pittsburgh—didn't hesitate to sign Hendricks.

"He's a guy who might help us win a game somewhere down the line that we might lose without him," reasoned Davis. "I think maybe some of our guys got a little complacent. Our only inflexible goal is to win, and we may use

flexible methods to do that. I'm not a guy who believes in wholesale housecleaning. I think you can upgrade in other ways."

Unquestionably, Hendricks liked the atmosphere in Oakland where he wouldn't be hassled by dress codes or convention. In rejecting

offers from the Atlanta Falcons, Miami Dolphins, and the New York Giants, he demonstrated he preferred the Raiders' caliber of play.

"We've got so much depth on this team that I don't see any way we can miss making it to

Hendricks comes down hard on former teammate Kenny Stabler.

the playoffs," remarked Hendricks. "The fact that I knew Oakland was going to be in the playoffs did enter into any decision."

Although he had always played on the left side, the Raiders decided to play him at right linebacker. Since he had reported late, Hendricks wasn't exactly overpowering in the early exhibition games. Hendricks managed to come on near the end. In the next to last game against the Dallas Cowboys, Hendricks pressured punter Mitch Hoopes into shanking a short punt. It helped position an Oakland touchdown that didn't escape assistant coach Joe Scannella's eyes.

"We've never been a real good punt-blocking team," pointed out Scannella. "It has to do with our style of play. Our game is 'Don't make mistakes or give the other team a break.' That's why we don't go after the punter a lot. If we hit him, they keep the ball. I think with Ted we're going to do it more; and what we'll probably do, too, is let him go on his own when he thinks he can get there.

The rangy Hendricks chases Dallas quarterback Danny White.

"It's a knack some people have. Some guys have the ability to get sideward momentum so that they can sneak in there between people. Ted is very good at hitting and sliding. We hope he'll do the same thing here. Later in the season we'll design some stuff to help him. When you've got a special talent, you've got to do something to utilize it."

Hendricks derives a certain joy in blocking kicks. No linebacker is better at it. In his one and only season at Green Bay he blocked an unbelievable total of seven kicks. One came against the Colts, which gave him added satisfaction, having spent some unhappy years in Baltimore when the club's general manager at the time, Joe Thomas, didn't relate to Hendricks's way of doing things.

"They've mentioned to me that blocking kicks hasn't been a big factor in the Raiders' system," said Hendricks. "The same thing existed in Green Bay before I got there. I was just fortunate to get a coach like Devine and an assistant like Hank Kuhlmann with whom I could work and talk over the best approach. It turned out beautifully. As time went on, I got to work on it more and more.

"We were in Baltimore, and they were getting to punt. I tried to draw the opposing player offsides so they'd get a five-yard penalty, but when one of their players did move and I reached over to touch him, the officials called an offside against me. The penalty against us moved them into field goal range, so they brought in their field goal team—but I blocked it."

Minnesota kicker Fred Cox will never forget Hendricks. Cox was working on an extra point skein that had reached 199 straight. He never added to it. Hendricks was personally responsible.

"I had jumped offside prior to the snap," recalled Hendricks, "which killed the play. Cox went ahead and made it, but he had to kick it over, and I blocked it the second time around. Basically, it's beating the person in front of you and getting a lot of help from your teammates. When you're trying to get penetration into the line, that's where you need some help from your teammates. Usually, it's a two-on-one situation: two defensive

linemen against an offensive blocker. You usually can get penetration that way. Then you've got to get your hands up in the air. That's where my height gives me an advantage. If it's a low-trajectory ball, it's easy to get to."

Ironically, it was Joe Thomas who had a high regard for Hendricks before the 1969 college draft. Thomas, who was the personnel director of the Miami Dolphins, had seen the big, gangly Hendricks as a defensive end at the University of Miami. Although he was considered the top college lineman in the nation, NFL scouts were puzzled about what position Hendricks would perform at in the pros because he weighed only 215 pounds.

Thomas estimated that he would be able to draft Hendricks on the second round. So he made a defensive end his first-round selection and waited to pick Hendricks the next time around. He never got the chance. The Colts, who just a few weeks earlier had been upset by the New York Jets in Super Bowl III, grabbed Hendricks.

Don Shula, who was in his final year with the Colts before moving to Miami, and Upton Bell, the Colts' personnel director at the time, rated Hendricks highly.

"He has the intelligence and reactions to be as good as he wants to be," said Bell. "He's a winner with a real chance to be a star."

The Colts weren't sure where they would play Hendricks. When he reported to camp that season, he was issued number 83, which was a lineman's jersey. Since he was projected as a lineman, Hendricks thought it would be nice to wear number 89, his college number. It wasn't possible.

"I couldn't take eighty-nine," said Hendricks. "It had belonged to Gino Marchetti, and nobody else was about to wear it. In the end they didn't have anywhere else to put me but linebacker. At the beginning I was behind Mike Curtis, and that didn't give me any hope at all. Mike wouldn't even let me practice. I'd go in, and two plays later he would come running out and chase me off the field. He said he needed the work. I spent seven or eight games that year sliding around like a hog on ice."

It was quite a change from college where

Hendricks was such a strategic force. After his sophomore season Hendricks gained a national reputation. He had made an All-America team and would have made a lot more if Bubba Smith of Michigan State and Alan Page of Notre Dame weren't around. Charlie Tate, Miami's coach, felt he had the best in Hendricks.

"He could be anything he wants to be," exclaimed Tate. "That's the kind of potential he has. Why, he could even be governor."

In Hendricks's junior year Miami went to the Bluebonnet Bowl in Houston, but before he even got there Ted Hendricks reached a turning point in his career. Miami had been scheduled to play LSU in Baton Rouge earlier that season and the opposition's slogan all week on campus was, "We're gonna knock Hendricks out of there for Stokley." Stokley was then LSU quarterback. However, they couldn't manage to do it. Hendricks was all over the field. He kept pressure on Nelson Stokley and twice forced him to fumble at key

moments, and he saved his best for last. In the fourth quarter LSU had moved into field goal range. They were trailing Miami 17–15 and a field goal could win it. Hendricks dashed the Tigers' hopes as he dropped Stokley for a 14-yard loss that lost LSU a possible field goal and the game.

The turning point for Hendricks had come well before the game. Unknown to many, Walt Kichefski, Miami's defensive line coach, had benched Hendricks. While Hendricks was hurt by the move, he learned from it.

"He moved me down to second string, and he was right," recalled Hendricks. "I was approaching the stage of development where I knew more than the coaches did. I was playing my own game. Good old coach Ski taught me something right there, as he did throughout my college career. I discovered that he is a man of principle who does what he says he'll do. I give him a lot of credit for my development. Anyway, after he demoted me, I started looking within myself. I told myself I'd better get back to basics. By the time I got in the game, I was ready to play, all right."

His final year at Miami he was voted the Knute Rockne Memorial Award by the Washington, D.C., Touchdown Club as the outstanding lineman of 1968 and presented with a thousand-dollar diamond ring. All-America honors were everywhere.

By November in his rookie season with Baltimore, the Colts were struggling through their worst campaign since 1963. When Don Shula took over, he decided to make some radical changes. He moved Mike Curtis from outside linebacker to the middle, replacing Dennis Gaubatz. Then he inserted Ray May in Curtis's left side position. Finally, he sent Don Shinnick to the bench and gave his right side spot to Hendricks. It was a tough slot for the youngster, who wasn't at all familiar with playing linebacker.

"The play that was really tough was the run-pass where it will start out like a run and a halfback will come at you as if to block you. Naturally, you try to evade him. Then he runs past you, and you know it's a pass."

It didn't take Hendricks much time to learn. In 1970 he helped the Colts turn it around.

They were the AFC champions and went on to defeat the Dallas Cowboys in Super Bowl V. Hendricks was a standout in that 16–13 victory. By the time he started his third year as a pro, Hendricks was already considered to be an All-Pro. He substantiated it with another solid season with some outstanding games. One occurred on *Monday Night Football*, against the Los Angeles Rams. Early in the fourth quarter the game was tied at 10–10. Los Angeles's running back was carrying the ball when he fumbled on his own 31 yard line. The opportunistic Hendricks grabbed the ball and scored a touchdown.

"I don't know if the ball took a bounce or not," said Hendricks. "It was sort of hanging there when I caught it. All I know is that I saw that open field in front of me and was so excited I started running."

Just six days later he had New York Jets quarterback Bob Davis running. At that time

Hendricks when he played for the Baltimore Colts.

the Jets were leading 7–0. They were driving into Baltimore territory as Davis went back to pass. He rolled to his right and threw; Hendricks caught the ball and ran it back to midfield. Quarterback Johnny Unitas took over from there and got the Colts the tying touchdown.

"I knew there was a linebacker between me and the receiver," explained Davis, "but I've thrown over them before and didn't expect any trouble doing it this time. It's just that you don't have time to stop and think that it's Ted Hendricks, and he's six seven. All of a sudden he goes straight up in the air like a basketball player and makes the interception that turns the game around."

Hendricks wasn't finished for the afternoon. Baltimore was ahead 14–7 when the Jets scored another touchdown. Bobby Howfield came in to kick the extra point that would tie the game. Hendricks broke through a hole, stuck up his arm, and blocked the kick. It gave the Colts a 14–13 victory. When the game was over, Hendricks had taken part in 11 tackles.

Yet, it was the 1970 AFC championship game that was perhaps Hendricks's most memorable. It was only his second year in the league, and ironically, the game was against the Raiders. The week before the championship Baltimore had blanked the Cincinnati Bengals 17–0 in the opening playoff game, allowing them only 139 total yards. They would have a much tougher game against Oakland.

Defensively, the Colts had to protect against the bomb. Daryle Lamonica, the Raiders' strong-armed quarterback, liked to throw deep. He had two excellent wide receivers in Warren Wells and Fred Biletnikoff. They both lined up on the same side, which was still basically a new formation back then. Baltimore felt they could handle both Wells and Biletnikoff by doubling up on them with their four defensive backs.

Hendricks's primary mission was to cover tight end Raymond Chester. Hendricks flopped on both sides of the field, lining up opposite Chester. That's the way the Colts prepared for Oakland in the week before the game. However, once a game began, anything

could change strategy. This time it took an injury to do it. Early in the first period Lamonica took a hard hit from Bubba Smith and had to leave the game. He was replaced by forty-three-year-old George Blanda, which meant that the Raider attack would also change.

Rather than going deep, Blanda's strength was in the short and intermediate passing attack. The struggle became a classic passing duel between two students of the game—Blanda and Unitas. It was early in the fourth period when Blanda hit Wells with a 15-yard touchdown pass that trimmed Baltimore's lead to 20–17. Some five minutes later it took a 68-yard bomb from Unitas to Ray Perkins to seal Baltimore's 27–17 victory that got them into Super Bowl V.

"My play that afternoon wasn't that noticeable to the average fan," pointed out Hendricks. "However, as far as execution was concerned, I felt it was one of my best games. I was out there to prevent Chester from catching passes, and he ended up with only two receptions for thirty-six yards. It was legal to hit receivers more than once then, and that's what I did to Chester. When he would get away from me and move into the middle, then Curtis would lower the boom on him. We had him pretty well frustrated."

Several years later Hendricks himself would be frustrated with the Colts. Baltimore fell on lean years, and Joe Thomas left Miami to take over at Baltimore with a new owner. Thomas's immediate task was to rebuild the Colts to the championship form that they had enjoyed a short time before. Thomas encountered some problems with a number of the players, including Hendricks. Entering his option year in 1974, Hendricks asked Thomas to trade him, preferably to a warmer climate. It was a battle between two egos, each one strong-minded and confident of his abilities. When Hendricks threatened to go to Jacksonville and the WFL, Thomas reacted. He traded Hendricks after five years in Baltimore to Green Bay—definitely not the warm-weather city Hendricks desired.

"He put me in cold storage," quipped Hendricks. "I wanted out because Thomas had everything like basic training. I had no choice but to play out my option. I was ready to go to the World Football League in Jacksonville, but Thomas got back at me."

Hendricks isn't accustomed to the cold. He is probably the only Latin-born player in the NFL, having been born in Guatemala City, Guatemala. His mother, Angela, was of Austrian-Italian descent. His father, Maurice, is from McAllen, Texas. Both worked for Pan American and met while they were based in Guatemala.

"We lived in Miami for twenty-seven years, but I went home to Guatemala for the birth of my other two children," explained his mother. "I was surprised when Ted became a football player. He had never been an aggressive person. He avoided fights as a child. I can remember telling him to hit back, but he wouldn't. He's quiet, doesn't say much, but he has to be doing something all the time. He's so fidgety he doesn't even sit still when he's talking on the phone."

Hendricks's parents were supportive of his athletic endeavors while he was growing up. They never missed a home game in which he played, beginning with Little League football, where Hendricks played quarterback, through high school and college. His mother's 1967 Christmas present was a trip to Houston, where she saw the University of Colorado defeat Miami in the Bluebonnet Bowl. Although he was only a junior at the time, Hendricks was already a national celebrity. He was the first Miami player to be given unanimous All-America honors. As a result he appeared on the Ed Sullivan and Bob Hope television shows.

Some of Hope's droll sense of humor must have rubbed off on Hendricks. In 1972 Hendricks carefully plotted a course that would legally allow him to miss the first two weeks of Baltimore's training camp. He wanted to serve his two weeks of active duty with the Florida National Guard—in Panama, yet! It was his second attempt within a month. His first had been aborted when he forgot about taking some exams at Miami, where he majored in mathematics. He postponed his guard duty to take his final exams, which he felt were more important. Actually, Hendricks isn't much on details. When he got married several years later, he forgot two necessary items: the marriage license and the blood test. Realizing it was too late to rectify the matter before the wedding, Hendricks came up with a solution. He and his intended wife, Jane, jumped in his car and hurried to Folkston, Georgia, for a civil ceremony. They got back in the car and sped back to Miami in plenty of time for a church service and reception the next day.

"I had a deal worked out to miss the first two weeks of camp," revealed Hendricks about his 1972 escapade. "I think preseason camp is for rookies anyway, and owners, of course. I don't go into exhibition games willing to make the kind of physical and mental sacrifices necessary during the regular season. They couldn't fine me, either, whether I was signed or not. Besides, they can't fault a man for being in the Guard.

"The first time, I called Coach (Don) McCafferty at eight o'clock on a Sunday morning and woke him up. He's usually a mild-mannered guy, but I must have gotten him out of bed. His answers were extremely short. I wanted him to write a letter to the Army informing them that I would be needed in training camp, but later I remembered about my exams. I didn't want to jeopardize my situation at the university under any conditions. Besides, after thinking about it, going to Panama in late July was ideal. I'd not only miss the worst part of the preseason training, but I couldn't possibly be held accountable for it. Furthermore, I might not be signed by then. I wouldn't have to come to camp unsigned."

Hendricks and the Colts couldn't come to terms. The math-minded Hendricks figured he was worth a lot more than the Colts wanted to pay. His original contract he signed out of college was valued at $100,000 over three years and included a $25,000 signing bonus. He played his option year in 1973 with Baltimore, and when Thomas and the new owners came in, Hendricks was out. He played in Green Bay for one season, 1974, before the Raiders signed him as a free agent. Since he was an All-Pro, the price was high. It cost Oakland two number one draft choices, in 1976 and in 1977.

After his slow beginning in Oakland in 1975 it didn't take Hendricks long to get used to his new teammates. In reality it was the players that had to get acquainted with Hendricks. Oakland has always been classified as the haven for pro football's unwanted or misunderstood athletes. It is not an accurate characterization. The Raiders have allowed their players to be themselves—each a different personality. They prefer that their players operate as free spirits. In Hendricks they possibly have the freest spirit of them all. There is no telling what Hendricks will do at any given moment, although he confines his pranks to the practice field.

Once, during summer training camp at Santa Rosa, Hendricks was ready to report on the field. On the way he spotted a man riding a horse. He approached the rider and asked if he could borrow his horse for a few minutes. The man agreed. Hendricks mounted the animal and trotted on to the practice field

while everyone shook their heads. At midfield he pulled the horse to a halt, jumped off, and smiled at the coach, John Madden. When Madden retired a couple of years later, Hendricks thought he should have some kind of gift. On the way to Madden's house, Hendricks rammed a Yield sign, got out, placed it in his car, and then proceeded to give it to Madden.

On the walls of the players' locker room at the Raiders' training compound there is a large poster explaining what a legal tackle is. The poster took on a new look shortly after it was put up. Hendricks took a thick felt pen and made a drawing of himself executing his favorite tackle, the clothesline, which is, of course, illegal. It was Hendricks's way of protesting the rule change. One time at Halloween Hendricks didn't have a mask, so he asked a friend to get a pumpkin and carve it out in the shape of a helmet. When he got the pumpkin, Hendricks painted a black stripe down the middle and the Raiders insignia on the sides. When he got up to practice, he put the pumpkin over his head and walked on the field. He also has worn a Nazi helmet and a purple saucer-shaped hat with a large white feather to practice. Hendricks refuses to take any credit for the time a stripper streaked the practice field and did a complete lap around the field. Often during *Monday Night Football* games he dons a harlequin mask and mugs for the cameramen who are panning the sidelines getting close-up shots of the players.

"I don't like monotony," exclaims Hendricks. "I just consider myself a normal human being."

Yet, even a matter like paying dues is not a normal thing for Hendricks. The determined linebacker has never paid his National Football League Players Association dues. He is the only player in the league who doesn't. The reason is that Hendricks doesn't like the way NFLPA Executive Director Ed Garvey is running things, and it is his way of protesting. Garvey got technical. Before the 1980 season he notified the Raiders that Hendricks should be suspended for nonpayment of his dues. Garvey cited the fact that since this was in violation of the collective bargaining agree-

ment, the club would be held in violation. The Raiders had a quick solution. They paid Hendricks's dues, which amounted to $692.07.

"I've been in the league twelve years, and nothing has been accomplished except that the players have to pay their dues instead of being able to do it voluntarily," snapped Hendricks.

On the field his opponent paid. During the 1980 season Hendricks had 9½ quarterback sacks and 60 tackles. He holds the NFL records for safeties (4) and blocked kicks (21). He also has intercepted 21 passes and has who knows how many blitzes, which have resulted in quarterback pressures. Many called the 1980 season the best of Hendricks's twelve-year career.

"To me, as a linebacker, this year (1980) really was not my best year," claimed Hendricks. "I had better years in 1974 and 1971. I judge it on a technical standpoint—what you do on every play of a game. I graded myself out better in those years. Now that I'm older, I don't have the speed or endurance to cover the entire field. In those years I was making tackles on the other side of the line. Virtually anybody I played had no success on the left side of our defense, and I could cover anybody out of the backfield man-to-man, including tight ends.

"I guess I was a model for the blitzing we are doing with the team now. It has evolved gradually. They have to guess when I am going to go. Teams have to counter it. I believe my height has given me some advantages. I have more leverage, and although I may be giving up a little speed, I can make up for it with my range. One of the problems in the NFL is that coaches get too programmed. They thought I couldn't play the position at two fourteen. Well, that is really quite silly. If you're good, you're good.

"I look at it as a sixth sense. I study techniques a lot. I also look for clues. For example, when we played Houston, I noticed that Earl Campbell had a tendency to lean forward in the stand-up I formation when he was getting the ball. He was getting his momentum forward. They usually don't run him outside—just between the tackles, so you knew when he was getting the ball and where he was going.

"It reminds me of when I was still in Baltimore. They had a playbook with a page devoted to how to exit the huddle. They had it to the point where you had to make a right face on the command of 'Ready, break.' When I played in Baltimore, I'm not sure half the team knew my name."

His Raider teammates knew he didn't like the name, the Mad Stork, so a few years ago they named him Kickem. Hendricks actually earned the name on the practice field. He knocked out a teammate with a forearm smash.

"It makes it a lot easier when ball carriers know you're around," said Hendricks. "It encourages a little respect. The idea is to convince the offense to go to the other side so I can relax."

One way Hendricks relaxes is by collecting fancy cars and investing in real estate. Although he was named to the NFL's Team of the Decade, a high honor indeed, he still would like to make the Hall of Fame after he retires. He would also like a passing grade in abstract algebra so he can earn his college degree. Dealing with the abstracts interests him.

"I'm interested in satellites, Jupiter, the rings of Saturn," disclosed Hendricks. "I like to live in the future."

THE DEFENSE

The way linebacker coach Charlie Sumner looks at it, he has fourteen starters on defense. When he returned to the Raiders in 1979 after spending ten years with Pittsburgh and later New England, Sumner had to sell his 3-4 alignment not only to Al Davis but to Tom Flores as well. Both had been strong advocates of the conventional 4-3 defense until Sumner showed them how much more effective his method would be among the changing philosophies of pro football. Sumner emphasized the specific use of specialists, which is how he formed his theory about fourteen starters.

No one spends more time studying films than Sumner. He sits in the dark, puffs on cigarettes, and scribbles notes every time he discovers something. Then he'll rerun the film time and again to confirm his findings. Although he is listed as the linebacker coach, Sumner is much more. He is the one responsible for the Raiders' defensive game strategy. Amazingly, the Oakland defense never received the credit it deserved until the end of the 1980 season. By then they were known as "the Boys of Sumner."

Sumner devised two types of coverage. One was the normal 3-4, which in Oakland ver-nacular was the Orange defense. This was the regular deployment against the run. The other was the Pirate defense in which Sumner made use of his specialists in passing situations. In this alignment Sumner would take out three starters and replace them with specialists, namely Cedrick Hardman and Willie Jones at ends, and Odis McKinney or Monte Jackson in the secondary.

Normally in the Orange, the 3-4 configuration, the Raiders utilize the following personnel: on the line, middle guard Reggie Kinlaw; ends, John Matuszak and Dave Browning. Outside linebackers Ted Hendricks and Rod Martin; inside, Matt Millen and Bob Nelson. In the secondary, cornerbacks Lester Hayes and Dwayne O'Steen; safeties Mike Davis and Burgess Owens.

"If the goal is cohesion and coordination, it's possible to make too many changes," warned Sumner. "We like to think we're better off alternating two basic defenses; the Orange on first down and the Pirate on passing downs. The Pirates get more playing time than the starters. Second down and seven yards to go is a passing down. We'll usually put the Pirates in for that. Second and five is more like a running down. The gray area is second and six.

Defensive tackle Dave Pear.

We could either stick with the Orange defense there or sneak in the Pirates. Most good teams pass on third and three, and run on third and one. The third-down gray area is third and two. We would probably pick the Orange there.

"In a three-man front you need a lot of bulk and strength at the ends. With a four-man line the need becomes size in the middle and quickness outside. We shift Matuszak inside and put Hardman and Jones on the outside. The two Pirate pass rushers are quicker than the other guys. Normally on third and one we stay with the Orange. We just crowd everyone a little more tightly together."

Hayes is one who likes to play it tight. The colorful cornerback had been playing exciting defense in 1980. No one has played the position better. Certainly, no one played it with more flair for drama. In Oakland's basic one-on-one coverage in the secondary, Hayes was an artist. He would look at the enemy with his steely eyes and challenge him. Everyone in the stadium witnessed it since a cornerback is out there alone. Throughout the long season Hayes triumphed over his adversaries. He was as much a problem for opposing quarterbacks as for the receivers. Hayes intercepted 13 passes in the regular season: one short of the league record, which was set by Detroit's Hall of Famer, Night Train Lane, and has stood for so many years. He almost made history in the final regular-season game against the New York Giants. Hayes picked off three passes but penalites in which he wasn't involved nullified each one. In the playoffs he intercepted 5 more passes in three games. By then everybody knew about Hayes and his use of a sticky substance that he applied to his hands, arms, and uniform. Suddenly Hayes and his stickum were a focal point and Raider equipment manager Dick Romanski had to keep a plentiful supply of the compound on hand.

"I don't know if the stickum really helps me hold on to the football," disclosed Hayes. "Most of those passes I would have probably intercepted anyway. Anyhow, I think it psychs the other guys out. Receivers look at me all covered with the stuff and they think, 'How

Lester Hayes returns an interception for a touchdown.

can I beat the man? He's like flypaper.' "

A great many NFL personnel directors got stuck on the flypaper back in 1977 when Hayes at Texas A&M was considered to be the top defensive back in the country and the speculation was that he would be picked in the first or second round. There were even stories circulating that he would be the very first defensive back taken. Hayes had developed a reputation for being a quick, aggressive player in college. He had started as a linebacker but was switched to safety in his junior year and worked hard to master his new position. He got help from cornerback Pat Thomas of the Los Angeles Rams who had also gone to A&M. Thomas taught Hayes how to back pedal, how to react, and all the other intricacies involved with playing in the secondary. Hayes learned his lessons well. He set records at A&M that still stand. Hayes never forgot Thomas's help either:

"I call Pat Thomas my mentor because he taught me how to play strong safety before my junior year. He took time out from his summer schedule to teach me how to back pedal. He was the first guy to teach me the bump-

and-run. The next year I broke Pat's school interception record. He got fourteen in four years, but I got fifteen in two. What I know about being a defensive back I learned from him."

So, the morning of the 1977 NFL draft Hayes was sure he would be picked high on the list. He had all the physical characteristics—hands, speed, physique—plus the ability to hit and absorb punishment. Hayes waited for the phone to ring, but it didn't. He waited all day and finally early that evening he got a phone call from the Raiders. He was picked on the fifth round.

Most players would have been delighted. Hayes wasn't. He kept wondering why he hadn't been selected in the first or at least the second round as he and so many others had anticipated. He's never gotten over the disappointment. It remains deep inside him and gives him an edge that keeps him striving to become the best defensive back in football.

"I think about May third often," Hayes said. "I want to make twenty-seven teams wish they could go back to that day. There were fourteen defensive backs taken before me. I want to make them pay for that. I had seen all the scouting reports. They all said I was the number one safety in the draft. I heard the scouts and the coaches saying I'd go on the first or second round. Then I waited, and the phone didn't ring until six forty-five in the evening. I was heartbroken.

"It's a terrible thing to lie to a young man for five months like they did. I couldn't go to class for a week. I've got to make them pay for all that pain. I'll never forget it. That has always kept me going. I used it against them. Every one of them wishes they had me now."

There are two distinct possibilities why Hayes wasn't picked early in the 1977 draft. One centered around young Hayes himself, the other, around Al Davis. Hayes is now inclined to feel he was the victim of his own overconfidence. He came on too strong and gave certain people a negative impression, for like so many other Raiders he is a strong-willed, free spirit.

"They thought I was too cocky. I knew my value and wouldn't allow anyone to tell me

different. I felt I was going to be the first safety in the draft. On all the scouting polls I saw, I was always listed as the top safety in the nation. I didn't know if I could play cornerback, but I knew I could play strong safety. I was drafted fifth because I wasn't naïve. They

Defensive end Joe Campbell.

want college guys to be modest. But damn, that's not me. My college coach, Emory Ballard, stuck it to me. He said negative things about me. They try to set up a mold for black guys. They want you to have a smile on your face and say 'Yes, sir.' I was my own man."

Exciting cornerback Lester Hayes.

Defensive end Cedrick Hardman.

Defensive end Willie Jones.

Safety Dwayne O'Steen.

Defensive tackle Reggie Kinlaw.

Outside linebacker Jeff Barnes.

Outside linebacker Rod Martin.

The eagle-eyed Davis scouted Hayes in the Hula Bowl. As he saw it, Hayes would be better as a cornerback instead of a safety where everyone had him pegged. There were also whispers that Hayes wasn't smart enough to play pro ball.

"The label on him was that he wasn't intelligent," remembers Davis. "First you have to evaluate the intelligence of those who made the judgment. Hayes has a problem with stammering. He wouldn't talk because he was afraid people would think he was dumb."

At first Hayes thought the Raiders were dumb. When he reported to his first training camp, they told him that he was going to play cornerback. He played linebacker and safety in college, and now he was going to play yet another position. It didn't make sense to him. Hayes was suspicious.

"I wondered if it was some sort of plot," admitted Hayes. "How could they take the best safety in the entire draft and make him switch to corner? It wasn't even logical. I had made the transition from linebacker to safety, and now I had to make another one.

"I couldn't see myself doing it. I figured I'd been conned again. I told myself it was going to take a year or so, but someday I would make them pay. I hung in and learned I could play corner better than anyone in the NFL."

It wasn't until the 1980 season that Hayes was fully recognized for what he is—the best cornerback in the league—even though the year before he had intercepted seven passes to make him third in the NFL, which gave him the most interceptions of any cornerback in the AFC. That year Hayes was beaten by only three touchdowns—truly an outstanding year.

75

Nonetheless, Hayes never received any All-Pro honors or any AFC recognition. And he never forgot that season either:

"It baffles me how they pick guys ahead of me. Louie Wright and Mel Blount were the best once, but I outplayed them in 1979, and I wasn't even All-Conference. It is amazing, but the NFL has been amazing me since 1977. I had thirteen interceptions and five in the playoffs, but they kept throwing at me because they can't accept the fact that a guy who played guard, tackle, linebacker, and safety can play cornerback. They say, 'How can he play man-to-man defense on a par with such euphoric quality?'"

There was an incident early in his career with the Raiders that wasn't exactly terrific. Denver fans remember it. They won't let Hayes forget it, either. They hung the name Lester the Molester on him. Like Jack Tatum and George Atkinson before him Hayes learned how to hit hard. The one hit he did try but missed was a forearm smash to Bronco receiver Haven Moses in a 1978 game in Denver during Hayes's second year in the league. Hayes remembers the play although he regrets what happened. He doesn't mind talking about it so the public will understand the circumstances.

"I was still young, and Moses was a veteran," recalled Hayes. "He was turning me all around, beating me every time downfield. I couldn't deal with getting beaten like that. A couple of veterans told me to put 'the hook' on him. That was a forearm shot to the head like the one Atkinson put on Lynn Swann. I tried to do it to Moses right before the first half ended. The only trouble was—I missed. I swung at Moses, but he ducked. My arm went right over his head.

"Everyone in the stadium saw it. The Broncos started hollering, and the fans booed. That's when they gave me that name. I didn't like the name—I still don't. I don't think I'm a dirty player. I don't take shots like that anymore. I hit hard but clean."

There is no arguing the fact that Hayes is the most exciting defensive back in the NFL. He lines up closer to a receiver than any defensive back around. The excitement of

Cornerback Mike Davis.

Assistant coach Joe Madro makes a point at training camp.

watching Hayes begins after the snap of the ball. Within five yards Hayes will give his target a bump. Then he'll run with him step by step the rest of the way. Hayes is assigned more single coverage than any defensive back in the league.

"We let him play it because he can do it," said Flores. "I would say we play more single coverage than any other team."

It's not without its drawbacks. Hayes's style will always tempt a quarterback to throw his way, hoping he will miss the bump or slip on a turn. Hayes is aware of the pitfalls, yet the challenge of going one-on-one excites him.

"Playing the corner is like being on an island," said Hayes. "You see boats passing by, but you can't be helped. There is no rescue, but if they never threw the ball my way, I'd get bored. To me, that's the thrill of this game,

taking on a receiver man-to-man and beating him. There isn't a receiver around I can't beat.

"Being beaten sometimes is inevitable with our philosophy. It's only logical that when they see me in man-to-man coverage long enough, they will try to challenge me. It's inevitable that you'll be a target. If you're beaten, you have to forget it because there are too many other battles to be fought and won. Quarterbacks keep throwing in my direction figuring that eventually I'm going to break. I haven't broken yet."

Willie Brown, the Raiders' defensive backfield coach, knows all about winning and losing. He is considered one of the finest cornerbacks ever to play the game. Brown played the position sixteen years. The last 12 years he spent at Oakland. He holds the club record for interceptions with 38. His career total of 54

← Defensive end John Matuszak.   Defensive coach Willie Brown looks on as Sumner confers with Millen.

ranks among the all-time NFL leaders. He made a memorable 75-yard touchdown interception against the Minnesota Vikings in Super Bowl XI. Like Hayes he is a master at bump-and-run. Brown naturally appreciates Hayes's talents.

"Hayes doesn't need much improvement anymore," offered Brown. "When I was playing, I loved to have the ball thrown my way. When I see the ball thrown toward Lester, I love it, too, because I know he's going to break it up or intercept it."

Yet they still throw Hayes's way. Safety Mike Davis can't understand why.

"I guess they refuse to believe how good he is," reasoned Davis. "I guess they figure the law of probability will catch up with Lester, but it hasn't yet. He's the best I've seen. I think he should be All-Pro until he retires."

The Raiders' defense became a driving force in 1980 because of Hendricks, who had his best season leading the linebackers, and Hayes, who also had his biggest year. Together they solidified the linebacking and the secondary. The only area that remained was the line. It was no secret that John Matuszak, like Hendricks and Hayes, was having his finest season. Everything fell into place after that.

Matuszak earned his place in the Oakland limelight. He was voted the team's best lineman in 1980. He even tried to become a team leader. At twenty-nine Matuszak had come full circle. He settled in at defensive end and took hold of himself and his life. He had joined the Raiders as a free agent in 1976 with a cloud hanging over his head. He'd had a turbulent career.

It began in college. Matuszak was at the University of Missouri under coach Dan Devine. However, he lasted only one year. He got into a fight one night and hit a serviceman he claimed was annoying his girl. A plastic surgeon was needed to repair the damage. Matuszak left. He transferred to the University of Tampa. It wasn't so much the fight that prompted his move, but rather the realization that he and Devine would never get along. He says he knew it when he heard the coach's pregame speech one time.

"He said, 'I talked to God today, and we're going to win,'" recalled Matuszak. "We were playing Notre Dame that day, and I decided if God was going to be on anyone's side, it wouldn't be Missouri's."

Everything was fine at Tampa, at least for a while. Then Matuszak's temper flared again, this time during a basketball game in 1972. One of Matuszak's teammates allegedly submarined him and angered the giant. It later cost Matuszak $800,000 in an out-of-court settlement. It was the settlement not the punch that bothered Matuszak.

"I didn't beat him up, I just rearranged his face a little," exclaimed Matuszak. "I always did admire Picasso."

Matuszak was something else on the gridiron. With his size, six eight, and weight, 275 pounds, he was high on the list of the 1973 college draft prospects. The Houston Oilers, who picked first that year, didn't need much time to make Matuszak the first player chosen.

It all looked so promising: pro ball, the number one pick in the draft, and a city like Houston in which to play. He was an immediate starter and had made several All-Rookie teams when the season ended. However, the next year Matuszak left—quite dramatically, too.

Before the 1974 season began, the players' association voted to strike. It was a decision that Matuszak was in agreement with. One evening he invited Steve Kiner, an Oiler linebacker, to his apartment for dinner. He wanted to persuade Kiner to join the strike with the others. Kiner refused. Showing his displeasure, Matuszak got up, took the plate of spaghetti from Kiner, and dumped it into the sink. Kiner got up and quietly left.

Colorful defensive end John Matuszak, known as the "Tooz."

Inside linebacker Bob Nelson.

When the strike ended, the players reported to camp. After a 1-13 season in 1973, coach Sid Gillman had turned the Oilers around in Matuszak's rookie year, finishing with a 7-7 record. However, Gillman got under Matuszak's skin that summer.

"I respect the man as a great coach, but I can't stand him," said Matuszak. "When we came back off the strike, he put all the veterans in a separate little group and made us run an extra two or three miles after practice, while he let the guys who came to camp take showers. He treated us like dogs."

By August Matuszak had had enough. He left but didn't really go far. Despite having signed a long-term contract with the Oilers, Matuszak jumped in his car, hightailing it across town to the rival Houston Texans of the World Football League. It didn't take long for Matuszak to create excitement there. His first game with the Texans wasn't five minutes old when twenty sheriffs walked on the field and handed him a summons as he stood on the sidelines. They then proceeded to escort Matuszak off the field. Caught up in the significance of the moment, Matuszak had the crowd cheering as he waved the summons high in the air and left the field. Later in court Matuszak was asked why he would even consider making such an ill-advised move.

"I could do this," remarked Matuszak, "because this is the land of the free and the home of the brave."

Although the crowd in the courtroom cheered, Matuszak was ordered back to the Oilers. He didn't stay long. By mid-season they traded him to Kansas City for Curley Culp. It was paradoxical: Culp was a popular defensive lineman with the slumping Chiefs, who had fallen on lean years; Matuszak had been the cornerstone of a rebuilding program at Houston which had begun with so much hope.

Unfortunately Matuszak encountered marital problems after moving to Kansas City. One night in training camp Matuszak was walking to the dormitory after a team meeting. Steve Ortmayer, the Raiders' special teams coach, who was an assistant with the Chiefs then, was walking close by. Suddenly a car driven by Matuszak's wife came speeding out of nowhere, heading right for Matuszak. He just barely managed to get out of the way. In fact, as Matuszak ran up an embankment, the car followed, pursuing him. It crashed into a tree.

"It was kind of like the movies," exclaimed Ortmayer. "She would have hit him. She kinda bumped him. A big guard of ours, Ed Budde, reached into the car, grabbed the steering wheel, and bent it at a ninety-degree angle. The car might still be there. It wasn't going anywhere."

Matuszak reflects back on the incident without anger.

"I don't want to blame her," said Matuszak. "She's very beautiful, but very wild; very sweet but very dangerous."

A few weeks later he had another brush with death. One night at two o'clock in the

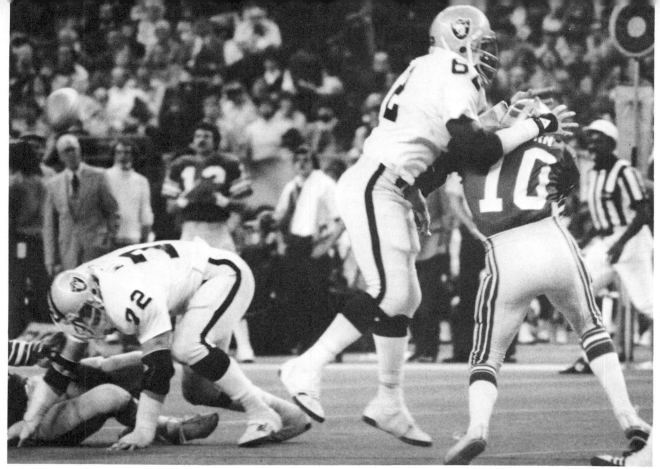

Defensive tackle Reggie Kinlaw.

morning his wife came running, screaming hysterically for Paul Wiggin, the Chiefs' head coach. Matuszak was unconscious in the car. The doctor had given Matuszak some Valium. Later he had had three or four beers and passed out. His heart had stopped.

Wiggins rushed out and began pounding on Matuszak's chest. He succeeded in getting his heart beating again. He quickly drove Matuszak to a small hospital in Liberty, Missouri, near the Chiefs' training camp.

"That was a very traumatic time for him," revealed Wiggin. "He was very lucky that the hospital staff knew exactly what to do. When the doctor came to me and said, 'I think he's going to live,' I was shocked."

Ortmayer had been just as shocked.

"Paul saved his life," Ortmayer said. "Matuszak was gone that night. When he was in Kansas City, he was a good guy. He'd always been one of the very best practice players I'd ever been around—very intense and full of speed. Paul Wiggin probably went further with him than he would have with anybody else. Matuszak had placed so much pressure on Paul regarding Paul's discipline structure on the team, that Paul almost had to do something

with him."

Matuszak still doesn't remember too clearly what happened that night. All he can remember is waking up in the hospital with several tubes in his body.

"I said, 'I'm sorry, coach. It was an accident,'" remembers Matuszak. "He said, 'Sorry, John.' I really thought it was my last shot."

It was his last shot, in Kansas City at least. Matuszak was traded to Washington. He didn't last long there, either. A week before the 1976 season opened Matuszak was cut by the Redskins. Matuszak hit a new low. He went back home to Milwaukee to think over an offer he'd had from Edmonton in the Canadian Football League. A few days later he learned that the Raiders were interested in him.

"When I got cut by Washington, I thought it was the end of the world," admitted Matuszak.

Oakland was something else again. The move gave Matuszak a fresh start. He was determined to make the most of it. He realized that Oakland was the last stop. It was a haven for unwanted players; for those who were ripe for another chance. That was Matu-

Outside linebacker Randy McClanahan.

Defensive end Dave Browning.

szak. However, he wasn't exactly greeted with open arms. He would have to earn his place on the squad.

"We had lost Tony Cline and Art Thoms from our three-man defensive line because of injuries. We only had three healthy linemen," said John Madden, who was the Raider coach that year. "At first I didn't want Matuszak playing for us, but there was nobody else available. To this day George Allen thinks I got one over on him by signing Matuszak."

Matuszak started at defensive end that year when the Raiders routed the Minnesota Vikings in Super Bowl XI. At last he had a new lease on life: he was only twenty-six and he had mellowed.

"I came into football as a number one pick, and I thought I would have everything going my way," explains Matuszak. "I've been through enough controversy for twenty guys. Now I have found the place where I can play. In the NFL images should be accented. We have an image on this team. We have a diverse blend of people, and it would be a step down to go to another team.

"They treat you like men here. You don't need to be rude or inconsiderate, but the guys on this team aren't going to kiss anyone's backside. I hated the Raiders before I got here, but that was because they were always winning. This has always been a controversial team, but they treat you right here. We have the highest salary rate in the league, and Al Davis is a quiet genius. I love the guy. That's one of the problems with the rest of the league; they treat you the wrong way. Some coaches worry that your hair isn't a certain length or that you don't wear a tie with your suit. If you treat a man like a boy, he'll play like one. I got my priorities straight. I try to keep the young guys out of trouble because, believe me, I've been there."

The mix of veterans like Matuszak and Hendricks with younger players gave the Raider defense a homogenous blend. In 1979 the Raiders made nose guard Reggie Kinlaw their number 12 pick in the draft. The players who made it at that low point in the draft could probably be counted on one hand—two

at the most. After appearing in sixteen games in his rookie year and gaining valuable experience, Kinlaw made the big leap to starter.

He is exceptionally quick. Despite the fact that he doesn't have overpowering size, Kinlaw at six two is strong enough with his speed to give opposing centers trouble.

"He has great leverage for a guy his size," said Sumner. "They've got to double-team him because centers can't handle him."

Much the same can be said about Dave Browning at the defensive end spot opposite Matuszak in the Raiders' 3-4 alignment. He was Oakland's number 2 choice in the 1978 draft. At six five he is perhaps a bit light at 245 pounds. He is on a special weight program that should add size and strength to his frame.

Browning is an intense competitor with good speed. He also possesses quickness and range. He started eight games his first season with the Raiders, the first rookie to start on defense since 1972. Browning has demonstrated he's dependable.

"He looks like he's still twenty years old, but he's really consistent," said Sumner. "He does his job without really sticking out."

The Orange defense wouldn't work effectively without outstanding play from the linebackers. Hendricks was only one of four in the solid quartet. Another Raider reclamation was inside linebacker Bob Nelson. He was re-signed by Oakland in 1980 after training camp opened. Originally, he signed with the Raiders as a free agent in 1978 after being drafted by Buffalo in 1975. He played with San Francisco in 1979 before rejoining the Raiders. He is strong against the run, which is the big reason Sumner wanted him back after reviewing films on him.

"I saw how Nelson took on blocks inside and held his own," disclosed Sumner. "I have a different concept than other linebacker coaches who want quick, run-around, pursuit guys. I like guys like Nelson who can hold up in there because he's facing offensive guards."

The biggest surprise among the linebackers turned out to be rookie Matt Millen. He was drafted on the second round in 1980 as a defensive tackle out of Penn State. The Raiders thought of him as a linebacker. At six two and

250 pounds, he's a big one. His strength, especially against the run, at inside linebacker is outstanding. Hendricks, who helped Millen learn the position, quipped: "He's a physical freak, just like me. I was never supposed to play linebacker, either."

Except for certain technical adjustments that were taxing at times during training camp, Millen didn't have any difficulties learning the position. He held the distinction of being the second rookie in league history to start a Super Bowl game at linebacker (the first having been Jack Lambert of Pittsburgh in 1975).

"He was a rookie who got fooled here and there, but he has the temperament not to let it bother him," said Sumner. "He comes back and makes a big play. He's strong and he can run."

The aggressive linebackers allowed the secondary to play tight. Hayes was the epitome of the man-on-man, bump-and-run style the Raiders prefer. When Monte Jackson was hobbled with a leg injury, Oakland turned to Dwayne O'Steen, another pickup from the Los Angeles Rams, to play opposite Hayes.

O'Steen was signed by the Rams as a free agent in 1978. He is aggressive and picked up the Oakland style of man-to-man coverage without difficulty. He accounted for three interceptions over the year and improved each week with experience.

"He is an alert, enthusiastic, and talented player who uses his head, too," remarked Sumner.

Another Raider pickup who also turned out to be a bargain was free safety Burgess Owens. The likeable Owens was unhappy with the Jets in 1979 after playing with them for eight years. He had started for them since his rookie year in 1973 and also played cornerback and free safety.

"The fun was missing," said Owens about leaving the Jets. "I wasn't having fun playing ball anymore. I began to actively think about retirement."

Sumner was glad he hadn't.

Owens worked in harmony with strong safety Mike Davis. Like Owens, Davis is a strong, sure tackler who comes up quick on

Safety Burgess Owens.

the run and is fast enough to defend against the pass. He was the Raiders' number 2 pick out of the University of Colorado in 1977, but he wasn't active that year.

"Mike is tough, and he has a strong desire to succeed," said Sumner. "He can't stand it when they catch a pass against him. He doesn't care whom you ask him to cover. He thinks he can stop them."

And that's just what the Raiders' defense did in 1980.

Inside linebacker Matt Millen.

THE 1980 SEASON

Something was different. The players could feel it. When the Raiders assembled at their Santa Rosa training camp to prepare for the 1980 season, some changes had been made. They weren't wholesale—only a few, but they were dramatic ones. The players had to adjust to the loss of a couple of superstars who had personified the team for so many years. Ken "Snake" Stabler, who had been the starting quarterback for the last eight years, and Jack "Assassin" Tatum, who had been a terror at safety for a decade, were gone. Also missing was linebacker Phil Villapiano. All three had been popular Raiders, not only with the fans, but with the rest of the team.

There was some apprehension among the coaching staff even before training camp opened. Oakland had prided itself on being known as pro football's most successful team over the last twenty years. However, two successive 9-7 seasons in 1978 and 1979 created concern. It also prompted the need for change in what was Tom Flores's second year as head coach. Oakland's thinking was to revert to the big-pass offense that had been missing the past two years. Although Stabler was still one of the game's most accurate short and inter-mediate passers, it was felt that he had lost his touch on the long ball. Al Davis didn't hesitate to trade the wily Stabler to Houston for strong-armed Dan Pastorini. In addition to having a stronger arm Pastorini was also four years younger. Several weeks later Tatum was also sent to the Oilers for little-known Kenny King.

In his first season with Houston, King only carried the ball three times as Earl Campbell's backup. The Raiders needed speed alongside Mark Van Eeghen, and they remembered that King was an exceptional runner at Oklahoma. In a third trade they sent Villapiano to Buffalo for veteran wide receiver Bob Chandler. That trade, too, had a particular meaning. Since Fred Biletnikoff's departure two years earlier Oakland's short and medium passing game had suffered. Granted, they were only three trades, but they were highly significant to the Raiders' offensive schemes.

"Sure we had doubts," admitted Ron Wolf, vice-president of personnel operations. "We're only human. We thought we had improved the year before, and we were surprised that we were not in the playoffs. People began to write about how bad we were, and we began to think, 'Maybe we are that bad.'"

There were some nagging questions that hung like storm clouds over the rooftops of the El Rancho Tropicana Motel where the Raiders have trained for eighteen straight summers. So serious were the doubts that the Raiders did not attract much support in all the preseason hoopla that usually surrounds a new season. The strongest prediction was for a fourth-place finish in the five-team Western Division. Some of the polls rated them fifth, with every expert already conceding the championship to the San Diego Chargers.

The experts were wary for the following reasons:

• The defense needed overhauling. It was one of the worst in the NFL in 1979.

• The running attack, even with the addition of King, wouldn't be as effective as in the past.

• The realization that back problems would diminish the effectiveness of thirteen-year veteran Gene Upshaw at left guard.

• Raider morale would suffer from the loss of Stabler more than the coaches thought.

• Davis's long-pass strategy wasn't viable because of the preponderance of zone coverages around the league.

Unquestionably, the Raiders faced their biggest challenge since 1963 when Davis had transformed a last-place team into winning material in just that one season. Since then the Raiders had had only one losing year—1964—but none in the past fifteen years. Yet, the probability of a losing campaign was a reality in view of not only a new offensive philosophy but a defensive one as well.

In 1979 the Raiders could not define their personality on defense. They kept experimenting with the 3-4 and the 4-3 alignments, partially because of injuries, but primarily because they didn't operate effectively with the 3-4 deployment that linebacker coach Myrel Moore brought with him from Denver. When Moore was fired, defensive backfield coach Charlie Sumner took over as linebacker coach and was responsible for the defensive scheme for 1980. Sumner was convinced the 3-4, as he coached it, would work. He completely scrapped the complex system which Moore advocated and installed a simpler approach relying on execution. The Raider brain trust decided to go with it.

"My philosophy is to let guys line up in one spot," revealed Sumner. "Last year Hendricks played on the left and on the right. This year Hendricks will see things as a left linebacker. This way, the other team may get to you for a few plays, but after a while you'll know what they're doing. I told the defensive players at our first meeting how far we could go if people didn't worry about individual goals and concentrate instead on playing consistent ball."

There were still eleven Raiders in camp who had played on the Super Bowl championship team of 1977. Upshaw, naturally, was one of them. Along with his other offensive linemates, he had to provide ample time for Pastorini to throw long.

"I don't think I've seen anyone who can throw the ball as far as Pastorini," smiled Upshaw. "He gives us that long threat we didn't have with Snake in the last years. We'll still have the short game, but the threat of the long game makes the short one go better."

Upshaw assured Pastorini that with the Raiders he would get time to throw the ball. Normally 3.0 seconds is accepted throwing time, with the very best teams providing 3.2 seconds. Upshaw was talking along the line of 4.0 seconds. Pastorini's eyes lit up.

"If you give any guy who can throw the ball four seconds, he'll win you a lot of games," exclaimed Pastorini.

During the preseason Oakland didn't win a lot of games: they split the four they played. However, when they lost, they looked terrible. San Francisco and Washington, both considered weak teams, defeated the Raiders handily. The defeats highlighted the fact that Pastorini was having a little trouble adjusting to the Raiders' system. Meanwhile, Jim Plunkett, who had sat on the bench in relative obscurity, was ready to play.

"Dan will be our number one unless he plays poorly," emphasized Flores during training camp. "If he does play poorly, then we're ready to go with Jim. We'll be better than most people think. *Playboy* picked us to win six games. We think we'll win more—quite a few more.

Owner Al Davis.

(Above) Coach Tom Flores at work, the playsheet checklist under his arm. (Right) Quarterback Jim Plunkett checking his end before he begins calling signals.

(Above) Ted Hendricks. (Right) Kenny King gets the call.

(Left) Mark van Eeghen gets hit. (Above) Catching the pass, Bob Chandler tries for extra yardage.

Jim Plunkett drops back to pass against Philadelphia in Super Bowl XV. (Inset) Victorious Raiders jubilant near conclusion of Super Bowl game.

Henry Lawrence, Art Shell, and Gene Upshaw.

(Above) The defense waits. From left, Reggie Kinlaw (62), Bob Nelson (51), John Matuszak (72), and Lester Hayes (37). (Below) Raymond Chester grabs a sideline pass against San Diego.

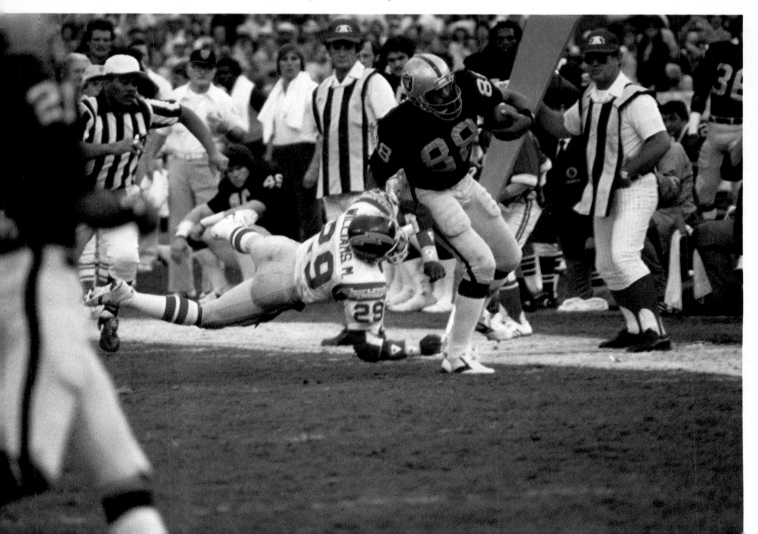

(Above) Lester Hayes, coiled for one-on-one and covered with "Stickum." (Right) Ray Guy booms a punt in AFC championship game against San Diego.

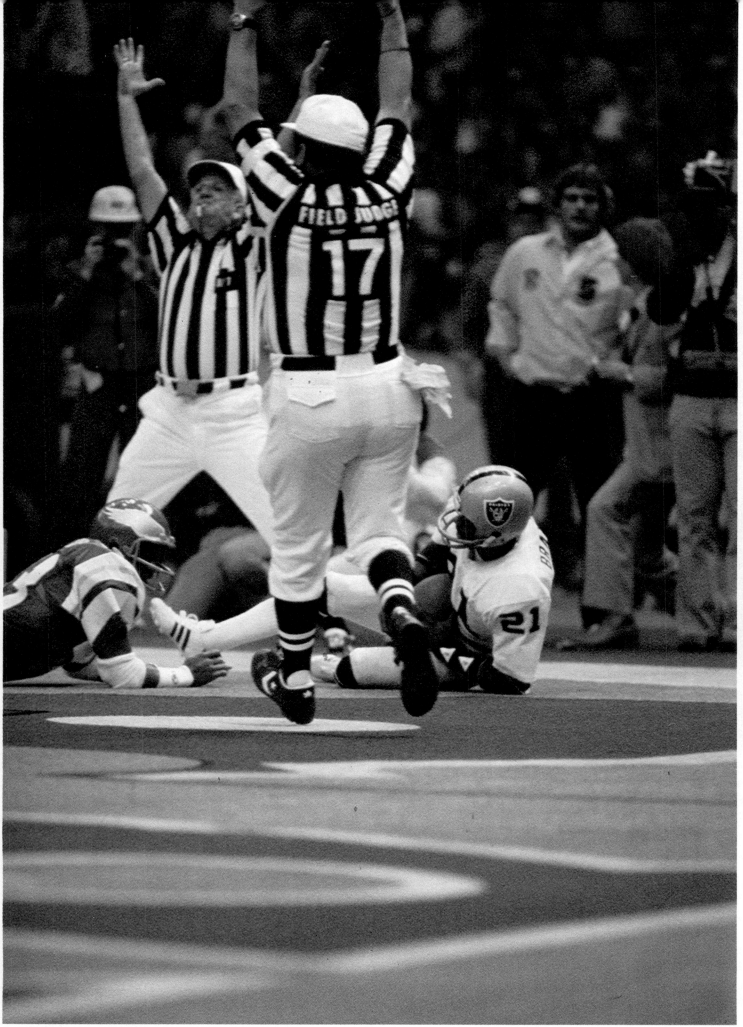

(Left) Super Bowl hero Rod Martin intercepted three passes. (Above) Mel Branch scores first touchdown in Super Bowl XV.

Plunkett and center Dave Dalby.

Running back Arthur Whittington catches a 55-yard pass against Kansas City Chiefs.

"We'll have a good offense." Flores continued. "Kenny King will be the much needed fast, strong halfback who can take advantage of misdirected plays. The offense will be strengthened by the trade for Bob Chandler. Pastorini is a great passer with an arm that will last four or five years. Stabler can't go much longer. Tatum has only one more year left—at the most, two. He's dealt out some powerful hits and has taken plenty. He's no longer a full-time player. Jack felt the criticism after the Darryle Stingley tragedy more deeply than he would outwardly admit, but what can you say? He was not the same player after that. Main thing is, I'm confident we can handle different situations. We intend to be flexible."

The regular season was scheduled to open soon. A lot of important questions would be answered then: Would Pastorini prove better than Stabler? Would Upshaw be plagued by back problems? Would Chandler help? Would King be the answer at halfback, and would Sumner turn the defense's performance around? How good were the Raiders, really?

Al Davis looked on with guarded optimisim: "We've got a chance to be good." How good he didn't yet realize. . . .

GAME ONE: KANSAS CITY

Oakland	7	0	14	6	27
Kansas City	7	0	0	7	14

Kansas City: 6:35, first period—McKnight, 7-yard run (Lowery, kick).
Oakland: 12:39, first period—Chandler, 16-yard pass from Pastorini (Bahr, kick).
Oakland: 11:59, third period—Van Eeghen, 1-yard run (Bahr, kick).
Oakland: 14:20, third period—Chandler, 32-yard pass from Pastorini (Bahr, kick).
Oakland: 2:11, fourth period—Bahr, 41-yard field goal.
Kansas City: 6:06, fourth period—Samuels, 4-yard pass from Fuller (Lowery, kick).
Oakland: 13:35, fourth period—Bahr, 39-yard field goal.

The Raiders with their new-look offense opened their schedule in Kansas City. The Chiefs were an old rival. In seven years, from 1966 through 1972, either Oakland or Kansas City had finished first in the Western Division. However, times had changed. Now the ex-

perts were picking either the Raiders or the Chiefs to finish *last*.

The game didn't begin too brightly. The first time Kansas City got the ball they pushed 70 yards for a touchdown. The eleven-play drive consumed 6:35. Pastorini then fastened his chin strap and impressively directed the Raiders on an 88-yard march in just twelve plays. The payoff was a 16-yard touchdown pass to Chandler, with Bahr's conversion tying the game at 7–7. Pastorini seemed in command as he completed 4 of 6 passes.

Both teams had scored quickly in the first period but ground to a halt in the second quarter. The Raiders had the ball four times and never really threatened. One second before the end of the half the crowd of 57,055 buzzed expectantly when Bahr came on to attempt a 61-yard field goal. It fell far short.

In the third period the Raiders broke through twice for touchdowns in the final four minutes: a 1-yard plunge by Van Eeghen climaxed a 69-yard drive; a second TD positioned by Matt Millen when he intercepted Steve Fuller's pass on the Kansas City 40 and brought it back to the 32. With forty-seven seconds left, it took Pastorini just one play to hook up with Chandler on a pass for the second time.

Another interception, this time by Hayes, gave the ball back to the Raiders on Kansas Ctiy's 36 yard line as the third period ended. When the drive stalled on the 23 early in the fourth quarter, Bahr booted a 41-yard field goal which gave the Raiders a commanding 24–7 lead.

After the Chiefs scored on the ensuing kickoff, the Raiders scored for the last time with just 1:29 left in the game. Odis McKinney intercepted Fuller a third time, which set up Bahr for a 39-yard field goal, giving the Raiders a 27–14 victory.

Pastorini's performance was quite promising in his first regular-season game. He'd completed 19 of 37 passes to seven different receivers for 317 yards and 2 touchdowns. Chandler had also made a fine debut, catching both touchdown passes as he led the receivers with five receptions for 85 yards.

"I'll never scare anybody with my speed, like Cliff Branch, but the patterns here are not dedicated that much to speed," said Chandler. "We receivers set each other up, and you know Dan will put it in there for you."

GAME TWO: SAN DIEGO

Oakland	3	7	7	7	0	24
San Diego	3	7	0	14	6	30

San Diego: 6:38, first period—Benirschke, 52-yard field goal.
Oakland: 12:22, first period—Bahr, 35-yard field goal.
San Diego: 14:12, second period—Jefferson, 4-yard pass from Fouts (Benirschke, kick).
Oakland: 14:54, second period—Branch, 48-yard pass from Pastorini (Bahr, kick).
Oakland: 6:54, third period—Jones, 11-yard fumble return (Bahr, kick).
San Diego: 3:25, fourth period—Winslow, 25-yard pass from Fouts (Benirschke, kick).
San Diego: 13:00, fourth period—Williams, 4-yard run (Benirschke, kick).
Oakland: 14:27, fourth period—Chester, 18-yard pass from Plunkett (Bahr, kick).
San Diego: 8:09, overtime—Jefferson, 24-yard pass from Fouts.

It didn't take the Raiders long to meet their first major test of the season. Playing for the second consecutive week on the road, Oakland faced the explosive San Diego Chargers, the team every expert picked to win the Western Division championship. There were only 727 no-shows as a crowd of 51,943 turned out in sunny San Diego Jack Murphy Stadium.

San Diego scored first. After the Raiders reached the Chargers' 33 yard line, Bahr tried a 51-yard field goal but failed. However, Rolf Benirschke sent the Chargers into a 3–0 lead when he kicked a 52-yard field goal. The Raiders then began a drive from their own 9 yard line before stalling on the Charger 17. Bahr came back to kick a 35-yard field goal and tied the game near the end of the first period.

In the opening minutes of the second quarter the Raiders lost an opportunity to grab the lead when Bahr missed a 30-yard field goal that went wide to the left. With less than a minute to play, the Chargers took a 10–3 lead as Dan Fouts tossed a 4-yard touchdown pass to John Jefferson.

There were only forty-two seconds left in the first half when the Raiders got the ball back. After Pastorini missed on his third pass, he connected for three in a row, the final one a 48-yard bomb to Branch with only twelve seconds remaining, pulling the Raiders into a 10–10 tie at halftime.

Oakland's defense took control in the third period. First, Mike Davis prevented a Charger touchdown when he intercepted a Fouts pass on the Raider 7 yard line. Minutes later Willie Jones sacked Fouts on the Charger 11. Fouts fumbled, Jones picked up the ball and ran it in for a touchdown. Suddenly the Raiders were ahead 17–10.

The Chargers came right back and threatened again, but Hayes intercepted Fouts's pass in the end zone. Near the end of the period the Raiders missed another chance when Bahr's 46-yard field goal attempt was wide. Amazingly, Fouts was intercepted for the third time in the period when Hendricks came up with a big play with less than a minute left.

On the second play of the final period Bahr attempted a 53-yard field goal. No good. The next two times the Chargers had the ball they scored. The first—a 15-yard pass from Fouts to Kellen Winslow. It tied the game at 17–17. Then the Chargers moved into a 24–17 lead when fullback Clarence Williams scored on a 4-yard run with only two minutes left in the game. One hundred and twenty seconds to go and the Chargers led 24–17.

The Raiders battled back. Pastorini drove them into San Diego territory, reaching the 16 yard line with one minute left on the clock. But Raider hopes dimmed when Gary Johnson sacked Pastorini on the 23. Pastorini, who had been hurt, had to leave the game and was replaced by Plunkett. Following a Charger offside Plunkett connected with Chester for an 18-yard pass in the end zone and the stadium went wild. Only thirty-nine seconds remained to be played. Bahr's conversion tied it up at 24–24 and the game headed into overtime.

The Raiders got the first opportunity to score and win the game, but Bahr's 5-yard field goal try was partially blocked. Fouts brought the Chargers back and on a third and 11 dramatically hit Jefferson with a 24-yard touchdown pass for a 30–24 triumph. It was a great satisfaction to Fouts, who was intercepted

five times, and a great disappointment to Bahr, who missed five field goals.

"I let everyone down," sighed Bahr.

GAME THREE: WASHINGTON

Washington	0	7	7	7	21
Oakland	3	7	7	7	24

Oakland: 6:38, first period—Bahr, 21-yard field goal.
Oakland: 9:37, second period—Casper, 20-yard pass from Pastorini (Bahr, kick).
Washington: 13:47, second period—Walker, 15-yard pass from Theismann (Moseley, kick).
Oakland: 7:52, third period—Whittington, 42-yard run (Bahr, kick).
Washington: 10:36, third period—Theismann, 4-yard run (Moseley, kick).
Oakland: 5:15, fourth period—Chandler, 5-yard pass from Pastorini (Bahr, kick).
Washington: 14:04, fourth period—Thompson, 3-yard pass from Theismann (Moseley, kick).

Raider fans got their opportunity to see their team for the first time at home against the Washington Redskins. On a warm, sunny, 75-degree day 45,163 fans turned out. It was the first time in six years that there wasn't a sellout crowd at the Oakland-Alameda County Coliseum.

The first time the Raiders went on offense they scored. They managed to drive to the Redskin 8 yard line but had to settle for a 21-yard field goal by Bahr, the only score of the first period.

After Bahr missed on a 5-yard field goal attempt, the Raiders scored the next time they had the ball. Pastorini moved them 52 yards with a 20-yard touchdown pass to Casper on a third and 4 call. Bahr's conversion upped Oakland's lead to 10–0.

With a little more than a minute left in the half, the Redskins finally got on the scoreboard. Joe Theismann hit his tight end Rick Walker with a 15-yard touchdown pass that put the finishing touch on a 59-yard drive. The Raiders went to their dressing room to cool off, with a 10–7 lead.

Ten minutes remained in the third period. Oakland got the ball back after Mark Moseley failed to tie the game with a 47-yard field goal. Two first downs got the Raiders to the Redskin 42. Running around the right end, Whit-

Mark van Eeghen and Gene Upshaw lead the way for Kenny King against Washington.

Dan Pastorini barks signals against Washington.

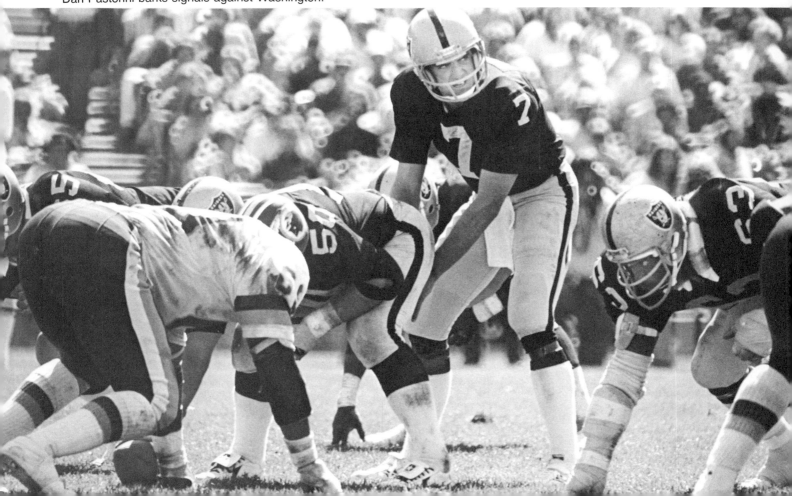

Mark van Eeghen became the Raiders' all-time leading rusher on this 15-yard run against Buffalo.

tington broke loose and raced into the end zone and moved the Raiders into a 17–7 lead. Predictably, the Redskins got tougher. Tony Peters intercepted Pastorini's pass on the Oakland 41 and got to the 4 yard line before he was pulled down. Theismann ran it in from there on first down to bring the Redskins to within 3 points when the period ended.

Oakland took control when the fourth period opened. The Raiders marched 90 yards for a touchdown in a drive that took fourteen plays and over five minutes to complete. On third down Pastorini found Chandler in the end zone with a 5-yard touchdown pass. The big play in the drive was a 30-yard run by King that got the Raiders to the Washington 25.

It didn't matter that Theismann hit Ricky Thompson with a 3-yard touchdown pass with less than a minute to play. The Raiders had won 24–21.

It was only King's third game as a Raider and he had had an impressive day: 136 yards on 25 carries, an average of 5.4 yards a run. It was his first 100-yard game since college.

"I'm overwhelmed," exclaimed King. "My last hundred-yard game was in 1978 in my senior year at Oklahoma, and it was against Colorado. Since coming here, I've quit looking to the past. My future is with the Oakland Raiders."

GAME FOUR: BUFFALO

Oakland	0	0	7	0	7
Buffalo	7	10	0	7	24

Buffalo: 14:45, first period—Brown, 4-yard run (Mike-Mayer, kick).
Buffalo: 3:11, second period—Cribbs, 1-yard run (Mike-Mayer, kick).
Buffalo: 15:00, second period—Mike-Mayer, 30-yard field goal.
Oakland: 2:06, third period—Hayes, 48-yard interception return (Bahr, kick).
Buffalo: 1:03, fourth period—Cribbs, 21-yard pass from Ferguson (Mike-Mayer, kick).

The Raiders went back on the road, the third time in four weeks. Meeting Buffalo, they were going against the unbeaten Bills, who had playoff aspirations of their own. The tenacious Bills were only one of two remaining undefeated teams in the American Conference. The other was San Diego.

On Sunday 77,259 fans showed up at Rich Stadium. Actually, all 80,020 tickets to the game were sold by Tuesday, one of the earliest sellouts in Buffalo history. Playoff fever was starting early.

The Bills set the tempo for the game as they went 81 yards, using almost nine minutes of the clock to score the game's first touchdown. Curtis Brown ran it in from the 4. Nick Mike-Mayer added the conversion to give wildly cheering Bills fans a 7–0 advantage. And they came right back again early in the second period. King had fumbled on the Oakland 16-yard line. In short order Joe Cribbs bolted over from the 1 yard line and the Bills were ahead 14–0. A little later they added to it when Mike-Mayer nailed a 30-yard field goal to provide the Bills with a 17–0 half-time cushion.

The Bills dominated the action in the first half in a practically flawless performance. Buffalo quarterback Joe Ferguson at one point completed 11 straight passes while the Bills' defense kept pressure on Pastorini.

Early in the third period Hayes gave the Raiders a lift. He intercepted Ferguson's pass and ran it 48 yards for a touchdown. Still the Raiders' offense couldn't get going and Buffalo clinched the game in the fourth period, catching the Raiders by surprise. Faking a reverse, Ferguson fired a quick 21-yard pass to Cribbs—who was all alone down the sideline—for a touchdown that put the Bills up 24–7. The Raiders didn't threaten the rest of the game and went down to their second defeat.

Oakland had been completely outplayed. Buffalo had the ball for forty-one minutes, limiting the Raiders to only 12 first downs and 179 yards. Pastorini had been sacked four times for 49 yards and was pressured for almost the entire game.

"It was the best pass rush I've faced all season," admitted Pastorini. "We couldn't get anything established so we could stick with our game plan."

Chandler, who played with the Bills in 1979, had another observation.

"It's easy to see the confidence the Bills have picked up this season," said Chandler. "They are not afraid to open up anymore, and they don't try to sit on a lead. They want more."

GAME FIVE: KANSAS CITY

| Kansas City | 14 | 17 | 0 | 0 | 31 |
| Oakland | 0 | 3 | 0 | 14 | 17 |

Kansas City: 5:26, first period—Spani, 16-yard fumble return (Lowery, kick).
Kansas City: 10:57, first period—McKnight, 2-yard run (Lowery, kick).
Kansas City: 9:57, second period—Lowery, 35-yard field goal.
Kansas City: 14:07, second period—Morgado, 1-yard run (Lowery, kick).
Kansas City: 14:21, second period—Paul, 32-yard fumble return (Lowery, kick).
Oakland: 15:00, second period—Bahr, 39-yard field goal.
Oakland: 2:10, fourth period—Branch, 10-yard pass from Plunkett (Bahr, kick).
Oakland: 4:52, fourth period—Chandler, 6-yard pass from Plunkett (Bahr, kick).

One month into the season and the Raiders were just holding their own at 2-2. They were returning home for a second meeting with the Kansas City Chiefs, who hadn't yet won a game. There were only 40,153 fans to welcome the Raiders back home, the smallest crowd since Thanksgiving Day in 1968. Then only 39,883 had showed up. And the fans were in a surly mood, at that. They were upset with the entire club's mediocre record but the target of their anger was Pastorini. Apparently they were still fuming over the trade that originally brought him to Oakland. It took on added significance in view of Pastorini's tough start.

On Oakland's opening drive Pastorini hit on 5 of 6 passes and positioned the Raiders for a 44-yard field goal which Bahr missed. The next time the Raiders had possession, Pastorini was blitzed. He fumbled and linebacker Gary Spani scooped up the ball on the 16 and ran unmolested for a touchdown.

Midway through the period Pastorini went down on a hit by cornerback Gary Green. He never got up. He was carried off the field with a broken leg and replaced by Jim Plunkett. Sadly enough, the new quarterback from Houston, the Raiders' great white hope of the new season, was booed as he was taken off the field to the dressing room. When the first

period ended, the Chiefs had scored again and led 14–0.

They extended their margin to 17–0 as Nick Lowery kicked a 35-yard field goal with 5:03 left in the second quarter. After Casper caught a pass, linebacker Whitney Paul stole the ball right out of his hands and ran 32 yards for a touchdown that ballooned Kansas City's margin to 31–0. The fact that Bahr booted a 39-yard field goal with no time remaining on the clock meant nothing to Oakland fans who were livid over the 31–3 score.

A scoreless third period reinforced their fears that the Raiders would slip even further. It wasn't until the opening minutes of the final quarter that finally the crowd had something to cheer about when Plunkett hit Branch for a 10-yard touchdown pass. The Raiders scored again a few minutes later following a blocked punt when Plunkett threw a 6-yard touchdown pass to Chandler. Nonetheless the Raiders took a 31–17 beating, their second in a row.

Pastorini was expected to be sidelined the rest of the season and the fans' reaction to his injury openly rankled Upshaw.

"Cheering Pastorini when he gets hurt, that's terrible," Upshaw said disgustedly. "The fans have always been great here when things have been going well but, as far as I'm concerned, they have destroyed all that in the last couple of games. If that's the way they want to be, I don't care if they never show up for another game here."

GAME SIX: SAN DIEGO

San Diego	7	3	7	7	24
Oakland	7	10	7	14	38

Oakland 2:19, first period—King, 31-yard run (Bahr, kick).
San Diego: 9:34, first period—Cappelletti, 5-yard run (Benirschke, kick).
Oakland: 1:46, second period—Bahr, 42-yard field goal.
San Diego: 5:30, second period—Benirschke, 25-yard field goal.
Oakland: 7:30, third period—Van Eeghen, 3-yard run (Bahr, kick).
San Diego: 9:33, third period—Jefferson, 25-yard pass from Fouts (Benirschke, kick).
San Diego: 0:34, fourth period—Fouts, 1-yard run (Benirschke, kick).
Oakland: 0:57, fourth period—King, 89-yard run (Bahr, kick).
Oakland: 1:08, fourth period—Christensen, fumble recovery, end zone (Bahr, kick).

Mickey Marvin gets ready to clear way for Kenny King.

The season was only five weeks old and the Raiders were already involved in a crucial game against San Diego. The Chargers, with a 4-1 record, were two games ahead of Oakland, who were 2-3. A loss now would just about destroy any hopes the Raiders had of winning the Western Division.

Plunkett was getting his first start as a Raider. He'd sat on the bench his first two seasons behind Ken Stabler so it was an important game for him, too. He would be the club's quarterback for the rest of the season and 44,826 had come to see what he could do.

The Raiders scored the first time they had the ball as King opened up around left end and ran for a 31-yard touchdown. San Diego tied the game with 3:34 left as they moved 82 yards in eight plays and John Cappelletti went in from a yard out.

Early in the second period the Raiders assumed the lead when Bahr booted a 42-yard field goal. The stubborn Chargers answered back to deadlock the game at 10–10 as Benirschke kicked one from 25 yards. However, with a little over four minutes left Plunkett fired a 43-yard touchdown pass to Branch. The half ended that way with the distinct possibility that both teams would wind up in another overtime struggle.

In a controlled drive the Raiders scored following the second-half kickoff as Plunkett directed them on an 86-yard march that required thirteen plays and consumed 7:30 of the clock. Scoring from 3 yards, Van Eeghen stretched Oakland's lead to 24–10.

The Chargers quickly came back the next time they got the ball. Fouts hit Jefferson with a 25-yard touchdown pass to cut Oakland's margin to 24–17. When the third-period action ended, San Diego was on the Raiders' 5 yard line and knocking on the door.

Three plays later the Chargers tied the game as Fouts on fourth down dove over from a yard out. Overtime seemed a certainty. The Raiders got the ensuing kickoff in deep—the 11 yard line. Suddenly, King brought the crowd to its feet. He shook loose over left tackle and went down the sidelines with the Chargers in pursuit. They never caught him. His 89-yard touchdown run was the longest in

Oakland's history and put the Raiders in front, 31–24.

On the kickoff the Raiders struck again: Chuck Muncie fumbled on the 5, the ball rolled into the end zone, and Todd Christensen pounced on it for a touchdown. It was the final one of the game. The Raiders had snapped back with a 38–24 victory.

"Our special teams were the key," said Flores. "We overcame a lot of adversity and kept coming back. Jim Plunkett did an outstanding job mixing his plays, and King got us the game-breaker. Knowing we had to win the game helped a lot."

GAME SEVEN: PITTSBURGH

Oakland	7	21	7	10	45
Pittsburgh	10	14	10	0	34

Pittsburgh: 3:01, first period—Smith, 19-yard pass from Bradshaw (Bahr, kick).

Pittsburgh: 5:03, first period—Bahr, 18-yard field goal.

Oakland: 7:38, first period—King, 27-yard run (Bahr, kick).

Pittsburgh: 10:31, second period—Hawthorne, 1-yard run (Bahr, kick).

Oakland: 9:38, second period—Van Eeghen, 1-yard run (Bahr, kick).

Oakland: 11:55, second period—Martin, 34-yard fumble return (Bahr, kick).

Oakland: 13:38, second period—Bradshaw, 45-yard pass from Plunkett (Bahr, kick).

Pittsburgh: 14:50, second period—Smith, 13-yard pass from Stoudt (Bahr, kick).

Oakland: 2:24, third period—Branch, 56-yard pass from Plunkett (Bahr, kick).

Pittsburgh: 7:44, third period—Bell, 36-yard pass from Bradshaw (Bahr, kick).

Pittsburgh: 14:41, third period—Bahr, 34-yard field goal.

Oakland: 3:39, fourth period—Branch, 34-yard pass from Plunkett (Bahr, kick).

Oakland: 14:02, fourth period—Bahr, 36-yard field goal.

After evening their season record at 3-3, the Raiders faced another crucial game—Pittsburgh. Oakland would be facing the Pittsburgh Steelers before a national television audience on *Monday Night Football*. The Steelers, who had won two consecutive Super Bowls, suddenly found themselves struggling. They had lost to the Cleveland Browns the week before and had a 4–2 record.

The Steelers received the opening kickoff and took it in for a touchdown as Terry Bradshaw led them on a 67-yard drive in just six plays, hitting Jim Smith with a 19-yard pass for the score. When King fumbled on the

Chris Bahr hits the final field goal against Pittsburgh in wild-scoring game.

Raiders' first offensive play, the Steelers were in business again on the Oakland 19. At the 5 yard line the Steelers offense stalled and had to settle for an 18-yard field goal by Matt Bahr, Chris's younger brother.

Down 10–0 inside of the first three minutes, the Raiders fought back hard. King climaxed an 85-yard drive by circling the right end for a 27-yard run to keep the Steelers from pulling away. However, in the early minutes of the second quarter reserve running back Greg Hawthorne, playing in the backfield without Franco Harris, who was injured, dove over from the 1 yard line to cap an 84-yard sequence in ten plays. Pittsburgh led 17–7.

Hendricks gave the Raiders excellent field

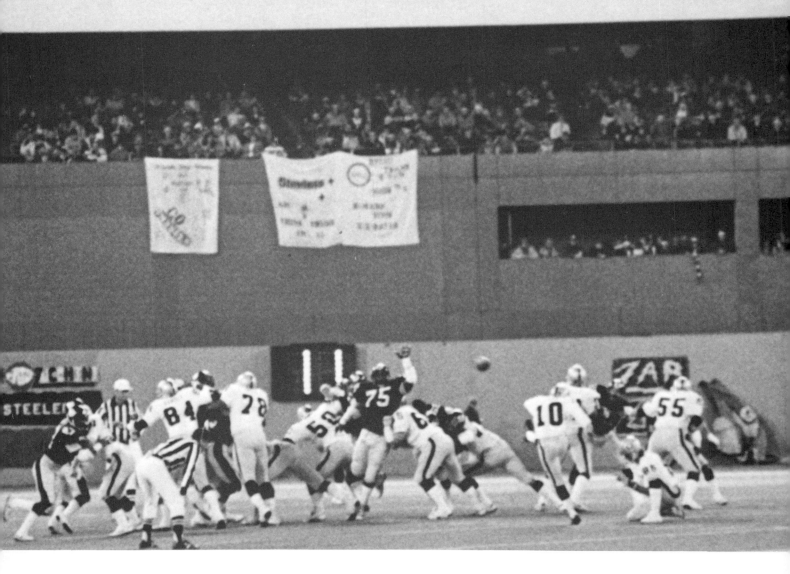

position when he intercepted Bradshaw's pass on the Pittsburgh 39. Seven plays later the Raiders scored their second touchdown as Van Eeghen plunged over from the 1.

On Pittsburgh's next series, Cedrick Hardman sacked Bradshaw on the Steeler 34 and he fumbled. Hardman lateraled the ball to Rod Martin who ran into the end zone, putting the Raiders ahead for the first time, 21–17. Bradshaw left the game limping.

Then Hendricks struck again. He intercepted backup quarterback Cliff Stoudt's pass on the Pittsburgh 49. Facing a third and six, Plunkett hit Morris Bradshaw deep with a 45-yard touchdown pass that sent the Raiders into a 28–17 lead. But just before the half

ended, Stoudt connected with Smith on a 13-yard Pittsburgh touchdown pass that trimmed Oakland's edge to 28–24 in an unexpectedly wild and high-scoring game.

The Raiders made the most of the second-half kickoff. After moving for the first down, Plunkett hit Branch with a 56-yard touchdown bomb to give the Raiders a 35–24 lead. Bradshaw returned to the lineup and led the Steelers on a 68-yard drive. The touchdown came on the eleventh play—a 36-yard pass to Theo Bell. Trailing 35–31, the Steelers got a 32-yard field goal from Matt Bahr to cut Oakland's advantage to 35–34 when the third period ended.

With Oakland's lead threatened, Plunkett steered the Raiders on an 82-yard drive. In eight plays he led his teammates toward the goal line. A 34-yard touchdown pass to Branch gave Oakland a 42–34 lead and Chris Bahr put the game away with a 36-yard field goal that gave the Raiders an exciting 45–34 triumph before a nationwide TV audience.

Plunkett had played a big game, completing 13 of 21 passes for 247 yards and 3 touchdowns.

GAME EIGHT: SEATTLE

Seattle	0	0	0	14	14
Oakland	3	3	10	17	33

Oakland: 13:16, first period—Bahr, 34-yard field goal.
Oakland: 4:01, second period—Bahr, 38-yard field goal.
Oakland: 3:13, third period—Bahr, 30-yard field goal.
Oakland: 6:50, third period—Chandler, 5-yard pass from Plunkett (Bahr, kick).
Oakland: 0:54, fourth period—Chandler, 12-yard pass from Plunkett (Bahr, kick).
Seattle: 4:08, fourth period—McCutcheon, 1-yard run (Herrera, kick).
Oakland: 6:09, fourth period—Chandler, 23-yard pass from Plunkett (Bahr, kick).
Seattle: 7:05, fourth period—Largent, 67-yard pass from Zorn (Herrera, kick).
Oakland: 12:16, fourth period—Bahr, 25-yard field goal.

The Monday night win over Pittsburgh was a big one. It gave the Raiders two successive victories over playoff contenders. The triumph over the Chargers two weeks earlier had broken a two-game losing streak; and now the Raiders had put together a modest two-game winning streak as they returned home to face the Seattle Seahawks.

This five-year-old expansion club had proved quite troublesome to Oakland. In the last two years the Raiders had dropped four straight games to the rambunctious Seahawks, who also had their hearts set on the playoffs. Besides, just about every preseason poll picked the Seahawks to finish ahead of the Raiders in the West.

Oakland scored the second time they got the ball in the first period as Bahr hit on a 34-yard field goal. In the opening minutes of the second quarter Bahr connected again, this time from 38 yards out, to give the Raiders a modest lead. Surprisingly, that was all the scoring in

the first half. The only other chance for a score came when Bahr missed a 43-yard field goal attempt. The Oakland defense had checked the Seahawks, who were adept at scoring points. The Seahawks never threatened seriously. Oakland limited quarterback Jim Zorn to only 98 yards passing and his entire offense to just 109 yards in the opening thirty minutes of play.

The Raiders received the second-half kick-

Cedrick Hardman collars Seattle quarterback Jim Zorn.

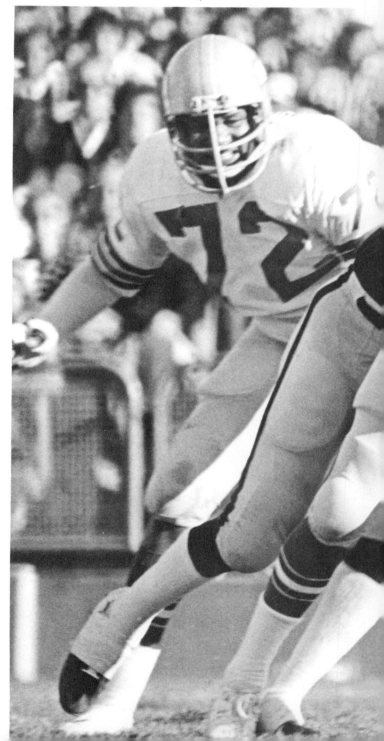

off and once again Bahr provided the action. He kicked a 30-yard field goal to stretch Oakland's lead to 9–0. Two minutes later Lester Hayes positioned the game's first touchdown when he intercepted Zorn, giving the Raiders the ball on the Seattle 27. Five plays later Plunkett tossed a 4-yard touchdown pass to Chandler to give Oakland a 16–0 advantage.

Most of the scoring came during the fourth period when a total of 31 points were logged.

The Raiders opened it when Plunkett hit Chandler with a 12-yard touchdown pass for a 23–0 lead. Seattle finally got on the scoreboard by taking the kickoff and going 80 yards. Lawrence McCutcheon punched it across from the 1 yard line.

Oakland came right back. For the third time Plunkett and Chandler hooked up—this time on a 23-yard touchdown pass that gave Oakland a 30–7 lead. Then it was Seattle's turn. Zorn didn't wait long, either. He threw a 67-yard touchdown bomb to Steve Largent. Four times between them the Raiders and Seahawks had the ball, and each scored each time. With 2:44 left in the game Bahr made a 25-yard field goal that completed Oakland's resounding 33–14 victory.

"Jim Plunkett used to tear us up when I was at Buffalo, and he was with New England," said Chandler. "He's turned this team around, and he's given us all a big lift."

GAME NINE: MIAMI

Miami	0	3	7	0	10
Oakland	6	10	0	0	16

Oakland: 6:13, first period—Chester, 13-yard pass from Plunkett (kick failed).
Miami: 0:03, second period—Von Schamann, 35-yard field goal.
Oakland: 4:44, second period—Bahr, 48-yard field goal.
Oakland: 12:04, second period—Chandler, 17-yard pass from Plunkett (Bahr, kick).
Miami: 5:52, third period—Robiskie, 2-yard run (Von Schamann, kick).

The pesky Miami Dolphins were 4-4; the Raiders, a respectable 5-3. The Dolphins failed to move following the opening kickoff. The Raiders struck. They covered 51 yards in eleven plays. The payoff was a 13-yard touchdown pass from Plunkett to Chester. Bahr missed the conversion and the score stood at 6–0. The first period ended that way, even though the Dolphins were threatening after intercepting Plunkett's pass deep in Oakland's territory. The Dolphins had to settle for a 35-yard field goal by Uwe von Schamann that cut the Raiders' lead in half, 6–3. Five minutes later Bahr came back with a 48-yard field goal. That gave the Raiders a 9–3 lead.

With the offenses of both teams struggling, Randy McClanahan gave the Raiders an excel-

Arthur Whittington turns the corner against Miami.

Derrick Jensen protects ball from eager Dolphins.

lent chance to score with a little over three minutes remaining. McClanahan picked off Dave Woodley's pass on the Miami 27 before being brought down on the 20. Plunkett didn't squander the opportunity. Two plays later he hit Chandler on a post pattern for a 17-yard touchdown pass. Von Schamann's 21-yard field goal attempt hit the right goal post. The half ended with the Raiders ahead 16–3.

The Dolphins capitalized on a break to score in the third period. They recovered a fumble by Derrick Jensen on the Oakland 35-yard line. Four plays later Terry Robiskie, a former Raider, scored from 2 yards out to pull the Dolphins to within 6 points. The quarter finished that way. Both teams had failed to generate a scoring drive. In the final period neither the Raiders nor the Dolphins could move into each other's territory. When it was finally over, Oakland had won its fourth straight game.

The Oakland defense had performed exceptionally well. They'd held the Dolphins to only 10 first downs in limiting them to just 166 total yards. Throughout the entire game the Dolphins managed to complete only fifty plays. In the second half Miami produced a meager 4 first downs.

Chandler's sensational touchdown catch, when he tipped the ball then fell back as he caught it, had made the difference.

"I heard Dolphin defensive back Glenn Blackwood yell, 'Oh, no!'" Chandler said, smiling.

"I don't know how Chandler caught the ball," lamented Miami coach Don Shula. "I thought for sure we had an interception."

GAME TEN: CINCINNATI

Cincinnati 3 7 0 7 17
Oakland 0 14 7 7 28

Cincinnati: 7:04, first period—Sunter, 29-yard field goal.
Oakland: 2:39, second period—Van Eeghen, 2-yard run (Bahr, kick).
Cincinnati: 10:04, second period—Ross, 1-yard pass from Anderson (Sunter, kick).
Oakland: 13:55, second period—King, 7-yard run (Bahr, kick).
Oakland: 0:15, third period—Whittington, 90-yard kickoff return (Bahr, kick).
Cincinnati: 5:07, fourth period—Bass, 20-yard pass from Thompson (Sunter, kick).
Oakland: 9:32, fourth period—Plunkett, 4-yard run (Bahr, kick).

The Oakland defense was growing more assertive each week. By the tenth game of the season they were tied for the NFL lead in interceptions, 20, and quarterback sacks, 34. When they took to the field against the Cincinnati Bengals in Oakland, the Raiders and the Chargers were tied for first place in the West with 6-3 records.

Cincinnati took the opening kickoff and drove straight downfield far enough for Ian Sunter to connect with a 29-yard field goal. The Raiders came back, but Chandler fumbled on the Bengals' 9 yard line after grabbing a pass from Plunkett.

Oakland finally assumed the lead early in the second period as Plunkett directed a 66-yard, eight-play series with Van Eeghen running the final 2 yards for the touchdown. The Bengals took the next kickoff and marched 77 yards in fourteen plays. Ken Anderson's 1-yard pass to tight end Dan Ross gave them a 10–7 lead.

Taking the kickoff, the Raiders cranked up. Plunkett, completing 3 out of 4 passes in a ten-play drive, led the Raiders 75 yards. King got the go-ahead touchdown on an 8-yard run, and the Raiders were leading, 14–10, at halftime.

Plunkett had an excellent first half. He completed 11 of 13 passes, but even more impressive was the fact that he converted all the third downs he'd had.

The second half had barely begun when Whittington had the fans on their feet. He had settled under Sunter's kick on the 10 yard line and broke it for an electrifying 90-yard kickoff return. It turned out to be the only score in the period. The Raiders went into the final period leading 21–10.

On Cincinnati's second possession of the fourth quarter, Jack Thompson replaced Anderson at quarterback. He brought the Bengals close with a 20-yard touchdown pass to Don Bass that cut Oakland's lead to 21–17.

However, five minutes before the end Plunkett got an insurance touchdown. He moved the Raiders 49 yards in six plays, running the last 4 yards himself. Oakland had won its seventh game.

"I felt we had to do whatever was necessary

to get another touchdown at that point," explained Plunkett. "I didn't like the feel of the game, the way it was going. They kept getting breaks, and I wasn't convinced our four-point lead would hold up under those circumstances."

Hendricks had been outstanding with seven tackles, including a sack.

"I felt like I played two games out there," said Hendricks. "It seemed every time we had them stopped, something would happen to keep us on the field."

GAME ELEVEN: SEATTLE

Oakland	0	0	7	12	19
Seattle	0	7	7	3	17

Seattle: 14:37, first period—McCutcheon, 1-yard run (Herrera, kick).
Seattle: 6:08, third period—Doornink, 8-yard pass from Zorn (Herrera, kick).
Oakland: 7:57, third period—Whittington, 10-yard run (Bahr, kick).
Seattle: 0:04, fourth period—Herrera, 37-yard field goal.
Oakland: 4:32, fourth period—Hendricks, safety, blocked punt through end zone.
Oakland: 6:30, fourth period—Van Eeghen, 1-yard run (Bahr, kick).
Oakland: 14:04, fourth period—Bahr, 28-yard field goal.

To everyone's surprise, when the Raiders appeared on their second *Monday Night Football* game of the season, they were in fiirst place in the Western Division. They had a 7-3 record while the Chargers, who had defeated the Chiefs the day before, were 7-4.

In meeting Seattle for the first time, the Raiders were playing their second Monday night contest on the road. The Seahawks were experiencing a disappointing season, losing six of their first ten games. They were picked by many to finish ahead of Oakland in the Western Division.

The teams played a scoreless first quarter. It appeared that the Seahawks would be the first to score. They took the opening kickoff and started on their 15 yard line, driving all the way to the Oakland 28 where they were stopped. Efren Herrera tried a 46-yard field goal that fell short. The Raiders had no scoring opportunities, having possession of the ball only twice during the entire quarter.

Seattle continued to control the game in the second period. Oakland never got close enough to even attempt a field goal. Finally, twenty-one seconds from the end of the half, Seattle scored. Quarterback Jim Zorn took the Seahawks 81 yards in ten plays with Larry McCutcheon scoring the touchdown from 1 yard out to give Seattle a 7–0 halftime lead.

Plunkett couldn't get things going in the opening half. He completed only 3 of 9 passes for 12 yards. The Raiders could only produce 3 first downs with a ground game that netted just 56 yards. Their offense didn't elicit any praise from Howard who, from the television booth, was quite critical of the Raiders.

Oakland couldn't do anything after receiving the second-half kickoff. When the Seahawks got the ball for the first time, they scored. Zorn led them on a 56-yard drive in eight plays, putting Seattle ahead, 14–0, with an 8-yard pass to Dan Doornink.

The Raiders finally scored when they got the ball back. They drove 81 yards in six plays with Whittington running the final 10 yards for the touchdown. However, they needed a break to do it. Oakland's attack stalled, and Ray Guy was sent in to punt on fourth and 2 on the Raider 27. Instead of punting, Guy took off around right end for a 24-yard run before he was knocked out of bounds.

When the fourth period opened, Seattle added to its lead. Herrera booted a 37-yard field goal to send the Seahawks into a 17–7 lead. The Raiders needed a spark to get them going, and they got one—from the defense.

With just over ten minutes left in the contest, the Seahawks were forced to punt from their 28 yard line. Herman Weaver never got his kick off. Hendricks, who once again displayed his remarkable ability to block kicks, rushed in, blocked it, and chased after the ball as it rolled out of the end zone for a safety that narrowed Seattle's lead to 17–9.

Oakland then marched 59 yards in five plays after the free kick with Van Eeghen scoring from a yard out to pull the Raiders to within one point, 17–16. There were still eight minutes to play. With only fifty-six seconds remaining, Bahr gave the Raiders a 19–17 victory by kicking a 28-yard field goal.

"If there's time on the clock, we'll find a way to win it," exclaimed Upshaw triumphantly.

Jim Plunkett scrambles for a four-yard touchdown against Cincinnati.

GAME TWELVE: PHILADELPHIA

Oakland	0	0	0	7	7
Philadelphia	0	0	3	7	10

Philadelphia: 7:54, third period—Franklin, 51-yard field goal.
Oakland: 2:37, fourth period—Branch, 86-yard pass from Plunkett (Bahr, kick).
Philadelphia: 12:04, fourth period—Montgomery, 3-yard run (Franklin, kick).

The Raiders' lethargic showing against Seattle was perhaps attributable to the fact that they were looking ahead to the Philadelphia Eagles. The high-flying Eagles had won ten of eleven games and needed only one more victory to clinch a playoff spot. A large crowd of 68,535 turned out in Philadelphia's Veterans Stadium to see if the Eagles would do it.

Philadelphia won the coin toss and received the opening kickoff. They moved from their 25 to the Oakland 43 yard line before Ron Jaworski threw three incomplete passes in a row. The Eagles were forced to punt.

The Raiders had a good drive going after Max Runager's punt went out of bounds on the Oakland 18 yard line. Plunkett quickly had them downfield with three big pass completions, one to Branch for 16 yards and two to Chester, the first for 20 and the second for 22. That brought the Raiders to the Eagle 10 yard line. On second down from the 8, Plunkett hit Chester with a short pass on the 5. Chester fumbled as he was hit, and Jerry Robinson recovered the ball for the Eagles.

With less than four minutes remaining, the Raiders threatened again. Bahr got a bad break on his 45-yard field goal attempt when his kick hit the right upright. The quarter ended with no score.

The defenses continued to dominate in the second period. Only the Raiders came close to scoring. The first time, Plunkett's pass was intercepted in the end zone. The second time, the Raiders reached the Eagle 39 as the half ended in a deadlock.

Plunkett had a rough time. Although he managed to complete 6 of 19 passes for 111 yards, he nevertheless was sacked 6 times. The Oakland ground game was virtually nonexistent. Oakland's defense was outstanding, limiting the Eagles to only 4 first downs and a total of 70 yards.

John Matuszak, Willie Jones, and Cedrick Hardman **109** surround Philadelphia quarterback Ron Jaworski.

The tough defense continued during the third period. Finally, halfway through the stanza the Eagles scored. It took a herculean 51-yard field goal by barefoot kicker Tony Franklin to give the Eagles a 3–0 lead. It turned out to be the only score in the quarter.

Early in the fourth period the Raiders invaded. They swooped down quickly, too. Plunkett and Branch connected on an 86-yard touchdown pass less than three minutes into the period for a 7–3 Oakland lead.

It appeared they'd taken a firm hold on the lead. Relentlessly, the Eagles kept pecking away, searching out the soft spots until they'd put together a 71-yard drive that resulted in a game-winning touchdown by Wilbert Montgomery from 3 yards out. The big play that positioned the touchdown was a 43-yard pass from Jaworski to heavy-running fullback Leroy Harris. Philadelphia's hard-fought 10-7 victory broke the Raiders' six-game winning streak.

"We thought we could do a few things against them, but we didn't," said Plunkett, who was sacked eight times. "You usually control the game by shutting down the run and using a good pass rush. The Eagles had that today. We had a chance to score some points in the first quarter, but we didn't. We thought we could run the ball better, and we didn't. We thought we could throw it, and we didn't."

GAME THIRTEEN: DENVER

Denver	3	0	0	0	3
Oakland	0	0	6	3	9

Denver: 9:19, first period—Steinfort, 41-yard field goal.
Oakland: 3:01, third period—Plunkett, 8-yard run (kick failed).
Oakland: 1:54, fourth period—Bahr, 44-yard field goal.

It was to be the Raiders' third *Monday Night Football* game of the season. No team had appeared more in this prime-time slot during the 1980 season than Oakland. As always seemed the case, Oakland was faced with another crucial game.

The Raiders were to meet the rugged Denver Broncos for the first time. Two weeks later they were scheduled to meet the Broncos again in Denver. And the Broncos were hot, winning three consecutive games and aver-

aging 29 points over that span. Their winning streak pushed the Broncos into a contending spot in the Western Division. They had a 7-5 record, while Oakland and San Diego still remained tied for the lead with 8-4 records.

Oakland couldn't capitalize on a first-period turnover when Burgess Owens intercepted Craig Morton's pass. Starting on their own 43 yard line, the Raiders reached the Broncos' 35 before stalling. Upon getting the ball back, Morton took the Broncos from the 15 yard line to the Oakland 24 before missing on a third-down pass. Fred Steinfort, an ex-Raider, booted a 41-yard field goal to give Denver a 3–0 lead.

Beginning a drive near the completion of the first quarter, Oakland had reached the Denver 5 yard line as the second period opened. Suddenly, after moving from their own 28 yard line, the Raiders were stymied. On third down Plunkett was sacked for an 8-yard loss, and Bahr came in to attempt a 31-yard field goal that would tie the game. However, he missed it.

As it turned out, that was the only serious scoring situation for the rest of the quarter. Neither team could get close enough to score any points, and the half ended with Denver on top, 3–0.

The Raiders collected the second-half kickoff and didn't stop. They drove 77 yards in only seven plays. Plunkett scored the touchdown himself. On first down he ran a bootleg around right end from 8 yards away to give Oakland a 6–3 advantage. Bahr couldn't increase the lead because his conversion attempt had hit the left post. The Broncos were only a field goal away from tying the game.

Oakland's defense kept them away. Three times the Broncos had the ball in the third period, and three times they went three downs and out. The Raiders missed a chance to increase their lead when Bahr went wide on a 26-yard field goal try with less than a minute left in the quarter.

However, the fourth period was less than two minutes old when Bahr was dispatched to attempt a 44-yard field goal. This time he connected and lifted Oakland's margin to 9–3. The Broncos were still only a touchdown away

Matt Millen makes sure Denver's Jim Jensen doesn't go anywhere.

from grabbing the lead.

They never even got close. The Raiders' defense didn't allow the Broncos to cross midfield for the rest of the game. They couldn't afford to give up a touchdown. Bahr missed two more field goal attempts, and Oakland held on to a 9–3 win.

GAME FOURTEEN: DALLAS

Dallas	7	9	3	0	19
Oakland	7	3	3	0	13

Oakland: 4:59, first period—Chester, 6-yard pass from Plunkett (Bahr, kick).
Dallas: 11:53, first period—Dorsett, 20-yard run (Septien, kick).
Dallas: 2:29, second period—Septien, 52-yard field goal.
Dallas: 4:14, second period—Springs, 2-yard run (kick failed).
Oakland: 8:31, second period—Bahr, 22-yard field goal.
Dallas: 3:05, third period—Septien, 34-yard field goal.
Oakland: 13:52, third period—Bahr, 38-yard field goal.

There was some concern before the Raiders faced the Dallas Cowboys in Oakland. Flores was wondering whatever happened to his offense. In the last three games the Raiders had only scored 35 points. To make matters worse, the offense had produced a paltry 16 points in the last two games. Against the powerful Cowboys that kind of showing wouldn't be nearly good enough.

The first time the Raiders got the ball all doubts were dispelled; they cashed in quickly. A short punt by Dallas gave the Raiders excellent field position on the Cowboy 34. Seven plays later, Oakland scored a touchdown when Plunkett hit Chester with a 6-yard pass in the left corner of the end zone.

The Cowboys tied the score when they took over. Quarterback Danny White led them on an 80-yard drive that took twelve plays. The payoff was a 20-yard burst up the middle by Tony Dorsett. The period ended that way: 7–7.

Less than three minutes after the second quarter had begun, Dallas took the lead. Rafael Septien booted a 52-yard field goal to give the Cowboys a 10–7 lead. It didn't take them long to increase it, either. Keith Moody fumbled the kickoff, and the Cowboys recovered it on their own 46. Moody had almost broken away for a touchdown when he was stripped of the ball on the Dallas 48. Five plays later the

112   Raymond Chester catches a six-yard touchdown pass against Dallas.

Cowboys scored on a 2-yard run by Ron Springs. However, the score remained at 16–7 when Septien's extra-point kick hit the right post.

Oakland managed to get back on the scoreboard following the kickoff. Plunkett had a good drive going, which began from his 30 and reached the Dallas 4 yard line before stalling. Bahr then kicked a 22-yard field goal to trim Dallas's lead to 16–10. He missed a chance to trim it even further with an aborted 41-yard attempt at the end of the half.

Three minutes into the third period the Cowboys added another field goal. O'Steen recovered Robert Newhouse's fumble on the Dallas 16. When the Raiders failed to get a first down, Bahr kicked a 38-yard field goal to bring Oakland to within a touchdown again, 19–13, as the third period ended.

Throughout the final quarter the Dallas defense continued to frustrate the Raiders. Four times the Raiders began an offensive series, and only once did they come close to scoring. It occurred less than two minutes from the end when Oakland reached the Dallas 30 yard line. Throwing on first down, Plunkett's pass was picked off in the end zone, and Dallas prevailed, 19–13, to give the Raiders their fifth loss.

"We just made too many mistakes against a good football team," explained Flores. "We had our share of opportunities, but we just didn't take advantage of them. We're still in first place, though. We can still win the division, but we'll have to do it ourselves."

GAME FIFTEEN: DENVER

Oakland	7	10	0	7	24
Denver	0	7	7	7	21

Oakland: 5:56, first period—Owens, 58-yard interception (Bahr, kick).
Denver: 0:04, second period—Preston, 2-yard run (Steinfort, kick).
Oakland: 9:05, second period—Bahr, 44-yard field goal.
Oakland: 14:20, second period—Chandler, 11-yard pass from Plunkett (Bahr, kick).
Denver: 13:32, third period—Odoms, 11-yard pass from Morton (Steinfort, kick).
Oakland: 0:48, fourth period—Chandler, 38-yard pass from Plunkett (Bahr, kick).
Denver: 3:52, fourth period—Preston, 9-yard run (Steinfort, kick).

Cliff Branch looks for more daylight against Denver.

Cornerback Lester Hayes goes one-on-one with San Diego's Charlie Joiner.

Deadlocked with San Diego for the Western lead with a 9-5 record, the Raiders began the first of two season-ending road games in Denver against the Broncos. Nothing comes easy in the Mile High City, and the Broncos were kicking up their heels after a sluggish campaign to even their record at 7-7. What the Raiders needed was a stronger showing offensively since the Broncos always represented a challenge over the years with their famed Orange Crush defense.

It took the Oakland defense to get things started. Only 5:56 had elapsed in the opening period when Burgess Owens picked off Craig Morton's pass and ran it back 58 yards for a touchdown to give the Raiders the early lead. The period ended with the Broncos threatening to tie the game.

They did so on the first play of the second period. Matt Robinson, who had replaced Morton, directed an 80-yard drive that took nine plays, with Dave Preston getting the final 2 yards for the tying touchdown.

The Raiders came back after the kickoff with their own drive, only to be denied. Beginning on their own 11, they had advanced to the Denver 18 before Plunkett missed on two passes. Bahr then tried a 26-yard field goal that was low and wide to the right. However, he came back on the next series and booted one 44 yards to give Oakland a 10–7 lead. With less than a minute remaining, Oakland struck again. Plunkett connected with Chandler for an 11-yard touchdown pass that provided the Raiders with a 17–7 halftime advantage. They had already scored more points than in each of their previous three games.

When the second half opened, Morton came back to direct the Denver offense. Less than two minutes before the third period ended, Morton brought the huge crowd of 73,974, the largest to see the Raiders play all year, to its feet. He completed three consecutive passes of 22, 33, and 11 yards. The final pass was caught by Riley Odoms, who scored a touchdown to narrow Oakland's margin to 17–14.

Early in the fourth period Plunkett answered back. He completed two passes in a row: the first to Derrick Ramsey for 17 yards; the second, a touchdown pass to Chandler that covered 38 yards. There were still fourteen minutes left when Oakland stepped into a 24–14 lead.

Denver came right back. Morton took them 87 yards in just seven plays, hitting on 5 of the 6 passes he threw before Preston burst

through the middle for a 9-yard touchdown run. With 11:08 left on the clock, there was still plenty of time. The Broncos still had a chance to tie the game with 2:30 remaining. However, Fred Steinfort, who used to kick for the Raiders, missed a 37-yard field goal attempt.

"We've won ten games now and have a chance to do something in the playoffs," said Flores. "We are in control of our own destiny."

GAME SIXTEEN
NEW YORK GIANTS

Oakland	10	10	7	6	33
New York	0	10	0	7	17

Oakland: 6:28, first period—Bahr, 41-yard field goal.

Oakland: 10:33, first period—Whittington, 7-yard run (Bahr, kick).

New York: 4:34, second period—Danelo, 47-yard field goal.

Oakland: 8:31, second period—Branch, 31-yard pass from Plunkett (Bahr, kick).

Oakland: 12:08, second period—Bahr, 38-yard field goal.

New York: 14:15, second period—Perry, 11-yard pass from Brunner (Danelo, kick).

Oakland: 12:05, third period—Chester, 37-yard pass from Plunkett (Bahr, kick).

New York: 14:38, fourth period—Taylor, 1-yard run (Danelo, kick).

Oakland: 14:44, fourth period—Jensen, 33-yard kickoff return (kick failed).

Only one game remained. The Raiders had to win that Sunday to keep the pressure on the San Diego Chargers who were scheduled in the final *Monday Night Football* game of the year on the very next day. It wouldn't come easy since the Raiders were making their fourth transcountry trip of the season, playing the New York Giants in East Rutherford, New Jersey.

Although the game was a sellout even before the 1980 campaign began, a record number of 15,447 no-shows kept the actual crowd to 61,287. It reflected the disappointment of local fans who were disgusted with the Giants' 4-11 record, their eighth consecutive losing season. Still, the Raiders had to guard against being overconfident.

Oakland opened the scoring when Bahr booted a 41-yard field goal midway through the first period. Five minutes later they added to their lead. Hendricks positioned the Raiders for a touchdown when he deflected Dave Jennings's punt. It wasn't ruled a block but a

1-yard punt instead and gave the Raiders possession on the New York 11 yard line. On second down Whittington scooted around right end to give Oakland a 10–0 lead.

Joe Danelo opened the second-period scoring with a 47-yard field goal to reduce Oakland's margin to 10–3. The Raiders took the kickoff and went 79 yards in nine plays with Plunkett hitting Branch with a 31-yard pass for a touchdown and a 17–3 advantage. Three minutes later Bahr added to it with a 38-yard field goal. The Giants scored just before the first half concluded as Scott Brunner threw an 11-yard touchdown pass to Leon Perry to keep the Giants in the game at 20–10.

That was as close as it got. Plunkett made certain there wouldn't be another opportunity for the Giants to become overconfident as he tossed a 37-yard touchdown to Chester, giving the Raiders a 27–10 bulge just three minutes before the end of the third quarter.

Scoring slowed down until twenty-five seconds before the end of the game. In that twenty-five seconds two touchdowns were scored. The first was by the Giants when Billy Taylor ended a seventeen-play, 80-yard drive by diving across the goal line from the 1 yard line.

The touchdown gave the Giants hope to try an onside kick. Danelo was short on his first try, and the Giants were penalized for illegally touching the ball on the second attempt. When Danelo tried a third time, Derrick Jensen picked up the ball on the New York 33 and ran untouched through the Giants' defense for a touchdown. Bahr's extra-point try was wide, and the Raiders ended their surprising season with a 33–17 conquest. At last, Oakland was playoff-bound. The Raiders' 11-5 record was their best since their Super Bowl season of 1977 when they finished 11-3.

"I don't think anyone would have given us any odds that we'd be in this position at the end of the year," said Flores. "Everyone was saying we'd be lucky to win four to finish out of last place. It's a real tribute to the whole team. They've hung tough week after week after week."

There was still a new season with four weeks to go. . . .

Bob Nelson (51) and Reggie Kinlaw (62) stop Giants' Billy Taylor.

HOUSTON PLAYOFF

The reality of making the championship playoffs didn't allow the players quite enough time to savor their accomplishment. It was, after all, a new season. Finishing their regular season with an 11-5 record simply allowed them the opportunity to participate in the playoffs to determine the final two participants in Super Bowl XV. For the Raiders it was a long shot. Yet, they had been battling long odds all season long. It's just that in the playoffs the odds are more pronounced. The Raiders didn't need to be reminded that a wild-card team had never won a Super Bowl. It was not a concern. It was much the same five months earlier when none of the experts even remotely suggested that Oakland would somehow make their way into the playoffs. The consensus was that the Raiders were in decline and would finish no higher than fourth in the five-team Western Division. Even after a shallow beginning the team hung tough, overcame incalculable obstacles, and succeeded in reaching playoff land. They felt now that they had destiny in their hands. They could win or lose it themselves, and that's the way they liked it.

Just as during the regular season, none of the analysts gave the Raiders much of a chance. In the first place they still weren't convinced that Plunkett could provide the big-game performance necessary in games of championship caliber. Then, too, as a wild card team, the Raiders would play their remaining two games on the road should they succeed in defeating the Houston Oilers, the other wild card entry, in Oakland.

Actually, there was strong sentiment across the nation that the Oilers would eventually end up in New Orleans as the American Football Conference champion. When Al Davis swapped Stabler for Pastorini long before the 1980 season began, Oiler partisans were talking Super Bowl as early as March when the deal was finalized. A month into the season, after tight end Dave Casper was reunited with Stabler, Houston fans were certain of it. With ex-Raider safety Jack Tatum, they had what they felt was the nucleus of the winning Raider team down through the years. They were singing "Luv Ya Blue" all over Houston.

In Oakland linebacker coach Charlie Sumner spent a long night on Monday before the Houston game watching films of the Oilers, making notes, devising charts, and setting alignments. By nature Sumner is conservative. However, for this game he wanted a special

The Raider defense pressured Houston quarterback Kenny Stabler all afternoon. Lester Hayes began it with a sack.

defensive scheme, since he was well acquainted with Stabler's tendencies. He felt that if he could pressure the wily quarterback, he could upset the tempo of the Houston offense.

Sumner had a heavy challenge. Besides Stabler, who is a pure passer and knew the Raider personnel better than any quarterback in the league since he'd been a Raider for a decade, the Oilers also had Earl Campbell, who is perhaps the purest running fullback in NFL history. Sumner couldn't attempt to concentrate on one without falling prey to the other. He determined that the Stabler project was paramount.

The initial phase of Sumner's defensive plan was to have Matuszak drive hard on every down from his left end position. Matuszak's charge would undoubtedly occupy two blockers in an attempt to slow down his rush. Matuszak's penetration would then allow Hendricks and, at times, Hayes to blitz from the left side. It was something different all right. It has never been a Raider tendency to have a cornerback blitz—a safety, yes, but rarely a cornerback. Sumner figured that such an approach would frustrate Stabler.

"I consider myself a conservative coach," admitted Sumner. "Blitzing isn't my style, but I saw something this time."

Flores agreed with what Sumner detected. Perhaps better than anyone else, he knew Stabler's tendencies. He didn't hesitate to approve Sumner's plan.

"We've got to load up on him from our left side," revealed Flores, after the strategy was implemented to the defensive team later that week. "When Kenny drifts, he drifts to his right. He feels it gives him a better look downfield. We've got to make him uncomfortable out there. I've seen him carve up so many teams—just work them over. I remember on the Thursday before the 1977 Super Bowl, which was our offensive day, we went through a whole practice; and the ball only touched the ground once, and that was on a dropped pass. John Madden was standing next to me and said, 'What do you think, Tom?' I said, 'Throw a blanket over him and get him out of here. This is scary.'

"Look, we've seen Kenny and Casper on

Coach Tom Flores hugs Hayes near game's end.

film and television, and the fact that they are no longer here with us isn't strange anymore. It's probably going to be more peculiar for the fans than for the players."

It was ironic that the Raiders' first challenge in the playoffs was the Oilers. Stabler, Casper, and even the notorious Tatum were all popular with Oakland fans when they played there. In fact, all season long there were grumblings among the fans that the Raiders should never have traded any of them. Now they were returning to the scene of their past glory, as their adversaries certainly cried for revenge. Yet, it never showed in Stabler, who has always appeared cool as a professional gunfighter.

"It's just another game to me," remarked Stabler. "Really, it doesn't make any difference to me about playing Oakland. It'll be nice to see the guys I played with again, but this game doesn't have any special meaning or anything like that. The main thing about our situation now with the playoff is not to get caught up in all the rhetoric about going back to Oakland. I've always gotten along with the fans in Oakland. I don't know what to expect, but I don't picture getting booed. I might . . . but I didn't play that bad when I was there.

"I think the key to the Raiders' winning this year is that they're playing better defense than last year. They don't gamble as much. They're a little more aggressive. They simply have better personnel defensively."

Tatum agreed. He had kept his friends on the Raiders ever since the trade. Like Stabler, Tatum was liked by the Oakland players.

"They play a very physical game," said Tatum. "That's the way the Raiders teach you to play. It's an organizational thing. Plus, guys like Ted Hendricks who have been around show the way, and it automatically rubs off. We had good defense when I was there, but I don't think we really had a great pass rush like they have now. We might have started the season that way, but we always seemed to have injuries.

"I'm really not surprised at what Oakland has done. I am, though, surprised at the year Jim Plunkett has had. He gave them a great year. He gave them exactly what they traded for to get Pastorini. I'll say one thing, the Oak-

land fans are pretty loyal, so getting booed wouldn't surprise me at all."

On the other hand, Casper was not at all popular with his Raider teammates. Casper, a free spirit, was a loner much of the time and really never cultivated many friendships. Many of the players considered him an outsider. After an early-season loss to Kansas City, the Raiders' record dropped to 2-3. At the time one of the players stood up and shouted, "If there is anybody here who doesn't want to be a part of this, you can leave." Reportedly, Casper left the room. A week later he was traded to Houston.

Casper managed to fall further out of favor with his ex-teammates. He took a hard verbal shot at Gene Upshaw, the team's elder statesman, several days before the game. Casper regarded Upshaw as the worst offensive lineman on the Raiders, calling him an underachiever who seldom worked up a sweat. "He's the Michelin Man in his white suit; he never falls down and never gets his uniform dirty."

"I was happy to get out of Oakland," added Casper. "The only time I thought of Oakland was when I got knocked out in New York. When I woke up, I thought I was on the Raiders. It was a bad dream, but I was okay after I found out I was still on the Oilers."

While Upshaw bristled, his teammates made light of Casper's remarks. Still, Upshaw didn't get caught up in the emotion. He kept his cool and kept things in perspective concerning the return of the ex-Raiders.

"We have to guard against thinking only about stopping them," cautioned Upshaw. "We have to see the big picture, which is beating the Oilers."

Upshaw's words were important to strong safety Mike Davis. His assignment was to take Casper in certain passing situations. Davis was cool.

"The thing you have to remember is that you can't wage any personal battles on Sunday," pointed out Davis. "It's eleven-on-eleven. I know I'll be playing Casper one-on-one part of the time, and I know I must play my best because he can make you look foolish if you don't. He and Snake work well together. You have to stop their free-lancing because they can adjust their patterns to take advantage of your defense. You never know what the hell they'll do.

"We realize the key guys on offense—Campbell, Stabler, and Casper—are nearly unstoppable; but you have to approach them as stoppable. Earl and Stabler are the keys to the Oilers. We know that. Everybody is talking about how we feel about those three guys coming back. Why don't they talk about the Raiders coming back? Why don't they talk about how we weren't expected to be here and how we made it anyway?"

Davis's teammate in the secondary, Lester Hayes, was looking forward to the Oilers, who were 3-point favorites to beat Oakland. Hayes, who led the entire NFL with 13 interceptions,

expected a busy day. Stabler had never been bashful about throwing. He had that much confidence in his passing ability. Hayes was ready.

"I love the fact that Houston is in the playoffs," remarked Hayes, "because I like to play against receivers with five-flat speed. Besides, Stabler is not the same quarterback he was when he was here. His scheme has changed considerably. His receivers are running much shorter routes now, and he's not throwing to his outside receivers as much. He'll throw most of his passes to his tight ends and running backs. The basic reason is that his receivers don't have a lot of speed."

The only speed the Raiders were primarily concerned about was Kenny King's. The quick

Hendricks makes his presence felt.

running back had sprained his ankle two weeks before and hadn't played much against the New York Giants in the final regular-season game. King, a former Oiler, was quite excited about facing his old team.

"Nothing is going to keep me out of this game," exclaimed King, whose ankle wasn't completely healed. "There will be more emotion in it for me than there would be if I were playing Buffalo or Cleveland. I have a lot of friends at Houston, and I know they are going to be out to stick me. They won't be trying to hurt me, but they'll try to hit me as hard as they can.

"They run a pretty basic defense. If we can go out there and sustain some drives and keep the momentum, we'll have a good day against them. I know what I'm capable of doing against their defense. I'm about seventy-five percent. I made a cut on my ankle in practice just to see how it felt, and it was pretty good. I'm a lot better than I was in the Denver game. My ankle wasn't as good as I thought for that one.

"I feel like Marlon Brando. I don't mind all the questions because it's all part of the job. I just hate being hurt because I hate people saying: 'How do you feel? How do you feel?' time after time. I'll tell you how I feel. I feel like putting a sign on my chest that says, 'I'm fine.'

"I'm not complaining. It's a lot better than Houston. I didn't get any attention there at all. Oh, a lot of people looked at me all right. They had to. My locker was right next to

Rod Martin leaps through the air after the Houston quarterback.

Ted Hendricks zeroes in on Stabler.

Campbell's. If I left and went to take a shower, I couldn't get back to my locker. I'd come back and say: 'Excuse me. That's my locker,' and they'd say, 'Oh, yeah, sure.' "

Matuszak wasn't as inconspicuous when he was a member of the Oilers. In fact, he was their first-round draft choice in 1973 and the first player picked in the entire draft. He jumped the team the following year and signed with the Houston Texans of the ill-fated World Football League. The big end really didn't have any emotional ties with the Oilers except, perhaps, to Stabler. He'd roomed with the quarterback during his last year in Oakland in 1979.

"I'm just going out there and play clean, hard football," said Matuszak. "I'm going to help Kenny up if I get a chance to knock him down, and I'm sure he'll pat me on the behind. We both have great respect for each other."

"I'll tell you, the way I look at it we don't even deserve to be in the Super Bowl if we don't get past this team. This has got to be one of the greatest teams that Houston has ever had. If we beat them, we deserve to keep going."

The Oilers were somewhat of an enigma offensively. No other Houston team in the twenty-one-year history of the club ever moved the ball as effectively as this one. They finished second in the AFC, averaging 352 yards a game; yet, they couldn't score with the same effectiveness. The Oilers averaged slightly better than 2 touchdowns a game during the regular season.

Stabler himself was a paradox. He threw more passes than he ever did, 457, and completed 64 percent of them, averaging 4 points higher than his career record, which is the best in NFL history. The telling statistics were that Stabler threw 28 interceptions and only 13 touchdown passes. It was the fewest in his eleven-year career.

On the other hand, Campbell had the best year ever in his short, three-year career. Despite missing several games with a deep thigh injury, Campbell rushed for 1,934 yards, just 69 yards short of tying O. J. Simpson's single-season record of 2,003 yards set in 1973.

With all the interest centering around Campbell and the return of Stabler, Casper, and Tatum, little attention was being given to Plunkett. Quietly, he prepared for the biggest game of his ten-year career. In all his years with New England and San Francisco, Plunkett had never appeared in a playoff game. He didn't allow the unusual interest the game presented to affect his outlook.

"I know the trades are fun things to talk about with this game coming up, but we're just playing the Oilers, and they have to play us," emphasized Plunkett. "That's all it really comes down to. This has to be played like a championship game. There can't be any concern for faces or friends.

"I'm looking forward to Sunday more than any other Sunday in my life. For the first time in my career I don't look at any other team with awe. We're as good as any of them."

Plunkett had stated it all succinctly. It was

the same thinking that management exercised. They wanted the players to remove themselves from all the emphasis being focused on Stabler/Casper/Tatum versus the Raiders. It was Oakland against Houston.

"We insulated the football team from all the distracting stories," said Al LoCasale, who is Davis's chief aide. "Their total concentration is on the game, and that's the way we want it."

Oakland fans couldn't have asked for a better day for football. The weather was perfect when both teams lined up for battle. The sky was clear, and although the temperature was 55 degrees, the humidity was 82 percent, which made it comfortable outdoors.

Stabler and Houston would get the opportunity to strike first. The Oilers won the coin toss and instructed referee Chuck Heberling that they would accept the kickoff. Bahr showed a strong leg. He kicked the ball to the Houston goal line, where Ronnie Coleman caught it and made his way back to the 24 yard line. For the first time in his career, Stabler walked on the field in Oakland as a visiting player. He looked strange in white.

He didn't waste any time in handing the ball to Campbell on the game's first play. The big fullback was hit hard by Reggie Kinlaw, and the ball squirted loose from his arm. An alert Davis recovered the ball on the 28 yard line for an unexpected turnover. The Raiders had a golden opportunity to score.

King tried the right side and couldn't gain anything. Van Eeghen went the same route and picked up 3 yards to the 25. A motion penalty set the Raiders back to the 30, where Plunkett had to convert a third and 12. He sent Bahr on a deep pattern in the left end zone but overthrew him. Bahr came back on the field, this time to attempt a 47-yard field goal. His leg was strong and accurate, and the Raiders jumped into a 3–0 lead after 1:27 had been played.

On the kickoff Carl Roaches, a dangerous kick returner, gave the Oilers good field position by reaching the 39 yard line. This time on first down Stabler went to his favorite receiver, Casper, and connected with a 12-yard pass to the Oakland 49. The combination brought back memories to Raider fans, only this time

Bob Chandler grabs on to one.

they weren't cheering. Switching to the run was futile. Campbell was stopped first for no gain and then gained 2 yards. On third down Rob Carpenter gained only a yard, and Houston had to punt.

The Raiders almost fell into serious trouble on Cliff Parsley's punt. Ira Matthews fumbled the kick on the 8 yard line, but fortunately recovered the loose ball on the 5. The misplay put the Raiders in a hole. After Van Eeghen pushed his way for 3 yards, Plunkett didn't hesitate to pass. He shot a quick one to Chester for a 10-yard gain to the 18. King got Oakland 5 yards on first down but could only get 1 the second time he carried. Plunkett wanted Chester again but missed him on the 45 yard line. Ray Guy made his first appearance but could only produce a 38-yard punt. When Roaches returned the kick 10 yards, the Oilers had excellent field position on their own 48.

Playing pass, Hayes figured correctly. He

blitzed from the left side and nailed Stabler for a 9-yard loss. The 52,762 fans went wild. Stabler then tried a quick pass over the middle to tight end Mike Barber, but Davis tipped the ball away. A third down pass to Carpenter produced only 9 yards, and Parsley returned to punt a second time. This time Matthews held onto the ball on the 7 and made his way to the 16 yard line. However, linebacker Randy McClanahan committed a clipping penalty inside the 10 yard line, and the Raiders were forced to begin play on the 5 for the second straight time.

Plunkett was cautious. He gave the ball three consecutive times to the sure-handed Van Eeghen. He advanced the ball 6 yards and 2 yards before being stopped for no gain on third down. Guy boomed a punt 53 yards to get the Raiders out of immediate danger. However, Roaches ran it back 11 yards to once again give the Oilers excellent field position on the Houston 45.

Campbell moved for 6 yards to get the Oilers into Oakland territory. Stabler's second-down pass to Casper was broken up by ex-Jet Burgess Owens on the 10 yard line. Stabler came right back with a pass, this time to Coleman, that was successful for 23 yards. Suddenly the Oilers were in striking position on the Oakland 26.

Campbell brought the crowd to its feet when he burst up the middle for 14 yards to the 12. It didn't end there. Stabler handed the ball to Campbell five straight times. Finally, the bruising fullback went over from a yard out to send Houston into the lead. Toni Fritsch, surprisingly, missed the extra point. An offside penalty on Dwayne O'Steen gave him another chance. He converted and Houston led, 7–3.

When the second period opened, the Raiders were in trouble again. Just before the first quarter ended, Plunkett was sacked for a 10-yard loss on the 8 yard line. After King failed to gain a yard, the period ended. On the first play of the second quarter Plunkett threw an incomplete pass to Branch. This necessitated another punt. Kicking near the end line of the end zone, Guy punted to the Houston 43. Roaches almost broke it. He sped 21 yards be-

fore being brought down on the Oakland 36.

The Oilers were in position to strike again. On first down Campbell got 6 yards; then he carried for 4 and a first down on the 26. Twice more the hard-working Campbell carried, first for 2 yards and then for 5. Stabler's third-down pass from the 19 was incomplete. On the play the Raiders accepted a 10-yard holding penalty that sent the Oilers back to the 29. When Carpenter gained only 2 yards, Fritsch was sent in to try a 45-yard field goal. His kick was short, and Oakland took over.

Still, Plunkett couldn't move them. King got 3 yards and then 4 more before Plunkett failed on a long third-down pass to Branch on the Oiler 23 yard stripe. Guy's fourth punt of the afternoon was a classic. It traveled 66 yards into the Houston end zone. On the kick Tatum was called for holding. The Oilers had to begin again from the 10 yard line.

Stabler depended on Campbell again. He went into the line three consecutive times for a total of 7 yards, with Hendricks in on two of the tackles. Campbell kept sliding in and out of the slots on the line. Parsley's weak 34-yard kick gave the Raiders an opportunity in Oiler territory for the first time since the opening minute of the game.

King gained 2 yards to the 39. On the next play the fans sprang to their feet, yelling. Plunkett sent King deep on a pass play down the right sideline. King, showing his exceptional speed, made a sensational catch while leaping and falling backward on the 2 yard line. Suddenly, on a single play, the Raiders were ready to assume the lead again. Derrick Jensen, who replaced King, was stopped for no gain. When Van Eeghen could gain only a yard, Plunkett had a big call to make on third down. With a full backfield, he fooled the Oilers by flipping a 1-yard pass to reserve tight end Todd Christensen for the go-ahead touchdown. Bahr made the conversion, and the Raiders moved into a 10–7 lead.

The Oilers couldn't do anything after the kickoff. Hayes put them in a hole by sacking Stabler for a 10-yard loss. Three plays later Parsley had to punt.

Beginning on their own 36, the Raiders, on a second-down pass from Plunkett to Arthur

Whittington, had a first down on the Oiler 44. They didn't get much farther. On third down from the 48 Plunkett tried to go deep to Chester in the end zone with only 2:38 left in the first half. However, Vernon Perry intercepted, and Houston took over on the 20.

After Carpenter gained 4 yards, Dave Browning made a big play. He dropped Stabler for an 8-yard loss to mark the third time the ex-Raider was sacked. Two plays later Parsley was called upon to punt. When, however, the Raiders failed to run out the clock, the Oilers got the ball back again, following another fine 56-yard punt by Guy.

There was only 1:01 showing on the clock as Stabler prepared to take the snap on the Houston 25 yard line. He could work magic with the clock. There was no question that he would utilize a hurry-up passing attack. His first pass to Mike Renfro gained 12 yards. After an incomplete toss, he collaborated with Carpenter up the middle for a 14-yard gain to the Oakland 49.

Just twenty-seven seconds remained. Stabler quickly hit Billy Johnson for 11 on the 38. An offside penalty on Matuszak placed the ball on the 33 yard line. There were only eleven seconds remaining. Stabler dropped back to pass again. He discovered Renfro on the 15 for an 18-yard gain. Only six seconds were left when the Oilers called time out. Fritsch trotted onto the field to get the game-tying field goal. However, on the snap, the Oilers were off side and were penalized 5 yards to the 20. There were only two seconds left when Fritsch lined up to boot a 37-yarder. He looked up, then down at the ball. Matuszak broke through

suddenly, stuck up his huge arms, and blocked the ball. The dramatic play preserved the Raiders' 10–7 halftime lead.

Although Oakland finally got decent field position when the second half opened, they couldn't do much. Three runs netted only 8 yards, and Guy was asked to punt for the sixth time. His kick was downed by McClanahan on the 9. After three downs that only gained 6 yards, the Oilers were forced to punt.

When the Raiders got the ball back, they were thwarted for the second straight time. Following Guy's punt, the Oilers tried to get going from their 37. Stabler lit the spark. On a first down he connected over the middle with Renfro for a 39-yard play that was finally stopped on the Oakland 24. The Oilers seemed primed to strike.

Campbell ran right for 5 yards and then left for 6 for another first down on the 13. He tried the left side again but could only find 2 yards to the 11. Stabler then faded to pass. The enterprising Hayes read the play and intercepted a pass intended for Renfro, 5 yards deep in the end zone. He tried to run it out but was brought down on the 1 yard line. It was the worst possible spot.

After a couple of first downs the Raiders stalled on the 28. Guy once again had to get them out of danger. He did so with a 63-yard punt all the way down to the Houston 9 yard line. When it looked as if the Oilers might get started again after a 33-yard aerial from Stabler to Barber, Mike Davis struck. He dumped Stabler for a 12-yard loss to the 33. It didn't matter that Stabler completed an 11-yard pass to Barber on the next play. The Oilers had to

Hendricks lands on Stabler as Matuszak rushes in for support.

punt once more. The third period ended on a high for the Raiders when Plunkett delivered a third-down 33-yard pass to Branch on the Houston 44.

Plunkett wasn't finished. On the first play of the fourth period he sent Whittington deep out of the backfield. He looked to his left and then threw long to his right into the end zone. Whittington and the ball got there at the same time. The little scatback reached up and pulled the ball down for a touchdown. Bahr's kick sent Oakland to a 17–7 edge.

On the ensuing two Houston possessions the Oakland defense frustrated the Oilers. When the Raiders got the ball back, they were on their 25 yard line with 9:17 left in the game. They attacked quickly. First, Plunkett passed 21 yards to Van Eeghen. Then King broke loose around right end for 27 yards, all the way to the Houston 27. In two plays the Raiders had advanced 48 yards and were threatening.

Following a 1-yard pickup by Whittington, Plunkett looked for Bob Chandler in the end zone. An interference penalty on J. C. Wilson,

who was guarding Chandler, gave the Raiders a first down on the 11. On third down linebacker Gregg Bingham gave Oiler fans hope when he decked Plunkett for a 10-yard loss to the 20. Bahr, unruffled by the play, calmly booted a 37-yard field goal to stretch Oakland's margin to 20–7.

Oakland's chances for a victory seemed bright. There was only 6:13 left in the game when Stabler brought his offense back onto the field. On second down he was victimized on a 9-yard sack by Hendricks. Stabler's dilemma was now a third and 20 on his own 2 yard line. He had to throw. Hayes realized it as Stabler passed to his left. The larcenous cornerback intercepted the ball on the 20 and raced into the end zone untouched for a clinching touchdown. Bahr's kick ballooned Oakland's margin to 27–7. Victory was imminent. With only 5:19 remaining, Stabler gave it one more try. He got all the way down to the Oakland 4 yard line on his final gasp. A sad bunch of Oilers walked off the field, their season ended.

A crestfallen Stabler was sacked 7 times in

one of the most frustrating days of his career. Hayes, the young cornerback, had 2 of the sacks along with 2 interceptions. He admitted that the defensive strategy the Raiders employed was new.

"This was the first time I blitzed all year," disclosed Hayes. "I didn't do it against other teams because they seem to adjust to it. They slide-block, they zone-block, they pick it up. Houston doesn't. The Oilers' offensive scheme is out of the forties. Brute strength. I kick your butt, you kick mine. Vince Lombardi football with Jim Taylor and Paul Hornung running the power.

"They never made the kind of adjustment another team would have made. They didn't make the moves needed to combat what we were doing. There was no change of venue, no tomfoolery. They just stayed with that brute strength concept. That last pass to Renfro looked like a moon shot. It was just beautiful the way it hung up there. It was as pretty as Hollywood Park. So beautiful, such a softly thrown pass.

"Every time I was standing on the same side as Mike Barber, I knew I had a clean shot at Kenny. As soon as Barber let go, that left only a back to pick up on Hendricks and nobody to get me. We tried it four times, and it worked four times. It was the first time that I had sacked a quarterback since I played linebacker at Texas A and M in 1974."

The low-keyed Sumner was the architect of the defensive game plan, and Flores had the courage to let it happen. He was a silent hero, but still he worried a little during the game.

"I told the team early in the week that I noticed something in the films," revealed Sumner. "I showed it to them in the films so they could take a look at it. Wednesday was our defensive day, and we tried a few things. We decided to keep it in for the game.

"Our big worry was that Stabler would hand off to Campbell, and he would pop it on us. We had never blitzed our cornerbacks or safeties, but if we picked the right spots, maybe on first downs, we would still have safe coverages."

Houston's colorful coach Bum Phillips didn't mince any words. He didn't make any excuses. His club was soundly beaten, and Phillips was the first to admit it.

"Today we were outplayed and out-coached," lamented Phillips. "The Raiders played as good today as anyone I've seen play in the ten or twelve years I've been in this league. It wasn't Stabler's fault. We had a malfunction in our pass protection that we just couldn't correct. They were rushing better than we could block. Kenny didn't have time to get his arm up, much less look for receivers."

Stabler echoed the feelings of his coach. He, too, is not one to belabor a point.

"Sometimes we didn't have the right protection, and sometimes we made physical mistakes," offered Stabler, the sweat pouring off his face. "They didn't do anything we hadn't seen before, somewhere. We just didn't handle it very well."

Upshaw, his uniform marked with dirt and grass stains, was compassionate. He definitely got dirty today.

"Now that it's over, I feel sorry for Snake," he said. "He's really a part of the Oakland Raider tradition. He really knew how to win. I didn't want him to get hurt, but there was still a good feeling inside me.

"But Casper is something else. In all my years in football, I've never heard one player talk about another that way. When I showed up at the pregame meal, all my teammates started calling me Mr. Michelin. A few of them asked me if I could get them a good deal on tires. I'll tell you, I wish I'd been out there for a few plays on defense today."

But Upshaw isn't one to carry a grudge. Besides, there wasn't any time. The Cleveland Browns were next. . . .

Oakland Raiders 3 7 0 17 27
Houston Oilers 7 0 0 0 0

Oakland: 1:45, first period—Bahr, 47-yard field goal.
Houston: 13:15, first period—Campbell, 1-yard run (Fritsch, kick).
Oakland: 9:25, second period—Christensen, 1-yard pass from Plunkett (Bahr, kick).
Oakland: 0:07, fourth period—Whittington, 44-yard pass from Plunkett (Bahr, kick).
Oakland: 8:35, fourth period—Bahr, 37-yard field goal.
Oakland: 9:31, fourth period—Hayes, 20-yard interception return (Bahr, kick).

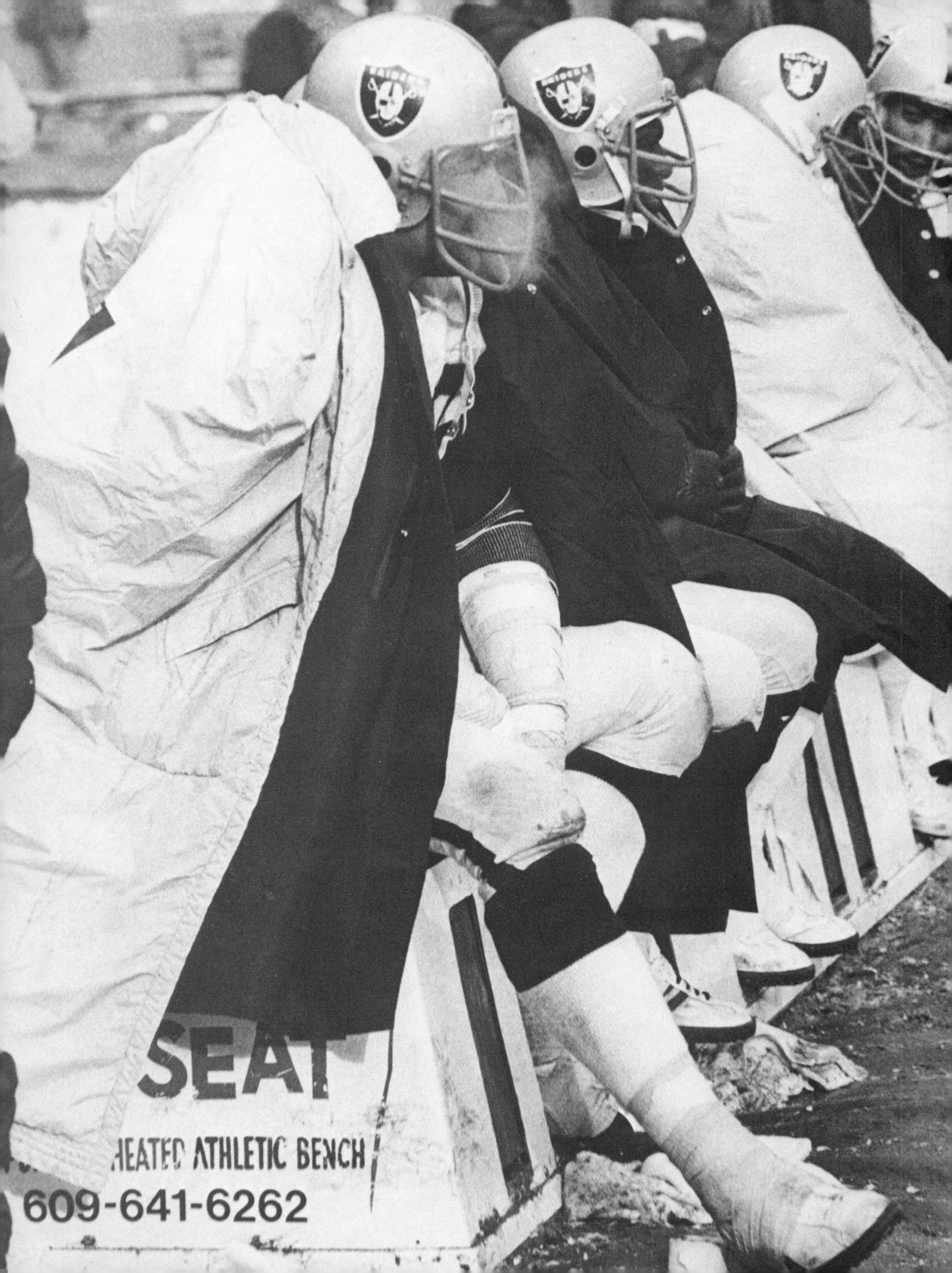
SEAT
HEATED ATHLETIC BENCH
609-641-6262

CLEVELAND PLAYOFF

It was a new experience for him. He felt uncomfortable. By nature he is quiet, soft-spoken. He much prefers to work in the background, leaving the limelight to others. That's how he always operated in the eighteen years he had been coaching. Now, suddenly, almost overnight, Charlie Sumner was being hailed as a defensive genius after the annihilation of the Oilers. He may be listed as the Raiders' linebacker coach, but Sumner is more, much more. In essence he performs as the team's defensive coordinator, and it was Sumner who finally implemented the defensive game plan that completely confused and frustrated Houston.

Still, he shunned the accolades. He tried to keep his visibility guarded as the Raiders began serious preparations for the Cleveland Browns at the club's training facilities in Alameda. Those who covered the Raiders all season long, and the new members of the press who were assigned to follow the team on its playoff excursion, wanted to know more about Charlie Sumner. It was all strange to Sumner. He nervously smoked one cigarette after another, shrugged at some questions, and sheepishly smiled at others. He was polite as could be, attributing the success of the Raid-

ers' defense to the players themselves.

"I feel I've been a pretty good coach all of my life," said Sumner. "I've had success elsewhere. That's why I don't think one game makes you any better or worse than you already are. We start out making our defensive game plans in the beginning of the week, and we make adjustments right up to game time.

"In fact, we make adjustments during the game at times. The veteran players like Hardman and Hendricks come up with some ideas, and if they fit into our system, then we'll use them."

Sumner's soft, open policy works. The players were comfortable with his approach. They respected Sumner's knowledge and honesty. Sumner didn't demand performance; he expected it.

"You know, he doesn't care where the credit for the defense's success goes," revealed Hardman, a veteran pass-rushing terror. "So I know he'll be perturbed about my saying anything real great about him. He'd rather stay low-key, but I'm going to spill the beans. He is one . . . great . . . coach.

"Not playing as much this year, I've learned more about football than any other year, just by talking to Charlie on the sidelines. I've

Art Shell and Gene Upshaw relax on plane ride to Cleveland.

It was that cold.

asked him a lot of questions, and I can see why certain decisions are made. He's so effective it's unreal. He'll blow up sometimes on the sidelines because a guy is not thinking with him out on the field. He's always aware of what's going on around him. It's just a joy to be with him."

Sumner's concern now wasn't what happened last week. All he had on his mind was Cleveland. He didn't for a minute lose sight of that priority.

"That's the only concern now," remarked Sumner. "It's obvious we'll have to get a good pass rush on Brian Sipe. He has excellent receivers, the kind that San Diego has. We might add a few things, but once again, we're going to go with our basic stuff."

Sipe was the Raiders' chief target. He'd had an amazing year, finishing as the NFL's number one passer and the league's MVP. In completing over 61 percent of his passes, Sipe threw for 4,132 yards. Only two quarterbacks in the history of professional football ever achieved the distinction of passing for more than 4,000 yards—Dan Fouts of San Diego, who did it two years straight, and Joe Namath of the New York Jets. More important, Sipe has the ability to come up with the big play. Throughout the season, Sipe dramatically threw a winning touchdown pass in the final seconds of play to avoid almost certain defeat. (The Browns' many exciting last-minute victories accounted for their being known as the Cardiac Kids.) Sipe completed 30 touchdown passes and was intercepted only 14 times. In that respect he presented more of a threat than Stabler had the preceding week.

Flores had nothing but admiration for Sipe.

"Brian Sipe is extremely intelligent. He knows how to run a game," Flores said, praising the quarterback. "He knows how to go after a weakness. He knows how to set the tempo of a game. It's up to us to disrupt him."

It was easier said than done. Sipe, who sets up quickly, also has a quick release. He is not an easy quarterback to trap. Sipe was sacked only 23 times all season, a far cry from Plunkett, who was dumped 47 times. Getting to Sipe presented a problem indeed, as some of the players well knew.

Dave Dalby checks to see if the paint will remain on the icy field.

"He's a very competitive quarterback," emphasized Mike Davis. "He's just the type of quarterback you'd want on your side of the field. He will run with the ball if he has to. He's a gutsy guy. He gets rid of the ball real quick, which is one of the reasons he was sacked so few times."

It remained to be seen whether the Raiders could exert pressure up front the way they did against Houston. That thought was on Reggie Kinlaw's mind.

"We just have to play reckless football like we did last week," pointed out Kinlaw. "It's going to be important for our four-man line to get off the ball and get Sipe before he starts gathering confidence. This is going to be a good test for us in both the four-man and three-man lines. I'll have to play the best game of my life against their center Tom DeLeone."

Sipe's effectiveness made fullback Mike Pruitt that much more dangerous. Not only had Pruitt gained 1,034 yards, but he was also the team's leading pass catcher. Pruitt caught 63 passes for 471 yards. That gave the Raiders something else to think about without getting totally caught up in the Sipe mania sweeping Cleveland. They weren't calling it the Super Bowl, but instead, the Siper Bowl.

"I'm amazed that he has five receivers with fifty or more receptions," observed Lester Hayes. "I really don't think his receivers are that good, but they have a real good passing scheme. All we have to do is put pressure on him and control the line of scrimmage. Hey, we stopped the best running back in the universe last week in Earl Campbell, so we can devise a defense to stop Sipe."

What the Raiders did to Houston didn't go unnoticed by Sipe. Since they had won the Central Division championship, the Browns drew an opening round bye. Sipe and the rest of his teammates had enough to do watching the Raiders on television as well as up close in game films. Sipe, more than anyone, saw the Raider blitz.

"I think they are capable of getting to me and putting a lot of pressure on me, but not in the same manner," disclosed Sipe. "They obviously saw a flaw in Houston's pass protection scheme, and they were taking advantage of it. I think it will be a physical game not so much for me, but for our receivers. I think it's the type of game where we need to have big plays to win the game.

"You win with defense in this league unless you're the Cardiac Kids. I don't know, we have a thing about winning games. It's not easy to put your finger on it. All I know is we know how to win football games around here. Maybe we did do it with a defense that gave up a lot of statistics, but when it came to the final score, we seemed to be a point ahead. I think we're a team with a lot of character. I don't know what else you can say about a team that's been involved in so many close games in recent years."

Like Plunkett, Sipe was a forgotten quarterback. When Sam Rutigliano took over as head coach of the Browns three years ago, Sipe was strongly rumored to be finished at Cleveland, where he had basically performed in a reserve role. Rutigliano had faith in Sipe's ability and stuck with him through endless hours of coaching, helping to turn Sipe into one of the game's premier quarterbacks. The reclamation project on Sipe brought Rutigliano his greatest satisfaction. Even Rutigliano didn't hide the fact that he was apprehensive about Sipe's ability at first.

"We needed a quarterback, and I didn't know if Brian Sipe was the guy," admitted Rutigliano. "Now, the principal reason for our success is Brian. I just don't think you can get it done unless you have the engineer under the center, and Brian is the number one quarterback in the NFL.

"He's like a duck on a pond. On the surface he's calm, but underneath, the legs are going a mile a minute. He's got a great release and a tremendous command in the pocket. I'd have to compare him to Joe Namath, Bob Griese, and Len Dawson in that regard. The tighter the fit, the better he plays. His greatest quality is his resourcefulness. He has great concentration, and he doesn't let the ball go until the last minute.

"We've been involved with teams all year long that in some way have tried to get to Sipe. We're a team that's 'thrown' to get here. Oakland is smart enough to realize that if they blitz us, it's going to hurt them. I think they'll blitz, but I don't think they'll come all out. We're not like Houston, a double tight-end offense geared to run just play-action passes."

A primary target of Sipe's passes, wide receiver Dave Logan, was ready to return to action. Logan, who led the Browns in reception yardage with 822, missed the final game of the regular season with a sprained left ankle and knee. With Logan in the lineup, he would attract attention away from the Browns' excellent tight end, Ozzie Newsome, and veteran wide receiver Reggie Rucker. Logan, greatly benefitting from the two-week layoff, was looking forward to playing.

"The Raiders are very adept at playing the bump-and-run," said Logan. "I'm sure that's how they feel they can beat us. It's an interesting match-up between what they do best and what we do best. That's how it should be. Hey, I know some of those guys, too. I went to school with Mike Davis and Odis McKinney.

"Their secondary really doesn't have many tendencies. All they do is keep lining up man-to-man with you, and that can throw you off your rhythm. Basically, they're the only team in the league that plays it the way they play it. The advantage to them is they hope to slow you down enough to create problems for you. You've got to have good people to cover, and they do.

"On our part, it requires a lot of work and timing in our pass offense. The advantage to us is that there's one man to beat, and that's it. There's usually nobody behind them. Should you beat him, it will probably be a long gain."

The weather conditions in Cleveland were perhaps of more concern than Oakland's defensive play. The city on Lake Erie was besieged by a cold front with howling winds blowing across the frozen lake into cavernous, old Municipal Stadium. The weather was not expected to warm at all for the crucial game.

The frigid cold also hampered the grounds crew at the stadium, making it difficult to work on the field. Close to ten inches of snow completely buried the tarpaulin that covered the field, making maintenance on the field practically impossible. Three giant heating units that were to aid in conditioning the ground sat idle. Brian Bossard, chief of the grounds crew, was grim.

The determined Van Eeghen cracked over for a touchdown.

"The field has had no watering in over two months, and the tarp has been on almost constantly," revealed Bossard. "Fans don't realize that the field is actually fifty feet below street level, and the whole place is on a landfill."

The weather and field conditions didn't sadden Rucker in the least. He strongly believed that Oakland's bump-and-run style of pass defense would provide the Browns with even more of an advantage.

"That type of coverage is hard to do in bad weather," mused Rucker with a smile. "In Oakland where they have good weather they can do that. If we have an icy field and the defensive back falls down, it's a touchdown. I'd like to see the same kind of weather on Sunday that we've been practicing in all week. The bad weather is part of our team's personality. It might as well be miserable, we're used to it."

It was indeed miserable. When the Raiders arrived in Cleveland on Saturday, the cold arctic air made Al Davis react quickly. He called the Browns' front office and asked them if they had planned on bringing in the special Hot Seat benches that were used earlier in the season when Minnesota played at Philadelphia. The Browns said they had no intention of doing so. Davis didn't hesitate. He made arrangements to have the seats sent to Cleveland by truck overnight. The total cost amounted to $3,700: $1,700 for the rental and $2,000 for shipping.

An NFL ruling states that each competing club is required to enjoy the same privileges. So Davis had to provide enough Hot Seats for the Cleveland players as well.

It was a wise move by Davis. On Sunday, the mercury stood at 1 degree. The day-long forecast was for bitter cold with fifteen- to

Chris Bahr adds the important conversion.

Mark van Eeghen did most of the running.

Lester Hayes picks off a pass intended for Reggie Rucker.

twenty-five-mile-an-hour winds. It was the coldest day for an NFL playoff game since the classic Dallas-Green Bay Ice Bowl in 1967 when temperatures were recorded at below zero. However, in measuring the wind-chill factor, Cleveland was almost as cold.

The Cleveland players got their wish. They had the cold weather they wanted, and 77,655 frigid fans dressed in every available form of cold-weather gear, warmed by the thoughts of a Super Bowl. It was the Browns' first appearance in a playoff game since 1973, and Siper Bowl signs quivered in the cold wind from the second tier of the antiquated stadium. It brought back memories of the legendary Jim Brown.

Oakland was the first to test the glacial conditions as Todd Christensen returned Don Cockroft's short kick a mere 7 yards to the 31. Opening the game, Van Eeghen edged for-

ward for a yard. Plunkett didn't hesitate to utilize the pass. However, he was unsuccessful on attempts to Kenny King and Bob Chandler. Ray Guy punted the ball into Cleveland's end of the field.

Sipe's initial play was an incomplete pass. Veteran Calvin Hill, who is usually utilized as a spot player, ran for 5 yards to the 36. Head coach Sam Rutigliano gave the experienced Hill a rare starting assignment. He reasoned that Hill's experience and pass-catching ability would help compensate for any mistakes caused by the frigid conditions. However, Sipe missed again with a pass, and the Browns had to punt. Evans's kick rolled dead on the Oakland 28.

On first down Van Eeghen was stopped without a gain. A screen pass to King got the Raiders to the 33. Plunkett then decided to go deep to Chandler. Covering all the way, Ron

139

Kenny King tries to turn the corner.

Bolton successfully intercepted the pass and was immediately brought down on the Cleveland 27.

Now Sipe worked on the ground. Mike Pruitt carried three straight times, finally ending up with a first down on the 38. After Sipe missed with a pass for the third time, Pruitt was dropped for a 2-yard loss by Kinlaw and Hendricks. Sipe's first completion to Hill got only 4 yards. Johnny Evans had to punt again. His 50-yarder pinned the Raiders deep on their 11 yard line.

The first quarter was almost halfway over when Van Eeghen punched out a 3-yard gain. King couldn't get anything, and when he and Plunkett missed connections on a third-down pass, Guy was sent in to get the Raiders out of danger. Guy got off a 49-yard punt, but an 11-yard return by little Dino Hall gave the Browns excellent field position on the Cleveland 48.

Sipe couldn't wait to throw. His first two passes misfired. When he tried again, Hayes was ready. He beat Rucker to the ball and intercepted, giving the Raiders possession on the Oakland 36. Still the Raiders couldn't do anything on offense. King got only 3 yards on two rushes, and Plunkett's pass to Branch fell

incomplete. Guy's abbreviated punt went only 31 yards and was downed on the Cleveland 30 yard line.

Cleveland again failed to get a first down. After Hayes broke up a pass to Rucker, Mike Pruitt managed to accumulate 9 yards on a couple of runs, leaving the Browns a yard short of a first down. Evans's punt rolled unchallenged on the Oakland 27.

For the fifth time in the opening period the Raiders went to offense. For the fifth time their futile efforts resulted in a punt after three downs. They could only move 7 yards on a 5-yard advance by King and a 2-yard pickup by Van Eeghen. Guy's 46-yard punt was returned 20 yards by Keith Wright, giving the Browns fine field location on their own 40 yard line.

At 1:55 Sipe zipped a 20-yard pass to Rucker, and the Browns were quickly on the Oakland 40. Mike Pruitt collected 2 yards, and Sipe found Newsome for 6 yards. Pruitt then got 3 yards for a first down on the 29. The Browns were threatening now. On the last play of the quarter Sipe brought the chilled crowd to its feet. He had Rucker open in the end zone, only to see the veteran receiver drop the ball.

Sipe continued throwing when the second period began. However, he was repelled. Davis broke up his first pass to Newsome, and Hendricks knocked down his second one, intended for Greg Pruitt. On fourth down the Browns sent in Cockroft to try a 47-yard field goal but his kick was harmlessly short.

Throwing the first play on first down, Plunkett hit Chester over the middle for an 11-yard gain to the 40 for the Raiders' initial first down of the game. Dropping back to pass again, Plunkett didn't have a chance. He was sacked for a 9-yard loss by nose tackle Henry Bradley. To make matters worse, he fumbled, and defensive end Marshall Harris recovered for the Browns on the Oakland 23. The Browns were threatening for the second straight time.

Rushed on first down, Sipe slipped away and ran to the 13. Brown fans cheered, sensing that Cleveland was ready to score. After Cleo Miller managed to gain to the 12, Sipe went back to his pass patterns. However, Dwayne O'Steen rejected two potential touchdowns—the first to Logan and the second to Rucker. Cockroft lined up a 30-yard field goal. Cleveland fans groaned as his kick went wide to the left.

The Raider offense was again ineffective. After three downs, Guy came in to punt for the fifth time. Hall ran back Guy's 36-yard kick 5 yards, giving the Browns the ball on the Oakland 49. After producing a first down, the Brown attack stalled, and Evans punted out of bounds on the Raider 26.

Van Eeghen gained a yard, and Plunkett threw him a quick pass for 5 more to the 32. Needing 4 yards for a first down, Plunkett dropped back, looking for a receiver. He tried to connect with Chandler on the 42, but cornerback Ron Bolton cut in front of the Oakland receiver and intercepted. With nothing but open sidelines ahead of him, Bolton ran unimpeded for a touchdown, giving the Browns a 6–0 lead. It remained that way because Hendricks broke through on the point-after attempt and blocked Cockroft's kick.

There was only 6:01 left in the first half when the Raiders began an offensive series on their 26 yard line. Unconcerned with the cold air, Plunkett came out throwing. He missed on his first pass but then hit Chandler for 15 yards on the Cleveland 49. It was the first time the Raiders had gotten past midfield. A short pass to King got 4 yards and another short one to Van Eeghen added 5. Plunkett picked up the first down himself by running behind right guard Mickey Marvin for 3 yards.

With a first down on the 37, Plunkett switched to his ground attack. King got 7 yards, then 1; and when Van Eeghen broke loose for 4 yards, the Raiders had a first down on the 25. Just before the two-minute warning Plunkett tried to pass to Branch. It was broken up. After King lost 3 yards, Plunkett had to go

Raymond Chester leaps for a reception.

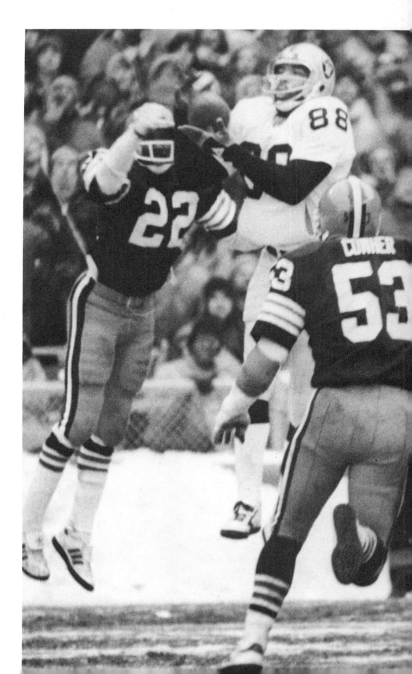

back to the air on third down. Looking over the field, he found Chester open and connected with a 26-yard pass to the 2 yard line. With only 1:03 left, Plunkett called time out.

Oakland fans got a scare as Van Eeghen fumbled only to recover his own miscue on the 1 yard line. Plunkett then tried a quick pass to Derrick Ramsey, the other end in Oakland's two-tight-end offense. He misfired. On a crucial third-down play, Plunkett called Van Eeghen's number in the huddle. The steady veteran came through and went over Marvin for the game-tying touchdown with only twenty-two seconds left on the clock. Bahr kicked the important extra point, sending the Raiders into a 7–6 lead. The half ended two plays later when Hayes intercepted Sipe a second time.

It was obvious at halftime that the cold weather would dictate a low-scoring game. Most parts of the field were frozen, and the receivers for both teams couldn't accelerate or employ their quick moves. Although Sipe was sacked only once, the Raiders had succeeded in exerting pressure on him. It reflected in his performance: Sipe could only complete 4 out of 18 passes for 48 yards. If the Raiders could continue to neutralize Sipe in the second half, they could control the outcome of the struggle to reach the AFC championship game.

Sipe's first pass in the third period was an 11-yard pop to Newsome, moving the Browns into Raider territory on the 49. On second down Hill, who doesn't run with the ball often, broke loose around right end for 18 yards to the 28. The Browns were driving. They were further aided by a penalty on the next play. Matuszak was called for a face mask infraction against Sipe, who had scrambled for a 4-yard gain. That gave Cleveland a first down on the 19. Two plays later Sipe faced a third and 3 on the 12. However, O'Steen frustrated the Browns' touchdown hopes by slapping Sipe's pass away from Logan. Still, Cleveland was within field goal range, and Cockroft sent the home team into a 9–7 lead with a 30-yard kick.

The Raiders were stymied after the kickoff, despite a fine 25-yard runback by Whittington

that gave them the ball on the 40. When the Browns got the ball back, they began to move again, this time from the 36 yard line after an 18-yard return by Hall. It was a typical Sipe attack, and it excited the crowd. He threw 7 straight passes, completing and getting the Browns to the Raider 18, before stalling. Cockroft came on the scene to try for another field goal. His holder, Paul McDonald, had trouble with the snap and the attempt was aborted.

The Raiders still couldn't generate any offense. Once again they had to punt, and for the third time the Browns came roaring back. A 21-yard Sipe-to-Logan aerial and a pass interference penalty on O'Steen gave the Browns a first down on the Raider 9. The Raider defense faced another challenge. They couldn't yield a touchdown which would put them 9 points behind.

After Greg Pruitt fought to gain only a yard, Sipe went back to his passing game. A sack cost him 4 yards, and on the third down he couldn't complete a pass to Logan. So it was time for Cockroft again, and he successfully kicked a 29-yard field goal to give Cleveland a 12–7 edge. The Raiders were still only a touchdown away.

Oakland got the ball back for the third time with only 2:30 remaining. They still couldn't do anything, and Guy had to punt once more. It was up to the defense to keep the Browns in check and disrupt Cleveland's momentum. They did, and when the Raiders got the ball back for just one more play before the period ended, it was obvious that they had to get the offense going. They had failed to produce one first down during the entire quarter.

The third period didn't end promisingly. Plunkett's short flip to King actually lost a yard to the 19. After conferring with Flores on the sidelines, Plunkett came trotting back on the field with his hands in his shirt pocket to protect his fingers from the bitter cold. It was up to him to spark the Raiders. The defense had given him time by holding Cleveland to just two field goals in the previous quarter, despite three deep penetrations into Oakland territory which could easily have resulted in touchdowns.

Jim Plunkett sets the offense.

After King sprinted for 7 yards, Plunkett was faced with a third and 4 decision on the 26. He teamed with Van Eeghen for a quick pass that produced 13 yards and a first down. Coming back with a 19-yard strike to Branch, Plunkett moved the Raiders into Cleveland territory for the first time since the closing minutes of the second quarter.

Plunkett had the Raiders driving. On second down he kept them moving with a 27-yard pass to Chester. Suddenly the Raiders had reached the Cleveland 15. Plunkett tried to hit Chester again after Van Eeghen gained a yard, but he was unsuccessful. The Raiders got a lift, however, when the Browns were off-side on the next play. Facing a third and 4 on the 9 yard line, Plunkett slipped a 6-yard pass to King, who circled out of the backfield for a precious first down on the 3.

Now Plunkett looked to Van Eeghen. He tried the right side and got 2 yards. He tried it again and was stopped cold. Plunkett called time out and went over to the sidelines to discuss the third-down call with Flores. They decided to stay with the dependable Van Eeghen. He didn't disappoint them. This time, he drove hard over Upshaw's spot and scored the touchdown that sent the Raiders into a 13–12 lead. A minute later Bahr extended it to 14–12 with his conversion.

143

With only 36 seconds left, cornerback Mike Davis sealed Cleveland's doom with a dramatic interception in the end zone.

Time was now becoming a factor. Plunkett had used up six minutes on the drive, and after both teams exchanged punts, Cleveland had the ball on its own 25 yard line with only 4:39 remaining in this tense game. Looking to pass, Sipe couldn't find anyone open and started to run. He was hit, fumbled, and an alert McKinney came up fast from his cornerback spot to recover on the 24. The Raiders appeared in control now.

Plunkett determined to carefully run down the clock. He assigned the task completely to Van Eeghen. He got a yard on first down and then broke loose around left end for 8 more.

It left the Raiders a yard short on the 15. Once again Van Eeghen carried, but he was stopped. The Raider huddle was tense. Should they go for it, or kick a field goal? Plunkett looked at Van Eeghen for the fourth time, disdaining the field goal and going for the vital first down with less than three minutes remaining. Fighting for their lives, the Browns lined up with practically their entire defense on the line of scrimmage. Again Van Eeghen tried for the elusive yard, and again he was denied.

The final drama still remained. With a scant 2:22 left to play, here was a choice opportunity for Sipe to mastermind still another of his exciting, eleventh-hour bids for victory. Everyone in the frozen stadium knew he would pass. It was something the Browns had lived or died with all year. Sipe missed the first one, but he delivered on the next—a 29-yarder to Newsome on the 44 yard line. After an incompletion Sipe kept the ball himself on what appeared to be a second-down mixup. He was spilled by defensive end Willie Jones for no gain. Sipe faced a big third down with 1:27 remaining.

The Browns got the break they needed. On an incompleted pass, O'Steen was penalized for holding. It was only a 5-yard penalty, but more important, it gave Cleveland a first down on the 49. With the Raiders playing Sipe's wide receivers tight, he sent little Greg Pruitt down the left sideline and lofted a 23-yard pass into his arms. None of Cleveland's fans thought about the cold now as they stood and cheered the unfolding drama.

The clock showed 1:06 when Sipe missed a first-down pass. He then switched strategy and gave the ball to Mike Pruitt, who turned the corner and scampered for 14 yards before Owens tackled him on the 14. Quickly, Sipe signaled for a time-out with 56 seconds on the clock as wildly cheering fans anticipated another last-second, epic victory.

Sipe discussed the crucial strategy with Rutigliano in front of the Cleveland bench. All the Raiders could do now was wait. The Browns were only a field goal away from winning. That was the way the Raiders were thinking when Sipe returned to the field.

They braced for the run and stopped Mike Pruitt after a 1-yard pickup on the 13. The Browns lined up as the clock showed 49 seconds. Sipe barked the signals, took the snap, and brought the crowd to its feet again as he surprised everyone by dropping back to pass. He looked to his right first for Logan, then to his left, and threw a pass in to the end zone where Newsome had cut across. Mike Davis wasn't fooled. He picked up Newsome, reached in front of him, and made a spectacular interception, thereby preserving a brilliant 14–12 Oakland victory. It was the biggest interception of Davis's career and one which sent the Raiders into the AFC championship game.

"Newsome lined up to my left split about four yards; I think Sipe thought Newsome was open, but I was on him. I jammed him, and he came across. We were surprised, but you have to watch how Cleveland plays to understand what they were trying to do. I saw the ball all the way. I saw it leave Sipe's hands. If I ever wanted anything in my life, that was it. I had to put my hands on it and catch it. It couldn't be incomplete then. It was too big. I knew I could pick it off. I was just worrying about catching the ball. It was so cold out there. God, I've never played in weather like that, and I just wanted to hold on to the ball."

"I kept thinking to myself that they were going to pass even though we figured they would run the ball up the middle and then kick it," beamed a happy Davis. "What they did though was baffling. I don't know why they did what they did, but I'm glad they did it. It was the biggest play I've made in my career."

It was an alert Raider secondary who actually turned impending defeat into triumph. The Raiders went with a Red Dog man-to-man defense which dictates that the two inside linebackers blitz; and the defensive backs are assigned single coverage on the receivers. The ill-fated play was designed for Logan to be the primary receiver. He lined up alone on the left side. Newsome and Rucker were split on the right side. Newsome's pattern was to take him into the end zone with Rucker, shallower, in front of him. Logan was then to cross to the right underneath both of them and catch Sipe's pass.

Owens upset the thinking. Instead of taking Newsome, he covered Logan. When Sipe saw Logan occupied, he then looked for Newsome who was the secondary receiver on the play. Since the strong safety was with Logan, Sipe felt certain that Newsome would be open, but Davis's quick reaction foiled Sipe's hopes.

"I took a gamble," explained Owens. "Instead of following the tight end through the middle, I went for Logan. I just had a feel."

Al Davis was feeling good, too. He was hugging his players who had brought him one step away from Super Bowl XV. He wasn't the least upset by the Browns' refusal to pay half the costs of the Hot Seats. As long as it provided some comfort to his players, he didn't care.

"They should have paid for half of it," snapped Davis, "but that's neither here nor there. I just wanted to win. This is the most courageous team I've ever had."

It wouldn't be long before his team would display that courage again. The next arena was San Diego. . . .

Oakland Raiders   0   7   0   7   14
Cleveland Browns   0   6   6   0   12

Cleveland: 8:50, second period—Bolton, 42-yard interception run (kick blocked).
Oakland: 14:42, second period—Van Eeghen, 1-yard run (Bahr, kick).
Cleveland: 3:31, third period—Cockroft, 30-yard field goal.
Cleveland: 12:20, third period—Cockroft, 29-yard field goal.
Oakland: 5:38, fourth period—Van Eeghen, 1-yard run (Bahr, kick).

AFC CHAMPIONSHIP SAN DIEGO

Before the Raiders became completely intoxicated by the euphoria of their Ice Bowl conquest of the Browns, Gene Upshaw gave the players a firm reminder. He told the squad that they hadn't won anything yet, that beating Cleveland only provided them with the opportunity to play next week in San Diego. Still, the Raiders were happy to get out of the tundra that was Cleveland, leaving Browns fans to talk all winter about whether Sipe should have thrown that ill-fated pass or whether he should have waited to kick what conceivably could have been a game-winning field goal. Cleveland fans had a long winter ahead of them indeed.

"I have never seen a town so against our team," remarked Upshaw. "There seemed to be an all-out campaign to do a number on us. Even the television stations kept addressing us and saying, 'The cold weather will kill 'em.'

"The cold wasn't that bad, but that was the worst footing I've ever played on. You couldn't dig in. We filed our cleats down. We tried longer cleats. We changed to turf shoes, which are tough to play in on grass. We searched and searched until we finally found something that worked."

Richard Romanski, the team's equipment manager, had judiciously packed a variety of cleats for the game. He had a bigger assortment than a shoe salesman at a national convention. It was needed, too. By halftime nearly every player had changed shoes. While the offensive linemen didn't experience any trouble pass-blocking, they had problems blocking for the run. Such was their concern moments before Van Eeghen's game-winning touchdown in the third period.

When Plunkett called the play in the huddle, the linemen voiced complaints. Wisely, the quarterback called a time-out and went over to the sidelines to consult with Flores.

"The offensive line didn't like the play," disclosed Plunkett. "It was pretty icy down there, and they wanted to go with a straight-ahead run instead of off tackle. What play did we end up running? The same one Tom sent in, in the first place. He simply said to go with it."

Lester Hayes learned one important thing: He couldn't go with stickum in the cold. As is his usual practice, Hayes applied the stickum to his hands and arms before the game. Unfortunately, by game time the sticky stuff froze, and Hayes had to crack the compound off his hands and arms. He then resorted to rubber gloves as insulation against the cold.

Raymond Chester made a dramatic reception in the first period that turned into a 65-yard touchdown that stunned the Chargers.

"It was just like having ice on your hands the way the stuff froze," said Hayes. "It was so difficult to get off. It's, well, psychological. If you think that it will help you, it probably will. I remember the first time I used it. I was starting my first game as cornerback against Houston in 1977. I believe I was covering Ken Burrough, and I had this one ball picked off, and I dropped it. I came to the sidelines, and Fred Biletnikoff had this jar of stickum, and he gave it to me."

Romanski hates the stuff. He hates it more than packing and unpacking the hundreds of pairs of cleats he was burdened with in Cleveland. Years ago only Biletnikoff used the stuff. Now other Raiders, notably Van Eeghen, use it. Nevertheless, it's annoying to Romanski.

"It gets everywhere," snapped the veteran equipment expert, who has been with the Raiders for eighteen years. "When guys take their helmets off, it gets on the helmets. My son Bob has to clean seventeen, eighteen helmets after each game to get the stuff off. When the players put their equipment in the traveling bags, the stickum gets on their shoes, shoulder pads—everywhere. Damn right I hate the stuff. It makes my job harder.

"Freddie Biletnikoff used it for one reason: to remember to hang onto the ball after he caught it so he wouldn't fumble. He could catch anything without it. Freddie used to make sensational catches without that stuff in practice. He used to wet his jersey with spray stickum because he felt the slick jersey numbers would make the ball slip through.

"It's a funny thing. When Biletnikoff went up to Canada to play, they put in a Biletnikoff rule prohibiting him from using stickum. They use only three balls a game in Canada. We use twenty-four a game and can clean the ball more often."

Having survived cleats, stickum, and arctic-like conditions in Cleveland, the Raiders were quite relaxed while getting ready for the Chargers. Romanski took comfort in the fact that he wouldn't have to pack all the extra cleats and thermal underwear, and Hayes wouldn't have to fret about his stickum freezing on his hands. San Diego was their kind of climate.

Because of the significance of the game against San Diego, the Raiders attracted more media to their Alameda compound than at any time all season. That's what winning does. Since the Raiders were winning against all odds, week after week, even their severest critics couldn't help but think that maybe, just maybe, these Raiders were a good football team, despite the fact that they were 4-point underdogs aginst the Chargers. It seemed that the Raiders were cast as the underdogs in every playoff game they faced. It gave them that much more satisfaction when they won and proved to the football experts how wrong they were.

For Plunkett it was quite ironic. He was, perhaps, the player most scrutinized by the critics. He was never given the edge against opposing quarterbacks in all the games he played during the long season. Yet all he did was win. The Raiders won eleven times in the thirteen games he started. Plunkett was the most publicized and interviewed Raider. Still, it was relatively new to him.

"How many television interviews have I done today?" Plunkett repeated the question put to him. "Let's see. Eight, I think. On a normal day I'd be home by now. I complain, but I accept it. I'd rather do it than be at home watching it."

Many wondered about the fact that Plunkett completed only 41.5 percent of his passes in the two playoff games, yet the Raiders managed to win both of them.

"The defense has been so good," answered Plunkett, "that it has forced a lot of turnovers and given us opportunities to score. We don't have to drive the length of the field."

Hendricks was having fun. He'd been exposed to such media attention before and felt the best way to handle it was not to take it seriously. That way everybody would stay loose. After all, a lot of Raider players were experiencing media attention for the first time.

The question was asked: "How can you shut down a great passer like Dan Fouts?"

"Well," answered Hendricks with a deadpan expression, "I broke his thumb once, and that seemed to slow him down a little."

Upshaw holds up the winning ball.

"Is there any way you can get a great receiver like John Jefferson out of the Charger offense?" someone asked.

"We could give him a ticket to Hawaii," quipped Hendricks.

"What about weight training?" another wanted to know.

"I do lift," claimed Hendricks. "I do it for one purpose. I want to look good when I go to Stinson Beach."

Earlier in the week when Dwayne O'Steen was being interviewed on television for being voted the team's best-looking player, Hendricks was in a prankish mood. O'Steen was talking away when Hendricks slipped behind the camera, made a face and dropped his pants. O'Steen broke up.

However, in a serious moment Hendricks posed a question.

"What I don't understand," he began, "is if we had the same record as San Diego and beat them by more points than they beat us, why are they the division champions?"

The Raiders and the Chargers were no strangers to each other—not at all. They had been keen rivals beginning back in the days of the old American Football League in 1960 when the Chargers had a quarterback like Fouts in John Hadl and a receiver like Jefferson in Lance Alworth. Hendricks's logic was based on the fact that the Chargers beat the Raiders the first time they played this year in overtime, 30–24; but when the two teams met again, the Raiders prevailed, 38–24. To Hendricks's way of figuring, the point differential was plus 8 for the Raiders. That was only one of the criteria which the NFL employs in selecting a divisional winner in the case of identical records, such as the 11-5 which both San Diego and Oakland produced. The primary reason the Chargers were named Western Division Champions was because they had higher net points in the division: 53–34.

The Chargers were the most exciting team in professional football to watch. Fans delighted in their high-octane passing attack, dubbed Air Coryell in recognition of the wide-open passing offense devised by San Diego's coach Don Coryell. Fouts had thrown

Raymond Chester gets open.

an unbelievable 589 passes, which weren't a burden on his arm. This was because in tight end Kellen Winslow (89 receptions), wide receiver John Jefferson (82), and wide receiver Charlie Joiner (71), he had the three top receivers in the game, each man gaining over 1,100 yards. (Jefferson had the most, 1,340, followed by Winslow, 1,290, and then Joiner, 1,132.)

For the second week in a row the Raider secondary would be severely challenged. Against Sipe they faced the NFL's top-ranking passer. In Fouts they were looking at the strongest arm in the business, one that accounted for a record 4,715 yards and 30 touchdowns. The midseason addition of fullback Chuck Muncie gave a decided lift to the

150

Lester Hayes concentrates on the dangerous John Jefferson.

once weak Charger running game. However, the primary concern was Fouts and his aerial circus. If Cleveland lived and died by the pass, then the Chargers were eternal. No other team throws more.

Still the Raiders managed to intercept Fouts 7 times during the two games in which they faced him. While the secondary respected Fouts, they were by no means intimidated by his presence.

"He's a strong quarterback," remarked Mike Davis. "He stands up in the pocket fearlessly. He stands tall. He has the ability to read defenses, too. You have to be on top of your game to defense this bunch. Yet Fouts has the tendency to force his passes. We have to have extra preparation for them. They do so many

things. They have an array of formations, and they try to get everyone into the offense. They spread the field out wide and put a man in just about every position on the field.

"I do have a stiff challenge defensing Winslow. They like to use him short and intermediate. He goes deep but very seldom. He definitely has a height advantage over most defensive backs. He has the size and the muscle to battle anyone for the ball. That's one of his main attributes. He also has the ability to split out like a wide receiver. He has a receiver's speed and quickness. If he catches the ball and he's running at you full speed, it's a nightmare.

"You can't completely shut down the Chargers' air game. You just have to hold it to a

151

minimum. You can't stop it. I feel if we get to Fouts, we'll definitely win, and if we don't get to him, we may win. We know each other so well it's no mystery what we're going to do against one another."

One look the Raider defensive backs can show is Cover One which is their tight man-to-man coverage. The other is Cover Three which is their zone defense. A combination of both wouldn't be unusual since it would serve to confuse Fouts and his receivers. In the long run most strategists felt it would come down to Hayes against Jefferson. It made for an exciting duel. Rightfully so. It was the best receiver versus the best defender.

"He's the hottest cornerback this year," said Jefferson. "I think he has more physical skills than any other defensive back. He's probably the best I've ever faced. He makes you work for what you get. He's willing to come up and gamble more. I concentrate more against him than anyone else.

"When you're going against Lester you have to have great leaping ability, which I have, because he's going to be there. It's just a matter of getting to the ball. In bump-and-run no one is better. Gary Green of Kansas City is fine, but basically Green plays zone. Lester is the only one who will go with you man-on-man all over the field. He's a Mel Blount type. He's willing to gamble more, and he's got the ability to get away with it.

"We have a lot of respect for each other. We talk to each other all the time during the games against each other. If I beat him, he'll say something like 'Nice catch.' Or if he knocks down a pass, I might say, 'Way to go.' But I don't think we'll be doing too much talking to each other this time. We'll be concentrating a whole lot more than usual, I guess."

The Jefferson-Hayes rivalry has some personal overtones. Both are from Texas, and when Hayes was at Texas A&M, the coaches tried to recruit Jefferson. However, Jefferson was looking for a college which was more pass oriented and went to Arizona State instead. That was five years ago. Now Hayes was confident about meeting Jefferson on Sunday.

"I fear Dan Fouts much more than I do Jefferson," exclaimed Hayes. "Fouts is crazy with the pass. Jefferson is a mere mortal; still, his hands are something else. What I will try to do is destroy the timing between him and Fouts. Most guys make me give one hundred ten percent out there, but Jefferson makes me give one hundred fifty. I fear his hands."

Fouts had two areas of concern: one was Hayes and the other was Hendricks. Each could decidedly influence his passing scheme.

"Hayes has better hands than just about any other defensive back," observed Fouts. "You don't necessarily like to go with your strength against the other team's strength. You like to look for the weaknesses and exploit them, but if your strength and theirs happen to collide, that's how you play it.

"You have to control Hayes and Hendricks some way. They're Oakland's big-play people. Whenever you throw the ball in their area, you have to be careful. Hendricks is a great football player. He's big, he's tough, and he's hard to block. The coaches give him freedom to do certain things, and he comes up with the big play time after time.

"I expect a very tough game. The key is not to make mistakes and to execute well. Determination will be a big factor. I don't expect this game to be decided in a half or in three quarters. I expect this one to go right down to the end. The team with more determination will win."

What Charger owner Gene Klein was determined to do was to try to publicly make Al Davis a "bad guy." In an unprecedented gesture he called a press conference just seventy-two hours before the game to launch a personal attack on Davis. It was an ill-advised move, simply because it could have an unsettling effect on his players, who were concentrating on their biggest game in a decade. Perhaps he was fearful that the Raiders were riding on the crest of an emotional wave that might very well sweep them over the Chargers and into New Orleans for Super Bowl XV. If it was an attempt at a psychological ploy, then it was even more of a mistake. In that area alone he couldn't compete with Davis.

At the press conference Klein was visibly upset. He held a copy of sportswriter Mel Durslag's column that appeared in the Janu-

Ray Guy booms Raiders out of trouble.

ary 5 issue of the *Los Angeles Herald Examiner*. It was titled: "The Owners Might Suit Up for the AFC Championship." Klein fumed that the column attempted to make it look as though the officials at last week's Cleveland-Oakland game nearly cost the Raiders the victory.

"I ask you people of the press whether this is fair, equitable, honest reporting, or is the writer in somebody's pocket and for what reason?" charged Klein. "I think it is an insidious attempt to intimidate the officials in this game on Sunday. It casts aspersions on the integrity of the National Football League from top to bottom."

Klein went further. He accused Durslag of being a mouthpiece for the Raiders. He also accused Davis of trying to sell his "big lie" through Durslag's column, dealing with Davis's allegations that Commissioner Pete Rozelle scalped Super Bowl tickets. He labeled Davis a "black eye" on the National Football League.

"They're not satisfied with saying the commissioner has stolen money by scalping tickets, rapping all the owners for being boneheads, and saying that the Rams' move to Anaheim was a heist," Klein continued. "Now they get down to insinuating that the officials may be crooked."

Davis wisely didn't acknowledge the comments. He didn't even attempt to retort. Frankly, he was accustomed to a season-long barrage of criticism in the press, centering around his public declaration to move his franchise to Los Angeles. His players were used to it and had somehow grown immune to it. It didn't affect their performance, otherwise they wouldn't have reached the AFC Championship. The off-field tirade, which had nothing to do with Sunday's game, was new to Charger players. It remained to be seen whether it would be distracting enough to affect their performance.

Al Davis must have laughed quietly. Essentially, Klein's rage put a damper on the city that was boiling over with Super Bowl fever. It diminished the purity of the game itself and added a hollow note to the disco song, "San Diego Chargers," which had blared on the radio all week long.

The Las Vegas bookmakers established the Chargers as 4-point favorites. They figured that San Diego, with its explosive offense, which ranked number one in the league, and its defense, which was rated third in the conference, and included a league high of 60 sacks, would be too much for the Raiders to overcome. Besides, the Chargers were playing at home, and the oddsmakers gave a big edge to Fouts over Plunkett. As some smart-money boys along the Strip in Las Vegas pointed out, the Raiders were a live underdog. Gary Austin, the biggest analyst in Vegas, warned those who felt that the Chargers were a sure thing.

"Nobody in the country ever imagined that the Raiders would ever get this far," said Austin. "Like everybody else, I wasn't too high on them at the beginning of the season, but I like what they've done. They know how to win, and that's important in playoff games. Everybody knocks Plunkett, but all he does is win. Anybody who feels the Chargers are a cinch might be surprised."

In his quiet way Plunkett put it all in perspective regarding his mediocre performance in the playoffs up until now.

"I haven't always performed as I did those first two games, but at least we got started and got a little more going," said the curly-haired quarterback. "I really feel good about myself overall. My enthusiasm is back, I've become a calmer individual. I used to get upset about what was happening on the field—this and that. Now I just wait for something good to happen—a turnover maybe."

Plunkett's offensive line, having survived the fierce weather in Cleveland, wasn't the least bit concerned about the Chargers' impressive statistics. Rather, they preferred to answer their critics as they had done up until then—on the field.

"Cleveland showed no respect for us by saying they were surprised Oakland knocked off Houston," recalled Art Shell. "They said Houston was their roadblock to the Super Bowl. They said Houston looked bad against us, and that's the reason we won. I'm proud of this team. Nobody believed in us except ourselves."

Upshaw, who had played in every one of the Raiders' playoff games going back to 1967, embellished on Shell's remarks. He had played alongside Shell for the last eleven years. It was hard to separate the two for comparisons and evaluations.

"When you get this far, it's like having two men on in the bottom of the ninth," remarked Upshaw, comparing it with baseball. "You don't want to strike out. It's like Tooz said on television the other day. He was asked what he was afraid of, and he said, 'Letting the other guys down.' I think everybody feels the same way."

Henry Lawrence did. While Shell and Upshaw hold down the left side of the line, Lawrence and Mickey Marvin secure on the right side.

"We are going to have to play the best game of our lives on Sunday and that means executing from the very beginning," emphasized Lawrence. "I guess you have to be a little lucky to win some football games. I haven't seen any game won without a little luck. Some games are won with just some great football playing. Well, I want to win this game with a lot of luck and some great football playing."

The luck part surfaced well before game time. On Sunday morning it was raining in usually sunny San Diego. Al Davis had to be chuckling to himself once more. Anyone who has ever played in Oakland always comes away claiming that Davis mysteriously manages to water down the field to make it soft, slowing down the opposing team's offense. Even on sunny days in Oakland the field would be soft enough in certain spots to provide the Raiders with a psychological advantage, if not a physical one. Yes, Davis had to be laughing early that morning in his San Diego suite. He had fond memories of the city where he had coached for two years as an assistant under Sid Gillman. Now Davis was thinking of Jefferson and Joiner and Winslow all trying to run their speed patterns on a muddy field. The best part was that he didn't have anything to do with the mud.

What the Raiders had to do once the game started was to try to score early and often. In that way they then could exert pressure on Fouts to upset the rhythm of his passing. It was determined that the best way to beat the Chargers was to break out fast on top. By winning the coin toss at midfield, the Raiders had the opportunity to do so.

Charger fans howled as Rolf Benirschke kicked off. Keith Moody caught the kick on the 8 and provided the Raiders with a modest return to the 29 yard line. As is so often the case, Plunkett opened the game with a run; Van Eeghen tested the right side for 4 yards. King followed the same route and picked up only 2 yards. It left Plunkett with a third and 4 on the 35 yard line. He expected the Chargers to blitz on an obvious passing down. So he called a quick pass to King over the middle. Plunkett was right. The Chargers blitzed, and Plunkett safely got his pass off to King on the 40 yard line. However, the pass was high. It went off King's fingertips and floated upfield. An alert Raymond Chester caught the ball on the 45 and turned to run down the right sideline. Charger fans leaped to their feet in disbelief as Chester ran untouched into the end zone. Bahr's kick left the Chargers stunned as the Raiders pulled ahead, 7–0, less than two minutes into the game.

Fouts and his aerial act came onto the field for the first time following the kickoff on the 17 yard line. On the very first play he brought the crowd to its feet again with a bomb to wide receiver Ron Smith. It covered 55 yards, all the way down to the Oakland 28. What a way to open the game! The tempo, however, died right down when Chuck Muncie was dropped for a 3-yard loss by Rod Martin. On the next play Fouts tried to hit Muncie with a pass but missed. Now Fouts studied a third and 13 on the 31. Everyone knew he would pass, and he connected with Jefferson on the 14 yard line.

Sensing a touchdown, Fouts went back to Jefferson but overthrew him. Again, for the third straight time, he looked to his dynamic wide receiver. The resourceful Hayes was looking, too, and quelled the noisy crowd by picking off Fouts's aerial on the 9 yard line and making his way to the 25 before he was tackled.

A 1-yard run by Van Eeghen and a 4-yard pickup by King left the Raiders with a third and 5 on their 30. This time Plunkett couldn't avoid the blitz and was spilled for a 10-yard loss by right tackle Gary Johnson. Guy's 60-yard punt got the Raiders out of any further trouble, and Fouts and his offense returned to the field on the San Diego 38 yard line.

Muncie tried to go around left end but was stopped after a 2-yard gain. When Fouts hit Joiner with a quick 12-yard pass, the Chargers had a first down on the Oakland 48. Fouts wanted Joiner again, only this time deep. As Joiner broke downfield, the crowd jumped to its feet to see him pull down a 48-yard touchdown pass. Anyone who left his seat for a beer would have missed it. Benirschke evened the game at 7–7 with his conversion.

It appeared that the Raiders were in trouble again when they got the ball back. After Plunkett misfired on a pass, he was sacked for the second time, losing 9 yards to the Oakland 15. On third down, in the face of a rush, Plunkett came up with a big play. He teamed with Cliff Branch for a 48-yard bomb to the San Diego 37 yard line.

The Charger defensive scheme was obviously designed to rush Plunkett. After Van Eeghen gained 5 yards, Plunkett could not escape a Charger rush and was tackled for a 1-yard loss by Louie Kelcher on the 33. On a third-down pass play Todd Christensen was interfered with, and the Raiders were allotted a first down on the 12. They were getting close. They got closer still when the Chargers were ruled off side, and the ball was spotted on the 7. King reached the 3, where Plunkett decided to pass. Finding no one open, Plunkett slipped across the goal line with the Raiders go-ahead touchdown. Bahr's kick gave Oakland a 14–7 lead.

When the Chargers couldn't do anything after receiving the kickoff, punter Rick Partridge made his first appearance. Ira Matthews returned his 41-yard punt 14 yards to give the Raiders excellent field position on the San Diego 49 with 3:08 remaining in the first period. Plunkett didn't wait. First he hit Chandler with a 16-yard throw to the 33. After King ran for 3 yards, Plunkett threw again, this time to Chester for a 9-yard gain and a first down on the 21. Plunkett was look-

ing sharp. He had completed 4 of his first 5 passes. His accuracy continued on the next play. He had Charger fans moaning when he connected with King for a 21-yard touchdown. Bahr added another point, and the Raiders extended their margin to 21–7. They indeed scored early, but no one anticipated that many points in the first quarter.

The sellout crowd of 52,428 couldn't have asked for more action, although the partisan

Burgess Owens makes certain Charlie Joiner doesn't catch one.

mob wished the score was evened. The period finally subsided a short time later with Fouts managing to get the Chargers a first down on a 20-yard pass to Joiner to reach the San Diego 47.

On the first play of the second quarter Mike Thomas got to the Raiders' side of the field with a 4-yard run. Then a trick play caught Oakland by surprise. Fouts handed the ball to Winslow on what appeared to be an end around, but Winslow stopped his run and threw a 28-yard pass to Jefferson on the 16. Illegal procedure then set the Chargers back 5 yards. A pass to Thomas only netted a yard. Fouts attempted to go deep to Jefferson. Burgess Owens anticipated it and intercepted the pass on the 1 yard line and brought it back to the 25.

San Diego's defense kept the pressure on Plunkett. After Van Eeghen and King both

RAIDERS

QTR	1	2	3	4*	SCOR
	21	7	3	3	34
	7	7	10	3	27

CHARGERS

TIME OF DAY
5:22

ran for 3 yards, Plunkett was dropped for a 3-yard loss. However, Guy thrilled Raider fans with a booming 71-yard punt that landed in the Charger end zone for a touchback, automatically positioning the ball on the 20.

Fouts combined with Thomas on a 5-yard pass play. Matuszak then repelled Thomas on a run up the middle. He hit Thomas hard enough to jar the ball loose, and Hendricks alertly recovered the fumble on the 29. The Raiders were making it happen with opportunistic football, producing their third turnover of the game. Charger fans were growing wary.

After Arthur Whittington was stopped for no gain, the Raiders were penalized 10 yards for holding. Plunkett's second-down pass wasn't good. He now looked over a third and 20 on the 39-yard line. Again he came up with the big play, a 24-yard strike to Branch that reached the 15. The Raiders were threatening to score for the fourth time. Moving behind Upshaw and Shell, Van Eeghen punched out 5 yards. Then he went up the middle for 2 more. On a key third and 3 from the 8 yard line, Plunkett delivered a 5-yard pass to Whittington for a big first down on the 3 yard line. The determined Van Eeghen didn't keep Raider fans waiting. He followed center Dave Dalby into the end zone for a touchdown. A stunned crowd watched as Bahr's extra point extended the Raiders' advantage to 28–7.

Oakland was on the verge of pulling away and turning the game into a rout. There was only 6:05 left in the half when Fouts came back to direct the offense. It was imperative that he get the Chargers some points, preferably a touchdown, to keep his team's hopes alive. Down 21 points, San Diego's chances for winning were slim at best.

He missed on his first pass when Hayes defensed Jefferson. He came back to Jefferson on the other side of the field for 10 yards and a first down on the Charger 46. Thomas then carried twice for a first down on the Raider 43. Three plays later San Diego had another first down on the 32. In two downs the Chargers could only get a yard. Faced with a third and 9, Fouts connected with Thomas for a 24-yard pass to the 7 yard line. Thomas then got to the 4 on a run. Fouts tried to pass on the next play and lost 4 yards when Hayes came up fast and dropped Thomas on the 8 yard line. However, Fouts hooked up with Joiner in the end zone, and the Chargers had the touchdown they needed. Benirschke added the conversion. Less than a minute later the half ended with Oakland in command, 28–14.

The much-maligned Plunkett made the difference. He had outplayed the heralded Fouts in the first half, hitting 7 of 9 passes for 188 yards, 2 touchdowns, and no interceptions. Oakland was only thirty minutes away from the AFC Championship.

San Diego needed to keep the momentum going after they received the second-half kickoff. Fouts came out throwing and hit Smith for 11 yards on the 35. On second down Mike Davis was called for pass interference, and the Chargers earned a first down on the Oakland 46. Following an 8-yard sack by Cedrick Hardman and an incompleted pass, Fouts had to convert a third and 18 on the San Diego 46. He did. He found Joiner with a 25-yard throw to the Raider 29.

It took Thomas two rushes to get another first down on the 18 yard line. When Hayes broke up another pass to Jefferson, Fouts turned to Smith for a 10-yard completion on the 8. The Chargers were getting close. Amazingly, Fouts stubbornly went to Jefferson three straight times, and three straight times he was thwarted. Instead of an impending touchdown, the Chargers had to settle for a 26-yard field goal by Benirschke that narrowed Oakland's lead to 28–17.

When Oakland failed to move the ball after the kickoff, the Chargers got the ball right back. Mike Fuller had provided the Chargers with prime field position when he returned Guy's punt 21 yards to the Oakland 41. A 4-yard run by Thomas and Fouts's 11-yard pass to Winslow got them to the 27. A motion penalty then set them back to the 32. Fouts cranked up again. He hit Thomas for 14 and Winslow for 10. Suddenly the Chargers were on the Oakland 8 yard line. Thomas tried the middle and got them 2 yards closer. Muncie then drew cheers when he swept around left end for a touchdown. The Chargers were right back in the game. Benirschke's kick brought them to within 28–24.

It was now up to the Raiders to stop the growing Charger momentum that had amassed 17 consecutive points. Their once-comfortable 28–7 lead had evaporated in the San Diego sunshine. There was 6:04 left when Plunkett regrouped his forces on the Oakland 23. After Van Eeghen gained 3, King broke loose for 8 yards and a first down on the 34. The speedy halfback was then on the receiving end of a Plunkett pass that collected 22 yards to the San Diego 44. Plunkett kept the Raiders moving with an 18-yard pass to Chester on the 26. The Raider drive looked good. King bolted for 8 yards and Van Eeghen for 3, and Oakland had another first down on the 15. Plunkett stayed with his ground attack. Running left, Van Eeghen got 3, and King, going the opposite way, picked up 4. However, on third down Whittington was dropped for a yard loss on the nine. Bahr came in for the first time to attempt a field goal and was successful from 27 yards to build Oakland's lead to 31–24 as the third period neared its conclusion.

Partridge's punt from deep in San Diego territory had given the Raiders the ball on their own 49 yard line when the fourth period began. A 14-yard burst by Van Eeghen put the Raiders in business on the Charger 37. After a 2-yard advance by Whittington, Plunkett went to his short passing game. He connected with tight end Raymond Chester for 5 yards and Branch for 6 for a first down on the 24. Plunkett missed with a pass thrown to Van Eeghen, who'd just gotten four yards. However, Plunkett converted on third down when he found Chandler for 11 yards on the 9.

The Raiders were closing in. Whittington moved for 2 yards, and Van Eeghen got 4 to the 3 yard line. That was as far as the Raiders got. Trying to pass, Plunkett was dumped for an 11-yard loss by blitzing Charger outside linebacker Woody Lowe. Instead of a potential touchdown, the Raiders had to think field goal. Bahr came through once again with a 33-yard kick that stretched the Raider margin to 34–24.

Time was now becoming a vital factor. Following the kickoff the Chargers lined up on the 20 yard line. There was no doubt that Fouts would rely increasingly on the pass. The Chargers needed to score quickly—not once but twice. Fouts missed on his first two passing attempts to Ron Smith but was successful on his third try, a 17-yard pass to Joiner on the 37. On the next play Fouts switched to the run and Muncie responded with an 11-yard burst to the 48.

It was time to pass again. Fouts's first two passes failed. He tried again on third down and delivered a 21-yard aerial to Winslow on the Raider 31. After Muncie got a yard, the Chargers picked up a first down on the 25 due to a face mask penalty. Two plays later the ball was still there on an exchange of 5-yard penalties. Muncie broke the monotony by shaking loose around right end for 16 yards to the 9. The Chargers were challenging for an im-

portant touchdown. The determined Raider defense stiffened. They tackled Muncie for a yard loss on a pass from Fouts. They then rejected Fouts on a third-down pass attempt to tight end Kellen Winslow. The Raiders walked off the field with the satisfaction that they had allowed only a 27-yard field goal by Benirschke instead of a key touchdown. The Raiders still had a touchdown lead, 34–27.

Time became an even more crucial factor now. It was up to Plunkett to control it. The scoreboard clock lit up 6:43 when Plunkett huddled on the 25 yard line following the kickoff. He had to run out as much of the remaining time as possible by making maximum use of his ground game. There was no question that the Chargers would brace for the run.

Plunkett would naturally depend on the sure-handed Van Eeghen to minimize the possiblity of a fumble. The countdown began as Van Eeghen got 5 yards up the middle and then 10 across left tackle for a big first down on the 40 yard line. On a third straight try Van Eeghen went right for 4 yards. When King could only manage 2 yards, Plunkett had to pass on third and 4. He carefully delivered a 6-yard pass to halfback Arthur Whittington for a first down on the San Diego 48. Just a few more first downs would put the Raiders into Super Bowl XV. Plunkett was making adequate use of the thirty seconds allowed in the huddle as Derrick Jensen gained 4 yards to the 44. On second down Van Eeghen could only find a yard, bringing up a third and 5. The anxious Chargers jumped off side, and now the Raiders had a first down on the 39 with valuable time ticking away. It was Van Eeghen again, and this time he drove ahead for 4 yards to the 35 as the two-minute warning was given.

Plunkett conferred with Flores. There wasn't any alarm. The two were just concurring to play it safe and not take any chances—just keep using the run to wind down the clock. There were no surprises when Jensen carried for 3 yards. Now it was Van Eeghen's turn, and he added 3 more to the 29. The Raiders were still short on third and 4. Plunkett called a pass but ran for 5 yards and a first

Coach Tom Flores has that Super Bowl look.

down instead to the 24. There was only 1:05 left when he gave the ball to Van Eeghen for the seventh time on the drive. He got down to the 20. It was all over. San Diego was out of time-outs. All Plunkett had to do was fall on the ball. He did so ever so carefully the next two times. He carried the ball off the field himself in what was probably the greatest game of his career. He had completed 14 of 18 passes for 261 yards, 2 touchdowns, and no interceptions. Jim Plunkett stood tall. Could his impossible dream come true? Who would say now that the Raiders couldn't win the Super Bowl?

The Raiders had clinched it with gutsy, old-fashioned football—nothing pretty, but nonetheless effective. Their three long drives consumed a total of sixteen minutes of perfect offensive football. The Raiders worked thirty-three plays, never once incurring a penalty. There weren't any missed snaps or blown assignments. Plunkett completed 6 of 7 passes and was sacked once. The other twenty-five plays were runs which produced 95 yards with the dependable Van Eeghen tallying up 62 of them. It was a proud offense in the pride-and-poise tradition of the Raiders. It was a much-maligned outfit with Plunkett as its prime target.

Before any of the media were allowed to enter the jubilant Raider dressing room, Upshaw called an impromptu team meeting to award the game ball to Al Davis. They cheered him on.

"The game ball goes to the one man in this organization who has taken more from the fans, the media, and the league than anyone in sports," shouted Upshaw. "If anyone deserves this game ball, Al Davis does. One thing that gave me great pleasure was coming down here and sticking it to Gene Klein. The only thing that's left is to win the Super Bowl, to stick it to our commissioner. I'm waiting for him to come into our locker room to present the trophy and find out what it's like to be booed.

"I'll tell you something else. Five days before the game Davis gathered the offensive line together for a talk. He pointed at us and said, 'You five guys have got to win it for us.' He talks to certain groups before each game; he

Equipment manager Dick Romanski does some repairs on Dave Browning's helmet.

knows which groups need to perform to produce a win. We knew we had to control the line of scrimmage. If we didn't we would lose."

They did control it. The last 6:43 was the most frustrating part for the Chargers. The Raiders' methodical execution was in sharp contrast to the flamboyant Charger personality. Henry Lawrence saw the forlorn looks on the faces of the San Diego players.

"When we were in our huddle, I'd look over and see how the Chargers' defensive linemen were taking it," revealed Lawrence. "One time I saw Louie Kelcher leaning over with his hands on his knees. They had to get Gary Johnson out of there. He was in pain with stomach cramps, I think. I could see their shirts heaving up and down, they were breathing so hard. They got frustrated. I heard Mike Fuller yelling, 'Come on, we've got to stop them,' and then they started getting disgruntled and griping at each other. I'll tell you, I loved it."

Nobody could have loved it more than

Plunkett. He had complete command out there. He had come up with numerous plays and had the respect of his teammates in fashioning the greatest game of his ten-year career.

"Believe it or not, I felt pretty confident at the end on those three drives," said Plunkett. "It was a very professional type of huddle, very calm. Guys were just thinking about which holes to hit, no offsides, no holding, knowing the snap count—that type of thing. During the last time-out I asked Flores about running a quarterback draw, and he said no. He gave me the routes, but when I dropped back, I saw the linebackers had fallen back in man coverage underneath. I saw the alley, and I took off.

"Our game plan going in was to throw to the open guys. The defensive backs were thinking I was going to go deep, and they were playing back. The passes to the sidelines and the ones in front of the linebackers were left open. Most people forget we had an offense. They kept talking about their offense against our defense."

Al Davis didn't. He put the team together with its own distinct personality both on offense and defense. He believed in his team all along. He had every reason to smile now.

"That Gene Upshaw knows how to make me feel good," smiled Davis. "He'll probably hit me for more money between now and the Super Bowl. I told a lot of players during the week that this was going to be like fighting Rocky Marciano. Whoever was left standing at the end was going to be the winner."

There was one more game to win. It was the same story. The oddsmakers had already made Philadelphia a 4-point favorite. For the fourth straight time the Raiders were cast as underdogs. Henry Lawrence shook his head when he learned about it.

"People just ain't smart enough," snapped Lawrence.

Indeed, the Raiders had to prove everyone wrong one more time. . . .

Oakland Raiders	21	7	3	3	34
San Diego Chargers	7	7	10	3	27

Oakland: 1:35, first period—Chester, 65-yard pass from Plunkett (Bahr, kick).
San Diego: 7:04, first period—Joiner, 48-yard pass from Fouts (Benirschke, kick).
Oakland: 11:14, first period—Plunkett, 5-yard run (Bahr, kick).
Oakland: 13:25, first period—King, 21-yard pass from Plunkett (Bahr, kick).
Oakland: 8:34, second period—Van Eeghen, 3-yard run (Bahr, kick).
San Diego: 13:55, second period—Joiner, 8-yard pass from Fouts (Benirschke, kick).
San Diego: 4:34, third period—Benirschke, 26-yard field goal.
San Diego: 8:47, third period—Muncie, 6-yard run (Benirschke, kick).
Oakland: 14:11, third period—Bahr, 27-yard field goal.
Oakland: 5:14, fourth period—33-yard field goal.
San Diego: 8:08, fourth period—Benirschke, 27-yard field goal.

Cliff Branch scored a touchdown that frustrated Philadelphia's Roynell Young.

A happy Rod Martin greets the press in the crowded Raider dressing room.

SUPER BOWL XV

An ominous cloud hung over Super Bowl XV. There were more intrigues, more accusations, and more off-field drama than had attended any other Super Bowl, with perhaps the exception of Super Bowl IV in 1970, also played in New Orleans. That year Kansas City quarterback Len Dawson's name was linked to a man from Detroit named Donald Dawson, who was under investigation by the FBI. The quarterback admitted having talked with him on the telephone when the alleged gambler called to offer his condolences upon the death of Dawson's father. Outside of that one call, Dawson had no other contact with him. The suspicion surrounding Dawson dramatically upset the team regimen. Kansas City Coach Hank Stram carefully shielded Dawson from the press to avoid further exploitation and pressure on him. He secretly assigned Joe Litman of Pittsburgh, a friend of Dawson's and the Chiefs', to act as a shield. "Pittsburgh Joe" Litman spirited Dawson through back doors and stairways to protect him from the horde of media types who inevitably descended upon the Fountainbleu Hotel, where the Chiefs were staying, when the news of the quarterback's alleged association broke on national television that Tuesday night.

It was a scene out of a Hollywood movie. When the writers and television announcers inquired about Dawson, no one on the Chiefs' staff would answer. Frustrated in their attempts to interview Dawson, the media decided to stake out the lobby waiting for Dawson to eventually show up. In the early hours of Wednesday Dawson remained hidden in the projection room where he and the other quarterbacks, along with Stram, viewed films of their opponents, the Minnesota Vikings. After three hours Litman carefully escorted Dawson to Stram's suite to avoid the press. Dawson stayed there for the night, sequestered in one of the bedrooms. The next day it was decided that Dawson would move into Litman's room rather than remain with safety Johnny Robinson, who was endlessly answering phone calls from people wanting to talk to the quarterback.

Stram was so determined to keep Dawson hidden that he even refused to let his quarterback leave the hotel and answer questions at the NFL headquarters in the Fairmount Hotel. Instead, with Litman standing guard outside the room, Jack Danahy, the league's director of security, came to the Fountainbleu to question Dawson. Still, the media had not gotten an opportunity to talk with Dawson.

When a rumor circulated that he was having dinner at a restaurant in the French Quarter, several dozen of them rushed there. All the while Dawson remained in an upstairs room at the hotel.

There was speculation that Dawson would not be allowed to play in Sunday's game and the pressure mounting at the Chiefs' hotel was at the breaking point. Finally, Jim Schaaf, the club's publicity director, prevailed upon Stram to let the media interview Dawson. After much discussion Stram agreed, but on one condition: Dawson would not answer any questions regarding the gambling allegations. The press consented to the conditions, and Dawson met them for the first time on Thursday. After this excruciating ordeal, during which he slept only nine hours in three days, Dawson played, starred, and led the Chiefs to an upset victory over the Vikings. Ironically, the Chiefs had reached the Super Bowl by defeating the Raiders, 17–7, in the American Football League championship game in Oakland. It was the last game played in the old AFL. After a colorful ten-year history, the AFL and the NFL would merge completely in 1971.

The drama unfurling a decade later didn't center on any particular player. Rather, it began some ten days earlier, before the Raiders ever arrived in New Orleans. In his long court battle against the NFL, Al Davis had testified that he believed that numerous owners were profiting by the scalping of Super Bowl tickets. He even went further to remark that Commissioner Pete Rozelle was well aware of the practice and that Rozelle, too, was involved. This incendiary remark broke on television and in newspapers throughout the country as a major news story. Contrary to what most people believed, Davis did not introduce the allegations. Instead, he was merely adding to the earlier admission by Howard Guiver, a former vice-president of the Los Angeles Rams, to the purchase of $100,000 worth of Super Bowl tickets in recent years.

Davis's testimony shocked the NFL's headquarters in New York. Rozelle vehemently denied the charges. Davis's remarks only added to his deteriorating relations not only with Ro-

The Raiders arrive in New Orleans.

zelle, but with the league's twenty-seven owners. The owners, incensed by Davis's year-long attempt to move the Raiders' franchise to Los Angeles, were further infuriated by his latest remarks. The battle lines were clearly drawn. Super Bowl XV was to be a conflict not only between the Raiders and the Philadelphia Eagles, but equally between Davis and the other owners. It was embarrassing enough, to the league as well as the owners, that the Raiders had made it to the Super Bowl against all odds. Rozelle, who earlier looked upon Davis as a rogue, now chastised him for violating the league's constitution in his attempt to move the Raiders to another city.

When the club left for New Orleans on Monday, a spirited group saw them off at the Oakland Airport. Flores and other members of the coaching staff had left the day before to check the facilities at the Gateway Hotel in Metairie, which was about eight miles west of New Orleans, as well as the team's practice facilities at Tulane University. Davis did not accompany the team. He was expected in New Orleans on Tuesday. Instead of staying with the team in Metairie, Davis had booked a suite of rooms at the New Orleans Hilton hotel downtown.

After a photo session at the Superdome on Monday afternoon, the players had a free night. It was their one and only night to be on their own. On Tuesday they would begin serious preparations for the Eagles, peaking with an offensive day on Wednesday and a defensive day on Thursday. The club would wind down for the final two days before Sunday's meeting.

Although he hadn't played since the fifth game of the season and wouldn't play in the biggest game of the year, Dan Pastorini had accompanied his teammates to New Orleans. The flamboyant quarterback was still a Raider, and although he hadn't contributed anything on the field for three months he still had friends on the squad. Every player, especially a quarterback, dreams of playing in a Super Bowl game. After nine years in Houston Pastorini was on his first championship team, only to be relegated to a spot on the sidelines by a broken leg that had since healed, but more by the success of Jim Plunkett, who'd replaced him.

The pain of frustration was clearly on Pastorini's handsome face. On Monday night he had stopped by to see his friend, Jimmy Moran, one of the city's most popular restaurateurs, in his Riverside Restaurant. Moran greeted him with a hug as Pastorini turned to introduce Mark Van Eeghen and Dave Dalby.

"How are you doing, Danny?" smiled Moran.

"Considering everything, I'm doing all right," answered Pastorini, but his disappointment was obvious. After sipping a glass of white wine, Pastorini left with his two teammates. Tuesday and practice would arrive soon enough. Philadelphia's coach Dick Vermeil didn't quite see it that way. He insisted on tighter discipline for his players, with a curfew every night, even going as far as having team dinners in the club's Hilton Inn headquarters next to the New Orleans International Airport, a half hour from downtown.

The cold weather in the early part of the week did not temper the requests for Super Bowl tickets. The event itself had reached such magnitude that it was the biggest ticket in sports.

Ticket scalping was, of course, illegal. The ticket-gouging story that broke ten days before prompted the NFL to bolster its security in policing illegal ticket sales. It didn't appear to deter the profit takers. They simply operated with more discretion and reaped their profits. A $40 ticket was getting as much as $400 on the sidelines and, in some instances, as high as $500 on the 50 yard line.

The chemistry between the teams this time was quite a contrast. It was almost a case of the good against the not so good. Quite naturally, the Eagles were projected as the "good guys," respected members of the professional football community. Vermeil's collegelike approach to training habits and dress code added to the clean-cut image. As in western movies, the "bad guys" wear black, which is one of the Raiders' dominant colors. Still, it was not just the color, but rather the casual style of a free-spirited group that caused others to look upon the Raiders with a critical eye. They enjoyed their notoriety but the "bad guy" image offended some of them. Veteran tight end Raymond Chester tried to explain the Raiders.

"We do a lot of crazy things, and our guys do hit the streets pretty hard at times," admitted Chester. "We wear what we want, and there are all kinds of outfits and lifestyles on this club. We do have an image, and it is a distinctive one, but it's misconstrued by the media and the public if they think of us as misfits and renegades or what have you. Don't let that fool you.

"First of all, I challenge the claim that any other team practices as hard as we do. The Eagles may practice longer, but I guarantee we put in more study time. I've been up watching films of our last Philadelphia game until two, three in the morning, and so have most of the other guys. The Raiders all have projectors in their rooms, and sometimes you've got trouble getting films because other guys are watching them.

"What outsiders must realize is that our management and coaches allow us to be individuals. They know when to back off. Look, we laugh and joke and play tricks on the practice field—until we hit the huddle. Then it's all business. It's just that being what we are and playing for the Oakland management allows us to bring out the athletic talent in us that would be suppressed somewhere else."

Unquestionably the Raiders appeared relaxed. Their mature approach and the fact that some of the veterans had played in the Super Bowl before seemed to be cohesive factors. Veterans like Art Shell were stabilizing influences on the younger Raiders who hadn't ever participated in a game of such proportions. Shell took it upon himself to caution the younger players.

"My reaction is, it's just another game," Shell said. "The last time we were here, John Madden had us prepared for what to expect. I talked to the younger guys myself. I told them that we had no curfew on Monday night, but that didn't mean they had to stay out late. I told them to go out and do what they had to do. Young guys think they can party all night. It's easy to get caught up in the partying atmosphere, but you have to remember what we are here for. We will have eleven o'clock curfews the rest of the week. We will spend a lot of time looking at films. I know in my spare time, I will take films to my room."

While much was made of Vermeil's work week during the season, little mention was given to Flores's tedious schedule. He admitted working a seventeen-hour day, disclosing the fact that the only time he sees his young daughter is when he kisses her while she's asleep at night and again the next morning when she's blow-drying her hair before going to school.

"Everybody prepares differently," remarked Flores. "I don't expect Dick Vermeil will change. He'll work his team hard. I only got about an hour of relaxation since beating San Diego for the conference championship. We had so much media coverage last week. You work on the press, you work on football, and there is little time for anything else."

However, Big John Matuszak always made time for other things. One of the Raiders' more celebrated partygoers, Matuszak is as big as life and relishes good food and good wine. Since New Orleans is famous for both, it was his kind of town. He knew he would enjoy it.

"I know Vermeil is a great coach, but I could never play for him," confided Matuszak. "I don't think he could coach for the Oakland Raiders. We have our own methods, and that's our way of being successful. A lot of teams around the league tend to treat you like little boys. That's the way they end up—playing like little boys. The Raiders treat you like men. Look, we all know what we're down here for. I'll personally see to it that nobody parties too much. If they do, they'll have to answer to the Tooz. I'll be the enforcer."

The Raiders appeared a natural for New Orleans. The eye patch on their insignia couldn't have been more appropriate. In earlier times the city had been a haven for pirates. Jean Laffite, one of the more prominent ones, often drank his rum in the French Quarter. One of the section's landmarks, the Old Absinthe House, boasts that Laffite and his brother Paul often frequented the musty bar which now is a haven for sports personalities all year round. Some of the Raiders ambled in and out of the Bourbon Street establishment greeting friends, staying a short while, and then leaving, ever mindful of the hour.

Late Wednesday afternoon Al LoCasale's busy work day was interrupted at the team's second-floor offices at the Gateway. The Gateway's switchboard had received a phone call warning that a bomb was planted on the eighth floor of the hotel where many of the Raider players were billeted.

At the time the players had returned from their workouts. However, quite a few of them were not in their rooms when a search began about five o'clock. In order not to alarm any of the players, no mention was made of the threat. Instead, Rudy Martin, an Oakland police officer looking after the Raiders' security in New Orleans, and the local police quietly knocked on every door without creating a panic. They searched the rooms that were empty making sure there was no bomb. Derrick Ramsey was taken by surprise.

Kenny King set a Super Bowl record, receiving an 80-yard touchdown pass that shocked the Eagles.

Linebacker Rod Martin with two of his three Super Bowl record interceptions.

John Matuszak made friends with the press and the police.

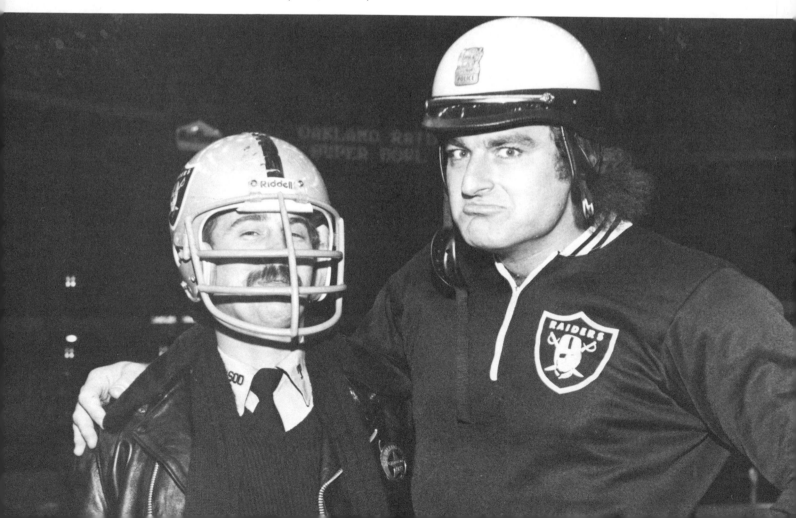

"I was on the phone when they came by and said they wanted to check the room," said Ramsey. "When they said something about a bomb, I said, 'Good-bye,' and got the hell out of there."

Fortunately, there wasn't any bomb to be found. "It turned out to be nothing, but it was something we had to check out," explained Martin. "It was disturbing to some of the players because they were asleep, and we woke them up. They wanted to beef up the hotel security, but I advised not to. It would probably upset these guys. They're a cool bunch of people, but there is no sense fooling with the stability factor."

Some of the visiting press corps made light of the matter. Many speculated that it was a good thing the bomb threat hadn't happened to the Eagles. If it had, most assuredly Davis would have been blamed. Then, too, others were questioning whether Davis would accept the trophy from Rozelle should the Raiders win on Sunday. Some were convinced that Davis would use the occasion for causing embarrassment to Rozelle and the league. Others joked that attorneys for each side would be the principals in the award ceremonies.

Through it all Davis kept a low profile. Late Wednesday night he dined quietly, accompanied by four friends, practically unnoticed by other diners. Although the game was still four days away, Davis already appeared to have his game face on. He seemed cautious and had a three-day growth of beard.

About the time Davis was having Wednesday dinner, Matuszak was finding it difficult to relax. He returned to his room by the 11:00 P.M. curfew but, feeling restless, went out again a short time later. Like a pirate of old, Matuszak began to unwide at the Old Absinthe House. He laughed and joked, his massive body dominating the packed room. All that was missing was a black patch over his eye tied to the back of his long curls. It wasn't until close to four o'clock that Matuszak sailed back into his room.

His plight was well known five hours later. Matuszak failed to show up for the player interviews which were being held for the last day at the Fairmount Hotel. His table, with the number 72 in the center, was ringed by newsmen but Matuszak was conspicuously missing. Finally, ten minutes before the end of the interview, Matuszak arrived, a blithe spirit through it all. For his escapade Matuszak was automatically fined $1,000. It didn't seem to bother him.

"I didn't go out Monday, and I didn't go out Tuesday," explained Matuszak, "but by Wednesday night I was really feeling the hair. I had to get out. It was my one night out. It was four nights before the game. I had to get it out of my system. Now all I have to think about is playing the greatest game I can."

"Yeah," one writer chided. "We thought you were going to be the enforcer, to keep everybody on the team out of the bars and in line."

"You got it, that's what I was doing," shot back Matuszak. "That's why I was out. I had to make sure that nobody else was out on the streets after the eleven o'clock curfew."

Matuszak sounded convincing. He brought a smile to Gene Upshaw's face.

"Tooz likes to go out on Wednesday nights," explained the veteran guard. "He'll be in bed on time the rest of the week. He got to the hotel before the curfew, but he went out again. That's an automatic one-thousand-dollar fine. We don't worry about the Tooz none."

Even rookie quarterback Marc Wilson was taking it all in stride now. Wilson, a Mormon, admitted he was concerned about joining an organization whose emblem is a feisty pirate with a patch covering one eye.

"One of the anxieties I had when I was drafted was that Oakland had a different reputation from most clubs," disclosed Wilson, "but I think it's overdone, overexposed, and mostly just an image. For example, I was driving down to San Diego before the AFC title game and I heard a guy on the radio say, 'All you mothers bring your kids in and lock the doors—the Oakland Raiders are in town.' I'm sure he doesn't say that when the Seattle Seahawks are in town."

But New Orleans was different, and this was the biggest game of the year. Everybody was saying that Sunday's game between the Eagles and the Raiders would be a low-scoring one. Bob Martin, the Las Vegas handicapper who establishes the point spreads for the nation's bookmakers, established Philadelphia as a 3-point favorite. It didn't surprise anyone. In Ron Jaworski they had the NFC's number one passer. They also had a big-game runner in Wilbert Montgomery and a big-play receiver in Harold Carmichael. Then, too, the Eagles were the top defensive team in the NFL, allowing only 222 points during the sixteen-game season.

A great deal of the pregame speculation centered around Carmichael and his duel with the exciting Raider cornerback, Lester Hayes. Both players were aware of each other, and each relished the challenge of going one-on-one against each other. Carmichael had been the Eagles' clutch receiver throughout the season. On the other side, Hayes was the Raiders' most vaunted defender, having devastated opposing quarterbacks with a league-leading 13 interceptions during the regular season and 5 more in the three playoff games.

"I don't expect to get beat," exclaimed Hayes. "If I can stop Carmichael, that will stop their whole passing scheme. Everything Philadelphia does on offense revolves around Carmichael. If Carmichael isn't functioning, Philadelphia's whole passing game is in trouble. He is the fuel that makes the Eagles' passing attack go. Seventy-five percent of their passing scheme is to Harold Carmichael. If he's not having his kind of day, it puts an awfully heavy load on Wilbert Montgomery. I'll probably play him the same way I played John Jefferson of the Chargers. I can't tell you how. That's a secret, but I'll be on him most of the time because our forte is man-to-man coverage. That's my forte, too, and I don't intend to change it for lack of being six foot eight. It's very cut-and-dried. If I keep Carmichael in check, it's almost impossible for those guys to score points."

Carmichael tried not to let Hayes affect him. He didn't want it to boil down to just himself and Hayes. Instead, he looked at the whole picture.

"It's not just Lester Hayes," remarked Carmichael. "I respect their whole backfield—Dwayne O'Steen, Burgess Owens, and Mike Davis. The Carmichael-Hayes duel is just a cog

in the wheel. They play physical, and we have to play as physical as we can. Of course, they get a better shot at me than I do at them. They catch me up in the air, and that's their job, but I don't think they are dirty or cheap-shot artists.

"Maybe they used to play that way but not many anywhere in the league play that way. Lester doesn't play with the forearm. That is, I've been in the league ten years and I've hit some guys where maybe I didn't have to, and maybe I've got paid back. You know this is a high-risk position from the moment you get into the league."

Flores gave Carmichael and the rest of the Eagle receivers more to think about when asked if the Hayes-Carmichael match-up could be a factor in the game. He wasn't about to be pinned into a corner.

"Man-to-man coverage is one of our big strengths," agreed Flores, "but we plan to mix it up so we won't get stereotyped. If Carmichael lines up on Lester's side, then Hayes will play him man-to-man. Lester isn't going to

Former coach John Madden interviews Lester Hayes.

shadow him. Both Hayes and O'Steen are big and strong and adept at playing receivers tight."

Still, the game revolved around the quarterbacks. Many experts felt the Eagles had the edge there. Most felt that Plunkett wouldn't hold up in a game as big as the Super Bowl, despite his outstanding game against San Diego two weeks earlier for the AFC Championship. They rationalized that Jaworski represented more offensive power than Plunkett because he was a more accurate passer who could get the ball off quicker. Yet, the mild-mannered Plunkett didn't appear to be affected by all the doubts about him. He was the most interviewed Raider all week long, and he handled himself well under what seemed to be an endless barrage of questions.

"I'm going to take it all in stride," beamed Plunkett. "I don't want to change anything that got me here. I'm excited about being here, but I also want to maintain my composure. You don't want to get yourself too up for any one game. We've played well this year. We've played a lot of good teams and we've beaten them, and I'm optimistic about Sunday.

"We're going to be as aggressive as we can be. Maybe field position might detract from that a little bit in some cases, but we intend to be aggressive both offensively and defensively. That's the style that got us here. Look, I'm excited as can be. This is something we all shoot for as professional players. It's eluded me for ten years. I can hardly wait for Sunday, but let me drop this thought: I think whatever team gets out on top might have an advantage because of the defenses we both have.

"The first time we played in November they knocked me around with some blitzes and stunts we hadn't seen before. Plus, I foolishly held the ball too long and set myself up to be sacked. This time we'll be prepared. We've seen something we can take advantage of—a little more motion and moving our split end closer to linebacker Jerry Robinson to occupy him, then getting our running game going. I'm sure we'll score more than seven points this time, and I think they'll score more than ten. Hopefully, not too many more than ten.

"The Eagles have the best defensive unit

Jim Plunkett and Mark van Eeghen enter the Superdome hours before Super Bowl XV.

we've faced. They managed to beat us the first time. If they get us in a pass situation, they come with four down-linemen in a tremendous rush. To avoid it, you don't get in long-yardage situations. We have to go out and attack—block well and run well. If we do enough of that, we'll come out on top."

While everyone quickly pointed to the Eagles' defense, it was, in fact, the Raider defense that was underrated. Although they gave up more points, 306, than Philadelphia, the Oakland defense began to jell the second half of the season. It was one of the chief reasons why the club managed to win nine of its last eleven games and all three playoff encounters. During the first half of the campaign the Raider defense surrendered 12 touchdown passes while accounting for 17 interceptions. In the last ten weeks, which included the three playoff games, the Raiders yielded only 7 touchdown passes while picking off 25 interceptions.

The defensive unit's performance brought a great deal of satisfaction to defensive coordinator Charlie Sumner and to line coach Earl Leggett. The first-year coach was a former member of the Chicago Bears, a rugged defensive team in the late fifties and early sixties, and had played with the likes of Doug Atkins, Bill George, and Joe Fortunato. The Raiders' ferociousness on defense reminded Leggett of those rough-and-tumble Bears who had been dubbed the Monsters of Midway back then. Leggett's style? Nothing fancy, no disguises, no deception—just plain hard and physical football.

"We just try to be physical," said Leggett. "This defensive team is very similar. The defensive line, the linebackers, and the defensive backs were all very big with the old Bears. We had a reputation of being big and bad. We have established the same kind of reputation here. We want players to be physical. We don't discourage it."

There was another similarity. The Bears revolved around Atkins, a Tennessee giant who stood six eight and weighed 275 pounds. Matuszak is just as big but weighs 5 more pounds.

"John's a brute," exclaims Leggett. "He sets things in motion."

It was Leggett's intention to let Matuszak stop the Eagles' running game. At times Matuszak can occupy two or even three blockers with his power and strength. The Tooz welcomes the battle in the pits.

"It's very tough to run on my side of the line," warned Matuszak. "Eight of ten plays they don't get anything. I don't have the quarterback sack total I want, but getting sacks in a three-four is difficult. Defensive lineman isn't a glory position. He is supposed to tie up as many linemen as possible in order to free the linebackers."

The Raiders have been very successful in stopping the run. Almost unnoticed is the fact that they have grudgingly given up only 107.9 yards a game.

"Yeah, it's been our strength," added Leggett. "Tooz has played like a Pro Bowler. Reggie Kinlaw has been tough in the middle. Dave Browning and Willie Jones have complemented each other, and Ted Hendricks . . . well, he excels every time he steps on the football field."

Jaworski was well aware of Hendricks. In fact, he worried the Eagle quarterback more than Hayes did. He studied Hendricks in film after film and still couldn't figure out his tendencies. He baffled Jaworski.

"I really believe the Oakland coaches tell Hendricks he can go anywhere on the football field he wants to go," snapped Jaworski. "I've looked at six games already, and I still don't know what he's doing. I really believe he just goes where he wants to go. They have such confidence that they can come in and play man-to-man defense on the wide receivers. They just let Hendricks rush wherever he wants to.

"The key to the game will be the first downs. We have to keep Hendricks from dictating what we do. If we have second and ten or third and long, we will be in for a long afternoon. If we can keep their nickel defense off the field and not give Hendricks freedom to go where he wants to, then I think we can dictate the game.

"Hey, look, I think Hayes will make some plays on Carmichael, but I think Harold will make some plays on him, too. What we have to do is give Hayes the opportunity to make the great plays. We can't concede defeat to him. We have to attack him. I don't think it will be a conservative game. If you play that way, you are playing right into their hands."

John Madden, who coached the Raiders two years ago, probably shook more hands around the press headquarters at the Hyatt Regency than anyone else, with the possible exception of Hank Stram. Madden guided the Raiders to their first Super Bowl victory in 1977, a 32–14 rout of the Minnesota Vikings. He still wears the ring from Super Bowl XI on his left hand. The affable blond was asked dozens of times for his opinion on the game. He knew most of the Raider personnel from having coached them, and he saw the Eagles play seven times from the television booth as CBS color analyst. It was a bit difficult to separate his heart from his head in analyzing the game, but Madden picked the Raiders to win.

"I like a team that's peaking. The Raiders are getting better every week, which is so dog-gone important this time of the year," began Madden. "They played as well as they have all year against San Diego. Is that my heart or my head talking? It's both.

"In order for Oakland to win, they must do two things: stop the Eagles' running game, something Dallas didn't do, and succeed offensively on first down in getting good yardage.

"In planning how to defense the Eagles, I feel the most critical element to defend is the run. You could almost gang up against the run. They do have a good passing game, but it's really not very effective if they can't run the ball. I would safely overplay the run on obvious running situations. By the same token, I wouldn't necessarily overplay the pass in obvious passing downs unless I was comfortably ahead.

"You know, the Eagles' three-man front is very good against the run, but it is not as effective against the pass. As a result I would anticipate throwing on first down more than usual. Oakland should aim to be successful on first down, either with the pass or the run, in an effort to pick up five yards. One thing they have to avoid is getting into predictable situations. That's the main reason why the Eagles were able to sack Plunkett eight times the first time they played."

All that was left was the game itself. Miles of stories emanated from New Orleans during the week-long preparations. Miles of video footage unwound on TV sets across the country, giving analyses and opinions on which team would win. Yet no one could be certain until Super Sunday when both teams would forget about all the reams of rhetoric by writers, announcers, ex-coaches, ex-players, and the pro football analysts who claim a select clientele of big-money gamblers. Professional football, even at Super Bowl time, can be very unpredictable.

Almost lost in the excitement of the Super Bowl game in New Orleans on Saturday night when the gridiron gladiators went to bed were two significant moments in recorded American history. The first took place earlier in the week, on Tuesday, when Ronald Reagan was sworn in as the fortieth President of the United States. A few days later the fifty-two American hostages, who were held in senseless captivity for 444 days in Iran, were finally freed. They were expected to land on American soil for the first time since their ordeal, on Sunday, only hours before Super Bowl XV.

Super Sunday dawned bright and sunny, unveiling a new look to New Orleans. All week long the skies had been cloudy and overcast, with a chill wind keeping the temperature below normal for the next-to-last week of January. The surprise of a gigantic yellow commemorative ribbon tied to the north end of the giant, saucerlike Superdome added to the festive mood.

It was a perfect day, one that begged for the game to be played outdoors, on natural grass with more than seventy-five thousand fans basking in the sunshine, yelling and cheering. The sunny skies were cloudless, and the 70-degree temperature made it ideal. Indoors, it would go relatively unnoticed. The revelers who had come to New Orleans would have one more shot at Bourbon Street. The game was scheduled for a five o'clock kickoff. Certainly there was time enough to enjoy the libations and vestiges of the storied French Quarter. If symbolism had any part in the event, then it should be a Raider day, with their pirate ancestors still alive in the spirit that is the Quarter.

Strangely enough, a good portion of the expected sold-out crowd of seventy-five thousand arrived at the Superdome early. More than two hours before the appointed hour they had begun to make their way into the arena. It was an Eagle crowd: when the combatants first came into view, the throng cheered more lustily for the Philadelphia players. It reached a crescendo when both teams emerged for the introductions of the starting lineups.

The Raiders weren't concerned when they lost the opening coin toss. Derrick Jensen had called heads, and the silver coin tossed by referee Ben Dreith came up tails. Flores had reminded some people earlier in the week that in ten of the last twelve games the Raiders won, they called the coin toss wrong.

It didn't matter that the Eagles elected to receive. Chris Bahr lined up his kick on the 35 yard line, looked across the field, signaled that he was ready by holding up his arm, and then proceeded to boot the ball to officially open Super Bowl XV. The crowd roared. Billy Campfield caught the ball on the 8 yard line and managed to slip a few blocks before being brought down on the 24.

On the first play from scrimmage Montgomery burst around his left end for 8 yards. Leroy Harris then picked up 3 yards over center, and in just two plays the Eagles had a first down. Feeling confident, Jaworski dropped back to pass. He tried to hit John Spagnola, one of the two tight ends, but linebacker Rod Martin read the play. He glided over the middle with Spagnola, stepped in front of him, and intercepted! Martin ran for 17 yards before he was pulled down by Montgomery on the Philadelphia 30. Within two minutes the Raiders were in position to strike.

Plunkett calmly opened the Oakland attack on the ground. Mark van Eeghen went over the right side for 3 yards. Kenny King went the same way but was stopped for a 1-yard loss. Plunkett now faced a third and 8, an obvious passing down. He tried to hit King near the goal line, but the pass was knocked away. However, Oakland had another chance. The play was called back because the Eagles were off side. Needing 3 yards for a first down, Van Eeghen churned his way for 4 yards to the 19. The Raiders were seriously threatening.

Plunkett didn't wait. On first down he fired a 14-yard pass to Cliff Branch on the 5 yard line. The Raiders were in an excellent position to score the game's first touchdown. Trying the right side again, Van Eeghen got 2 yards. He tried a second time but could only gain a yard. With the ball on the 2 yard line, Plunkett

faced a crucial third-down call. He decided to pass. Dropping back, he looked in the end zone and couldn't find anyone open. He started to run to his right, stopped when he saw Branch waving his arms, and calmly delivered the ball into his hands for a touchdown. Bahr's extra point was accurate, and the Raiders jumped ahead 7–0.

After the kickoff the Eagles put the ball in play on their 25 yard line. Montgomery could only manage 4 yards on two carries, and Jaworski's third-down pass was incomplete. Max Runager came in to punt, and the Raiders got the ball for the second time. Only now they were back on their 22 yard line. After King swept the left side for 6 yards and Van Eeghen gained 3 more, it appeared that Oakland would get a first down. Plunkett tried to pick

176   Plunkett runs from danger.

up the necessary yard but was stopped for no gain. However, Ray Guy got the Raiders out of danger by punting to the Eagles' 25. A neat return by John Sciarra gave the Eagles decent field positon on their 37.

On the first down Jaworski connected with his other tight end, Keith Krepfle, for 8 yards. Montgomery moved for 3 yards and an Eagle first down near midfield. When Hendricks dropped Montgomery for a 1-yard loss, Jaworski had to pass. Sensing a Raider rush, he wisely called a screen pass to Montgomery, who broke loose for 13 yards and a first down on the Oakland 40. The Eagles were in Raider territory for the first time. Less than four minutes remained in the first period.

This time Dave Browning stopped Montgomery for a 1-yard loss, which meant Jawor-

ski had to throw on second down. Pressured, he dropped a short pass to Harris which only gained a yard. On third and 10, Jaworski decided to go all the way for a touchdown. He sent Carmichael in motion to occupy the secondary and looked for Rodney Parker in the right side of the end zone. Parker reached up and pulled the ball down for an apparent touchdown. However, Carmichael was detected moving illegally and the play was called back. Jaworski tried Parker again, this time down the middle, but Odis McKinney knocked the ball away.

Runager's punt put the Raiders in a hole. Ira Matthews had to fair catch the ball on the Oakland 14 yard line. With only 1:06 left in the quarter, the Raiders couldn't take any wild chances. A quick, safe pass to Branch gained 4 yards. Then King ran for 2 more to the 20. Plunkett surprised everybody by fading back to pass on third down. Looking upfield, he couldn't find any of his primary receivers open. He started running to his left to hopefully scramble for a first down. Glancing at the left sideline, he spotted King. While still on the run, Plunkett uncorked a perfect pass to King, who caught the ball behind cornerback Herman Edwards. There was no one in front of King, and he sped the remaining 61 yards, untouched, for a touchdown. It was the longest pass play in Super Bowl history, covering 80 yards, and the suddenness of its execution shocked the Eagles. A minute later the Raiders stretched their lead to 14–0 as Bahr added the conversion point.

Eagle fans were still stunned when the second quarter began. On the opening play Montgomery gained 8 yards to the 34-yard line. Reggie Kinlaw thwarted Harris's first-down attempt by stopping him on the line of scrimmage. Undaunted, Jaworski reached back on third down and hit Spagnola with a 22-yard aerial for a first down on the Oakland 44. Suddenly the Eagles were in Raider territory again.

Jaworski tried for a touchdown to get the Eagles back in the game as he threw a bomb to Charlie Smith in the right corner of the end zone, but Hayes met the challenge. Jaworski came right back with a pass, finding Mont-

gomery open in the middle for a 25-yard gain to the 19. Now it was Philadelphia's turn to threaten. They needed some kind of score to break Oakland's momentum.

Montgomery then tried the left side and sped for 5 yards to the 14. Harris could only advance the ball a yard, and now Jaworski had to decide what to do on third and 4. Oakland reasoned he would pass and exerted pressure. Jaworski, forced to scramble to his right, tried to connect with Montgomery and failed. The Eagles had to settle for a field goal and Tony Franklin, the only barefoot kicker in pro football, hit from 30 yards out to narrow Oakland's advantage to 14–3.

The Raiders couldn't do anything after they received the kickoff at the 20 yard line. Plunkett overthrew Bob Chandler on a long pass, and Arthur Whittington was thrown back for a 2-yard loss. Trying another pass, Plunkett had to scramble, picking up 5 yards, before Guy came in to punt. He didn't quite get the distance he wanted, and Sciarra advanced his 42-yard kick 6 yards to the Eagle 41. Once more, it appeared that Philadelphia had good field position. However, a clipping penalty on reserve guard Ron Baker set the Eagles back to the 26.

Undaunted, Jaworski wasn't afraid to throw. His first, a screen pass to Carmichael, only gained 3 yards, as linebacker Bob Nelson reacted quickly. His next two throws were off target and the Eagles had to punt. Runager's 33-yard kick gave the Raiders the ball on the 37 when Matthews lost a yard on the return.

There was 7:23 remaining when the Raiders peeled off to the line of scrimmage. Working the right side, Van Eeghen moved for 6 yards and then came right back for 4 yards and a first down on the 47. Then, Plunkett went on top. His first pass to King was incomplete. However, he gingerly hit Branch with an 18-yard dart for a first down on the Eagle 35. The Raiders were moving into scoring range.

King got 4 yards to the 31. Trying to reach Branch on the 19, Plunkett's pass was broken up by Edwards. On third down Plunkett tried to throw again, but the Eagles' strong rush forced him to scramble for 4 yards to the 27, two yards short of a first down. Disdaining the

challenge, Flores decided to attempt a field goal for 3 points. However, Bahr's 45-yard attempt was short and off to the right.

The Eagles had only 3:34 left to score. Montgomery tried to sweep around the right side but was met by Matt Millen without advancing a yard. Thinking pass, Jaworski sent Carmichael down the middle. He overthrew his big receiver, and a surprised Burgess Owens dropped the errant pass that sailed right into his hands. On third down Jaworski came right back to Carmichael and connected with a 29-yard spiral and a first down on the Raider 44 as the big electric clock flashed 2:00.

Following the automatic time-out the Eagles hurried into their two-minute offense. After Harris ran for 3 yards, Jaworski went to his passing game. He threw down the right side to Carmichael for 14 yards and a first down on the Oakland 27. After two passes failed because of a strong Raider rush, Jaworski faced a third and 10. He successfully avoided the pressure of a third straight rush by connecting with Montgomery on a swing pass out of the backfield that gained 16 yards to the 11.

Calling a time-out with 1:07 left in the half, Jaworski talked over strategy on the sidelines with Vermeil. When action resumed, Jaworski came out throwing. However, the Raiders met the barrage. They rejected Jaworski all three times he passed—first Hendricks, then Mike Davis, and finally McKinney. All that was left on fourth down was that Franklin should kick a 28-yard field goal. The proud Raider defense wouldn't allow the 3 points. Hendricks penetrated, stuck up his long arms, and blocked the surprised Franklin's kick with just forty-three seconds showing. A group of disconsolate Eagles left the field trailing 14–3, knowing they had a lot to overcome and wondering if they could do so.

Oakland played a superb first half. Almost stereotyped as a team that runs left, Van Eeghen discovered continued success in running right, behind guard Mickey Marvin and tackle Henry Lawrence. As he had done all season, Plunkett made the big pass plays that resulted in 2 touchdowns. On defense Matuszak applied strong pressure up front while the secondary kept Jaworski off balance, not only by playing man-to-man on his receivers but by rotating into zone coverage as well.

When the second half began, there was strong sentiment that the Raiders would become the first wild-card team to win a Super Bowl. They played a solid first half and were in command throughout. The pressure was now on the Eagles to catch up.

Oakland's first possession in the second half was important. If they could add to their lead, then the Eagles' task would be that much more difficult; but if Philadelphia could stop Oakland's advance, then maybe they could swing the momentum in their favor. The crowd's emotions were high in anticipation of the opening confrontation.

Plunkett broke the huddle on the 24 yard line after Matthews ran the kickoff back 21 yards. Immediately, the Raiders were in trouble. Lawrence was signaled for holding on a first-down running play and the Raiders were penalized 10 yards to their 14. A mistake now would be costly. Plunkett handed the ball to Van Eeghen, and this time the solid fullback ran to his left for 8 yards. On second down Plunkett teamed with King for a quick pass that generated 13 yards and a first down on the 35. Smoothly, coolly, Plunkett maneuvered the Raiders out of danger.

With room now to operate, Plunkett called a deep crossing pattern to Chandler who would take off down the right side and then cut across the field to his left. Getting time to throw, Plunkett waited for Chandler to come all the way across and accurately dispatched his pass 32 yards to the Philadelphia 33 yard line. In just three plays Plunkett took the Raiders out of danger and had them threatening.

On the next play Van Eeghen went back to the right side and found 4 yards to the 29. On second down Plunkett called Branch's number. The speedster broke toward the right corner of the end zone. Plunkett's pass didn't appear to have enough power, and cornerback Roynell Young, who was playing Branch tight, seemed set to intercept at the goal line. Instantly reacting, the crafty Branch came back a yard, reached around Young, practically stole the ball out of his hands, then quickly turned and continued into the end zone with Oakland's third touchdown. It was a picture-book play, one that could be used in a training film on the art of catching a football aggressively. The Eagles appeared to be mumbling among themselves when Bahr's conversion pushed Oakland's margin to 21–3.

Philadelphia's quandary had intensified. The game was getting increasingly out of control. They seemed to lose their composure when rookie Perry Harrington tried to catch the kickoff while the ball was heading out of bounds. By touching it, the Eagles were mired on the 10 yard line. Jaworski tried to rally his forces. Montgomery advanced the ball to the 14 before Jaworski faded back to pass on second down. He drilled an 18-yard bullet to Carmichael for a first down on the 32. After Montgomery got 3 yards, the Eagles benefited from a pass interference call on Millen which gave them another first down on the 40.

Jaworski hooked up with Carmichael again, this time for 19 yards and a third straight first down on the Oakland 41 yard line. Two running plays got the Eagles to the 34, and Jaworski studied a crucial third and 3 situation. He felt the best percentage pass would be a short one to Spagnola. Martin figured the same way. He cut in front of the tight end and intercepted for the second time. Philadelphia's comeback hopes fell.

Beginning on the 32 yard line Van Eeghen made use of the right-side blocking for 5 yards to the 37. Attempting to pass, Plunkett lost a yard when he tried to scramble out of trouble. However, he was successful on third down, connecting with Raymond Chester for the first time for a 16-yard advance to the Eagle 48. Again, Plunkett indicated pass. This time he teamed with Chandler for 17 yards and another first down on the 31. Plunkett had the Raiders on the move again.

Running left this time, Van Eeghen picked up 5 yards to the 26. When Whittington lost 2 yards, Plunkett went back to the air. This time he missed when attempting to hit Chester on the 12 yard line. Flores sent in Bahr to try a 46-yard field goal. He didn't fail. His kick just made it over the crossbar to propel the Raiders into a 24–3 bulge. Oakland had scored the

only two times it had the ball in the third quarter. By now the Eagles were getting more apprehensive about their chances of winning.

A clipping penalty on the kickoff handicapped the Eagles on the 12 yard line. There was only 4:35 left when Jaworski set up. Despite the bad field position, he had no choice but to pass. His first sailed over the head of Montgomery on a deep sideline pattern. Under a tremendous rush, Jaworski slipped back into his end zone and let go a long pass to Smith on the right sideline. Smith caught the 43-yard aerial before stepping out of bounds on the Oakland 45. Hayes, who had positioned himself in front of Smith, momentarily gave up on the play when he thought that Jaworski was sacked.

The Eagle quarterback then switched to his ground game. Harrington gained 4 yards and so did Montgomery. On third down Mont-

gomery picked up 3 yards and a first down on the 34. After Harris ran for 3 more yards, it looked like the Eagles had been stopped. Reverting to the pass, Jaworski missed on two tries to Carmichael. Facing a fourth and 7 on the 31, the Eagles had to go for it. They desperately needed points.

Jaworski kept trying. He shot a pass down the middle to Parker for 19 yards and a first down on the 12 yard line. As the third period ended, Louie Giammona, the coach's nephew, snaked his way 7 yards to the 5. It was the farthest the Eagles had advanced into Oakland territory all day.

On the first play of the final quarter Montgomery was stopped for no gain. The determination not to allow the Eagles to score a touchdown was written on the faces of the Raiders' defensive unit. Montgomery tried again on third down and only got 2 yards to the 3. However, an encroachment penalty called on Hayes kept the ball on the 3 yard line, but it was still third down. Now the Eagles only needed a yard for a first down. Reacting too anxiously, center Guy Morriss was guilty of a false start. That moved the Eagles back to the 8, and it appeared that the Raiders would reject their bid for a touchdown. Unruffled, Jaworski fired a quick 8-yard pass to Krepfle for the Eagles' first touchdown. Franklin's conversion managed to bring the Eagles to within two touchdowns, 24–10. More important, it kept the Eagles' hopes alive.

It didn't last long, however. Plunkett kept the Raiders rolling despite going on offense from the 11 yard line after Franklin's kickoff. Twice Van Eeghen ran left, first for 8 yards and then for 5 for a first down on the 24. King could only manage a yard before Plunkett drilled an 8-yard pass to Chester. As Plunkett picked himself up off the ground, he derived some satisfaction in knowing that Claude Humphrey, the veteran defensive end, was penalized 15 yards for roughing him up. Humphrey protested and came dangerously close to being ejected from the game when he picked up the official's flag and tossed it away.

Starting a new series on the 48, Plunkett was unsuccessful on a long pass to Branch. He came right back with another pass, this one to Chandler, which gained 23 yards to the Philadelphia 29. Plunkett looked to Chandler again, this time for 5 yards. When Van Eeghen carried for 5 yards on the next play, the Raiders had a first down on the Eagle 19. There was no way that Plunkett was going to lose control of the game. Even a field goal at this point would seal Philadelphia's doom.

He tried a little pass to Van Eeghen but threw it short. Whittington then got 2 yards to the 17. On third down Plunkett tried to connect with Chandler in the end zone but missed. What remained was a 35-yard field goal attempt by Bahr. If he was successful, then the Raiders would be up by three scores. There wasn't that much time left in the game for that to happen. Bahr snuffed out the Eagles' last hope with an accurate kick that pushed Oakland's insurmountable lead to 27–10.

There was only 8:19 left on the game clock when the Eagles went back on offense from their 22 yard line. Hendricks dropped Montgomery after a 2-yard advance. Then Jaworski quickly went to the air. He passed to Smith for 16 yards and then to Montgomery for 19 more. Trying to run from the Raider 41, Harris was decked for a yard loss by Martin. When Jaworski fumbled the snap on the next play and Willie Jones recovered, the contest, for all practical purposes, was over.

Time was definitely the Raiders' ally now. When Plunkett led his offense back on the field, only 5:30 remained to play. It didn't matter that Guy came on to punt for the first time during the entire second half. No more offense was necessary. The Eagles had only 3:51 left, and with just three minutes showing, Martin made Super Bowl history by intercepting his third pass. All that was left now was to run out the clock. It was the Raiders' day all right, and all the ghosts of the old pirates must have been chuckling in the ancient buildings of the French Quarter.

The Raider dressing room was controlled bedlam. The area was actually too small for the horde of media types who were scurrying like ants to grab a quote in answer to a quick question. The heat from all the television lights in the room, coupled with the crowd, made it uncomfortably hot. Everyone was there, principally, to record the exact moment when Al Davis would accept the championship trophy from Commissioner Pete Rozelle. Standing on a makeshift platform under high-intensity floodlights, Rozelle and NBC announcer Bryant Gumbel patiently waited for Davis. In keeping with his style Davis kept them waiting. Some construed the practice as being intentional. It wasn't really. It's just that Davis, from his vantage point high in the press box, didn't want to leave the game until the final gun was sounded.

When he arrived, the Raider players shouted. Many of them stood on their stools and reached for cameras. They wanted to have their own photographs of Davis receiving the trophy from Rozelle. Davis didn't disappoint them. He accepted the trophy on behalf of the Raider organization while dozens of flashbulbs popped, adding that much more glare to the overilluminated room. Then Davis stepped off the platform, refusing any more comments, because he wanted to go around the room and personally thank all his players.

One player who had special meaning for Davis was Upshaw. The veteran guard was the only one who had played in all three of Oakland's Super Bowl appearances—in 1968, 1977, and now. The victory over the Eagles was especially satisfying to Upshaw who, at the age of thirty-five, was the oldest member of the team.

"What do you say, are you going to let me retire now?" asked Upshaw.

"It's up to you," replied Davis.

"Ah, hell, I can't retire," shot back Upshaw. "I've got a minicamp coming up in March."

Davis smiled as he walked away.

"No one expected us to be here, but we were," continued Upshaw. "It was the world against us, and everybody said we didn't have a chance. We knew we had to control the line of scrimmage, and we did. It might have looked easy, but it wasn't. I kept reminding our players during the playoffs that the only thing winning does is let you play next week, but unless you win the Super Bowl everything else is down. You can remember the Steelers

The Raiderettes make general partner Ed W. McGah feel right at home. From left, Anita Wheeler; Judi Wellens; Kristina Young; Betty Silva; and kneeling, Debra Johnson.

With executive assistant Al LoCasale holding the Super Bowl trophy, Al Davis talks to NBC's Bryant Gumble. In center is Tom Flores and at right is NFL Commissioner Pete Rozelle.

Chris Bahr's field goal sails through the uprights.

won four Super Bowls, but you never remember the teams they beat.

"We're not a bunch of choirboys and Boy Scouts. They say we're the halfway house of the NFL. Well, we live up to that image every chance we get. If Tom Flores sent home every guy on this football team who screwed up breaking curfew, he'd be the only guy on the sideline. Tom doesn't say a word if you screw up. He just cuts off your wallet. You see that stub in your wallet and you say, 'Well, I've got another tax deduction.' Yeah, we had guys break curfew this week; but when that door opened today, we were ready to play. We peaked at the right time."

The most celebrated curfew-breaker was Matuszak. He bristled at Vermeil's remark earlier in the week when the Philadelphia coach said that if Matuszak played for him he would have sent him home. He, too, enjoyed an extra helping of satisfaction and was quite vocal in his feelings about Vermeil.

"I'll tell you why the Eagles didn't win. It was because of their coach," blared Matuszak. "It wasn't their fault. It was his. They weren't ready for what we gave them today. They were overconfident, and he got them that way. He didn't let them go out all week. You can't treat a man like a boy and then expect him to play like a man.

"Wednesday night is my normal night to go out, so I went out, curfew or no curfew. I'll pay my fine. I walked out the front door. I had nothing to hide. Some guy said he heard the club had deputies to stand guard and try to stop me. If I want to go out, I go out. I don't care what kind of deputies they have. Vermeil can't understand that. Hey, use your head, buddy. I couldn't play for him in a million years, and I wouldn't want to."

Vermeil really didn't know the depth of Matuszak. He runs deeper than his mammoth six-eight, 280-pound frame, and his cocky bravado. Above Matuszak's locker was a newspaper clipping from a California paper. The big defensive end had tacked it up himself. It carried a picture of Matuszak with a bedridden boy who was near death. Matuszak dedicated the game to the youngster. He kept it a secret until now.

"My game jersey is going to that kid," snapped Matuszak as he left.

The triumph also meant a little more to Plunkett, the much-maligned quarterback. He was practically perfect in directing the offense, completing 13 of 21 passes for 261 yards and all 3 Oakland touchdowns, without suffering an interception. Modestly, he didn't dwell on his accomplishments.

"This is the greatest moment of my life as a pro football player," beamed Plunkett. "I can't say enough about our offensive line. What a great job those guys did. I was pumped up before we ever kicked off. I came off the field after warm-ups, and I was completely exhausted. We figured going in, if we could run the ball with a little success, our passing game would open up.

"Philadelphia's secondary played way off the ball. Branch and Chandler were able to curl back and make receptions under the coverage. We didn't run any route differently than we did the first time we played Philadelphia. The difference today was the protection I got from the offensive line, and the guys on defense did a tremendous job. We came up with a turnover when we needed it, or our secondary knocked down a pass when it looked like they were going to get rolling.

"I was looking for Chandler on the pass to

After the third one, Martin holds his prize high.

King. I had to scramble when Chandler was covered. That's when I spotted Kenny waving his hands at the thirty-nine. He did the rest. What can I say about the twenty-nine-yard touchdown to Branch in the third quarter. It was a great individual effort. He took the ball right out of the cornerback's hands."

The resourceful Branch looked as if he never broke a sweat. He was calm and spoke quietly without any sign of emotion. He's an intense performer who gets the job done.

"I believe the AFC dominates the NFC," remarked Branch. "It's tougher, more competitive. The AFC jams the receivers at the line. The NFC gives you a lot of room. I don't know why, but I enjoy it and hope they keep doing it. Today they gave me a lot of room. When I'm running and they don't touch me in the first ten yards, I can get open.

"The first touchdown was a hook pattern. Plunkett saw me get open; he scrambled and hit me. Chandler was the primary receiver. It was called Ninety-four Corner. I thought the first team to get on the scoreboard would win.

185

It would be a psychological lift. I think the second touchdown I scored was the turning point. It gave us a twenty-one–three lead."

Defensively, linebacker Rod Martin turned it around. It is almost unheard of for a linebacker to intercept 3 passes in one game, but to do it in the Super Bowl it has to carry that much more weight. Martin was all smiles at his instant celebrity status.

"I studied and studied all week," revealed Martin. "I sat in my bed after curfew and looked at film. They were trying to hit the short flat area. On the first interception Carmichael ran a streak pattern, and the tight end tried to hook behind me. They threw to my inside, and I caught the ball with my left arm. On the second one I just got a good jump on the ball. I knew with us in the lead they weren't going to abandon their game plan. They had to do something, and they weren't going to go to Hayes's side. The third interception was in a prevent. I had to stay along the hash lines."

As always, Flores was cool. He really didn't get caught up in the emotion, outside of being hugged by Davis along with some other players who congratulated him. That's how it was when he played and how it is when he coaches.

"It's hard to find words to express how I feel," said Flores. "I'm proud of the way that we did it. We were underdogs all year and went with a quarterback who hadn't played in three years. Making it to the Super Bowl as a wild-card team and winning all season under adverse conditions make it that much more satisfying."

The Raiders celebrated all night at a private party in the main ballroom of the Fairmount Hotel, the same room in which they had been interviewed all week. They deserved every moment. The day belonged to them, and the night was theirs, too. It's that way for winners, and the Raiders won the biggest prize of all against all odds.

Raider fans waited anxiously to greet their heroes on Tuesday. Despite a day-long rain, some twenty thousand lined the streets of Oakland and shouted at a ceremony at City Hall. When the first Raider bus arrived for the parade, Matuszak got off and looked around at a group of youngsters. They greeted him with shouts of "Tooz! Tooz!"

"I hope you guys got out of school today," remarked Matuszak.

The youngsters replied that they had.

"It's worthwhile then," smiled Matuszak.

It most certainly was. There will never be another year quite like this one.

The next day, the Raiders went home, and Mickey Marvin hugs his tired wife, Lisa.

Oakland Raiders	14	0	10	3	27
Philadelphia Eagles	0	3	0	7	10

Oakland: 6:04, first period—Branch, 2-yard pass from Plunkett (Bahr, kick).
Oakland: 14:51, first period—King, 80-yard pass from Plunkett (Bahr, kick).
Philadelphia: 4:32, second period—Franklin, 30-yard field goal.
Oakland: 2:36, third period—Branch, 29-yard pass from Plunkett (Bahr, kick).
Oakland: 10:25, third period—Bahr, 46-yard field goal.
Philadelphia: 1:01, fourth period—Krepfle, 8-yard pass from Jaworski (Franklin, kick).
Oakland: 6:31, fourth period—Bahr, 35-yard field goal.